THE POWER BRAIN

FIVE STEPS TO UPGRADING YOUR BRAIN OPERATING SYSTEM

ILCHI LEE

459 N. Gilbert Rd. Suite C-210
Gilbert, AZ 85234
www.BestLifeMedia.com
480-926-2480

First paperback edition: April 2016
Library of Congress Control Number: 2016935383
ISBN: 978-1-935127-86-4

Not only our pleasure, our joy, and our laughter, but also our sorrow, pain, grief, and tears arise from the brain, and the brain alone.

—HIPPOCRATES (C. 460 BC)

You must find your true self. And that true self has always been within you—inside your brain.

—SAM IL SHIN GO, ANCIENT KOREAN SCRIPTURE

TABLE OF CONTENTS

PART III: FIVE STEPS TO A POWER BRAIN 77

FOREWORD

The Wisdom of Brain Discovery

I believe that there is an important difference between knowledge and wisdom. As a mental health professional, I possess lots of knowledge. I know myriad psychological theories and dozens of therapeutic methods. As a hospital administrator, I know how medical institutions work and how to navigate the system. I use this knowledge every day in the work I do. Ilchi Lee, on the other hand, has built a career based on wisdom, and that is why I am grateful to be able to recommend this book.

Wisdom is the ability to make sound choices and to keep priorities straight. This, in essence, is what Ilchi Lee's Brain Education program teaches. Ilchi Lee guides people to use their brains wisely for more balanced, healthier lives. He has arrived at his understandings not just by studying facts and theories, but even more importantly through intuitive insight and practical work with thousands of people from all walks of life.

His method differs markedly from the approach traditionally taken by psychologists and psychiatrists. Why, then, do I recommend it? First of all, I have personally experienced the powerful benefits of this system. I know it works, because it has worked for me. Secondly, the Brain Education program complements current theories and practices within the mental health profession.

Until quite recently, mental health practitioners have largely focused on repairing weaknesses and understanding mental suffering. Increasingly, however, we've come to realize that people need ways to maintain a healthier state of being in everyday life, rather than waiting until difficulties arise. I believe Brain Education offers a strikingly practical way to do just that. Through its five-step process, people of all ages can nurture and develop their own internal wisdom and well-being as they gain a sense of meaning and purpose for their lives.

A Step-by-Step Approach

First, and perhaps most importantly, Brain Education effectively targets one of the biggest health problems of our time—stress. As Chief of Psychiatry of the Adult Mental Health Division of the Hawaii Department of Health, I myself am no stranger to stress. More than anything else, I've needed to learn how to quiet my thinking mind. Each night, I'd take my work home with me and replay the day's problems over and over in my head. At the end of a hard day, I'd often "reward" myself with my favorite comfort food—fried chicken. After practicing the Brain Education method for just a short time, I found that my mind had calmed significantly. I'm no longer dependent on caffeine for energy, and my cravings for unhealthy food have diminished.

The stress reduction techniques in Step One of the Brain Education system cultivate the trait of mindfulness, the ability to focus awareness in the present moment. The stress-reducing benefits of mindfulness have been confirmed in numerous scientific studies. Brain Education specifically works to develop sensory awareness—what in psychological terminology we call "interoception," the awareness and interpretation of signals originating in the body. The study of interoception is relatively new for Western medicine, yet interoception is now considered critical for personal well-being and motivation. Abnormal interoception contributes to multiple problems impacting public health, including addiction, depression, eating disorders, chronic pain, and post-traumatic stress disorder.

Step Two works on brain flexibility, helping us to accept change more readily. This step corresponds to the Western neuroscience concept of neuroplasticity. The work of multiple neuroscientists during the latter half of the twentieth century led to the current understanding that the adult brain is constantly changing, removing, and creating connections in response to its use. Exercise—especially low-intensity exercise like the Brain Education program suggests—produces neurotrophins, brain proteins that support the brain's ability to change its connections.

Step Three helps free the brain from unhelpful emotional patterns. In emotionally charged situations, normal individuals (those without psychiatric symptoms) show activation of the brain areas that process emotions, but they show even stronger activation of the areas involved in planning and decision-making. Unfortunately, many people suffer from unhealthy emotional reactions that don't allow them to access their planning and decision-making wisdom. Brain Education techniques help us to access and practice this ability, replacing knee-jerk reactivity with healthy problem-solving skills.

Over the past 20 years, numerous Western medical and psychological studies have demonstrated that meditation and spiritual practices, such as those in the Brain Education method, strengthen the structure and function of the brain's executive control and decision-making areas. In addition, a meta-analysis of studies on the psychological effects of meditation shows a meaningful reduction in anxiety and negative emotions. In other words, meditation improves the ability to recognize and consciously respond to emotions, freeing us from unhelpful responses.

Step Four focuses on integrating brain functions and unleashing our potential by revisiting and changing our responses to "core information," such as beliefs about ourselves and preconceptions about others and the world. This parallels the Western psychological concept of cognitive reappraisal—changing an emotional response by reinterpreting the meaning of the information that triggered the emotional stimulus in the first place. Often, our core information—what Brain Education calls our Brain Operating System—isn't consciously known to us. It only becomes apparent through our emotional responses, attitudes, and memories. By identifying and changing our negative responses, we can edit our core information through the miracle of neuroplasticity. Western research on cognitive reappraisal and decentering processes started only recently, so there's limited evidence to indicate whether mindfulness supports cognitive reappraisal and decentering. Anecdotal evidence, however, suggests promising potential.

Step Five of Brain Education trains us to use the brain's functions with intention. This is related to the Western psychological concepts of self-efficacy, self-control, and locus of control. Self-efficacy is defined as the strength of an individual's belief in their ability to complete tasks and reach goals. Self-control is the ability to control one's emotions, behavior, and desires in the face of external demands. Locus of control refers to the extent to which people believe they can control the events affecting them. Numerous psychological studies have demonstrated that high self-control and self-efficacy and an internal locus of control are related to a wide range of positive outcomes—greater overall well-being, healthier lifestyle choices, higher job satisfaction, greater success, and better interpersonal relations.

Unlocking Your Great Potential

As someone who has devoted my life to supporting people's mental well-being, I am gratified to see a method such as Brain Education helping people become healthier and happier. We doctors are not exempt from the struggle to maintain healthy, balanced lives. By following the methods described in this book, I've personally lost weight, improved my relationships, and modified many negative habits that I had struggled to change in myself.

The Power Brain is an accessible and engaging user's manual. I invite you to read it, knowing that practicing its five steps can forever alter your brain and thereby change your life for the better. Brain Education is a practical and sound way to help people find that sense of well-being that so many are seeking in today's complex world. It is my sincere hope that you will discover your brain's great potential in dramatic new ways as the pages of this book unfold—and that you will use this expanded potential for the rest of your days.

James Westphal
Chief of Psychiatry of the Adult Mental Health Division
of the Hawaii Department of Health

AUTHOR'S INTRODUCTION

Your Journey to Your Authentic Self

You can do anything, and you can be anything. Do you believe that? I assure you that it is true. The secret of becoming what you want to be lies in your brain. But to use your brain well, it must first become your best friend. This book is a guide for just that: becoming great friends with your brain so that you can reach your highest potential.

Without our brains, there is nothing we can do with our lives. Because you have a brain, you're able to see and hear and speak, and because you have a brain, you can think and work and have interactions with things and people. Your brain allows you to shed tears as you watch a touching movie. Thanks to your brain, you are able to tell someone, "I love you." And with your brain, you can ask, "Who am I?"

People are rightly amazed by the many wondrous things of the world—plants and animals, the stars in the sky, today's miraculous technology—but your brain is a thousand times more incredible than anything else you'll ever encounter. In that small space enclosed by your skull, there's a central control room, a space for meditation, and a healing center. There's also a school, a research facility, a chemical factory, and an amusement park.

The brain controls every thought, emotion, and behavior. It learns all the various forms of knowledge we need to function in our everyday lives. It observes objects and figures out how they work. It can heal the wounds of body and mind, big and small. It produces the chemical substances that mediate all of our mental activities and physiological functions, and it generates all manner of fantasies produced by our untamed imagination. It can understand the most complex philosophical theories and the most advanced mathematical equations. It is even capable of being conscious of infinite consciousness itself, the world beyond emotion and thought.

All great accomplishments—every feat achieved by humans throughout history—are the work of the brain. In fact, our brains possess infinite latent potential. So if you develop your brain's potential, and you use that potential well, you may affect much more than just your personal fate. Because of your brain, you have the potential to influence the entire future of humankind and to support the mending of the earth, whose future now hangs in the balance.

The journey toward full realization of your brain's potential starts with this recognition: "I have a brain with incredible capacities." If you know without a doubt that this statement is true, you can begin to put your brain to better use. As you do so, you can improve your life and pioneer great changes in this world. This book is meant to inspire you to this end and to provide you with the tools you need to do just that.

How It All Started

When I was young, I struggled with attention-deficit disorder. During class at school, I couldn't focus on my teachers' lectures or on anything in the textbooks. My mind wandered into thoughts like, "Who am I? Why was I born? Why do I have to live? Why does the universe exist?" I couldn't get a good grasp on anything else. Because my parents, teachers, and friends didn't understand me and thought I was strange, I was always lonely.

Even as I grew up, those kinds of questions didn't leave me. In fact, they made me ask even more intensely and persistently about myself and the human essence. In the process of finding answers to those questions as I passed through adolescence and entered adulthood, I developed new insight about myself, human beings, and the human brain. I became enlightened to the fact that my brain is my life—that it is everything. Whatever I may desire in my life—health, happiness, success, and even enlightenment—can only be achieved through my brain.

About 20 years ago, I compiled the brain development principles and methods that I had investigated and experienced into a comprehensive self-development system called Brain Education. These principles and practices have been used by all kinds of people seeking health and self-development. This system has been presented in various ways, including school educational programs and corporate training.

Today, Brain Education has become an academic discipline in its own right. A research institute and graduate university has been established in Korea to facilitate more specialized research, teaching, and dissemination of the program. The national government in Korea recognizes Brain Education trainers as a specialized profession. Furthermore, high school students are discovering their passion and self-worth through the Benjamin School for Character Education, an alternative school at which they mature and complete dream projects successfully using Brain Education principles and methodology.

This isn't the first time I've written a book about the brain. A few of the books I've written on brain utilization have even become international bestsellers. But this book is the most comprehensive of them all, containing updated, refined, and improved principles and methods of Brain Education. I've been refining this method for more than 20 years through research, development, and application in the everyday lives of hundreds of thousands of people all over the world.

This book doesn't seek to focus on the anatomical or neurophysiological functions of the brain. Rather, it explains how to use your brain to discover your value, to recreate the story of your life, and to claim a new destiny. I especially want to emphasize that improving your life through brain development is a skill that anyone can understand, practice, and apply to everyday life. By mastering this skill, you can bring fundamental changes to your life.

Your Brain Operating System

I view the brain as similar, in some ways, to a computer. Granted, the brain is far more complex and can be modified through self-directed intention, which is certainly not the case with computers. However, I think it is useful to think of the brain as having an operating system that we can change and upgrade. Like a computer, your brain processes information through an operating system—in this case, the system of beliefs and preconceptions through which you interact with the world. A central message of this book is that you have the ability to upgrade your brain operating system continuously so that your brain eventually achieves its full potential.

We get an owner's manual when we buy a car, a computer, or any other technological gadget, but unfortunately, we don't get one for our most complex technology—the brain. Wouldn't it be great if we could just look in a manual to find out how to manage our emotions, how to maximize our abilities, and how to find peace in a hectic world? In a way, though, we do have the owner's manual—but we must relearn how to read it. It exists in the form of the inherent wisdom that is every person's birthright. If we can just get out of its way, all of this wisdom is right there, written into the very nature of the brain itself.

My life has been a process of rediscovering, resetting, and upgrading my brain operating system. *Who am I? What is the purpose of my life?* Fundamental questions about life provided the turning point that made bright lights come on in my brain. And as I found the answers to these questions, my life changed drastically. Through intense self-reflection, I discovered the goal that I really want to achieve, and my brain helped me reorient my life toward this dream. Everything I've ever needed to achieve my dream, I've obtained through my brain.

No matter what it is you want right now, you can make it a reality. If you have a dream, don't hesitate. Choose that dream with courage. As you continue to have constant conversations with your brain, make those dreams come true. If you don't yet have a dream, confidently ask your brain to find one. Your brain will listen with keen ears and do its best to find what it is you really want. Considering the tremendous power hidden in your brain, what if you never used it fully? What if you lived a life of unsatisfactory days until you drew your last breath? Wouldn't that be a true tragedy?

No matter who you are, if you approach it with love and respect, your brain will throw its doors open for you. More than anything, I hope that through this book you will turn your brain into the most supportive friend imaginable. This friend could become the greatest strength for you on your journey toward actualizing your Authentic Self—who you really are. As you communicate and interact with your brain as if you were talking with a dear friend and kindred spirit, I hope that you awaken to the infinite value and potential that you have, and that you make it a reality.

As I've worked through the years to develop and spread Brain Education, the greatest gift I've received is the rediscovery of the greatness of the human spirit. It has been incredibly heartening to see many people recover their sense of confidence, courage, harmony, and peace through interaction with their brains; to see that blossom into understanding, respect, and love for other people and other life forms; and especially to see these changes in the younger generation. I believe that the way to address the challenges facing humankind and the earth is to awaken the greatest and most noble qualities possessed by human beings. We already know all too well that, if the human consciousness isn't mature enough to think of the whole earth and all humankind, even the most innovative technology could end up being a calamity rather than a blessing.

What makes humans truly great is our capacity to actualize the noble desire to help others beyond our immediate personal gains. These are the ultimate latent powers of the human brain. If we fail to create a peaceful and sustainable earth civilization despite having been given the power of this expansive and incredible brain, wouldn't that be a real disgrace? If we were to make these goals the number one priority of humanity, our brains would certainly accomplish that greatness. In that moment, the brain of humankind will go beyond simply being a "smart brain" to proving itself to be a true Power Brain.

Spring 2016
Ilchi Lee

1

Three-Pound Universe

CHAPTER 1

Welcome to Your Brain

Did You Bring Your Brain?

Did you bring your brain? It's a question I often ask attendees at the beginning of my public lectures. Everyone laughs, and they all respond, "Yes!" as if the answer were obvious. Then I ask them again, "Did you really bring your brain with you here? Really?"

When I ask again in this way, audiences start thinking, trying to identify my intent. And then, when I feel the time is right, I quickly add the following: "There is one condition for listening to this lecture: You have to make sure your brain is really present, here and now. If it isn't, please bring it here now."

The brain controls all our physical and mental activities, from the most important vital functions of our bodies to our high-level cognitive functions, but it doesn't have the sensory nerves to feel itself, and it doesn't have the motor nerves or muscles to move itself. Since it's contained in a hard skull, we can't see it with our eyes or touch it with our hands. Most of us live our lives mostly unaware of the existence of our brains.

Of course, everyone who comes to a lecture brings their brains, but most of them do so only physically. Attendees "consciously" bring their brains once I've asked them, "Did you bring your brain?" That's when they finally start to become "aware" of the existence of their brains.

Unless our head aches or our memory fails, most of us don't concern ourselves with our brains. We often think that they lie outside the realm of our influence. Although we know intellectually that the brain gives us the ability to enjoy our five senses, we forget about the brain itself because we can't directly experience it. We don't often think of it as part of our body. Moreover, we're often taught that the brain's intellectual capacity is genetically preprogrammed, sadly negating the notion that we might develop and transform our own brain. But the reality is that the brain never stops adjusting and rewiring itself. You can constantly develop and change it in a positive way.

The Most Extraordinary Thing

It's common to hear the human brain compared to a computer, and many people even suspect that computers and brains work in much the same way. Some even imagine that the sophisticated computers that send spacecraft to Mars, for example, far outstrip the abilities of the human brain. But in fact, no computer in the world is capable of your brain's extraordinary feats.

For example, no computer can create its own programs. Yet your brain not only manages the operation of your body but also constantly refines itself to meet the complex demands of the society in which you live. In addition, your brain readily adapts to different and changing environments, alters them when it needs and chooses to do so, and evaluates its own performance. The most advanced computers on earth are the products of the human brain, but even the human brain will never be able to fully replicate itself in the form of a machine. There will never be anything as powerful, sophisticated, and creative as the human brain—and you already own one! Doesn't it simply make sense to make the very most of it—and, in doing so, to enrich virtually every aspect of your life?

If you decide to maximize the full potential of your extraordinary brain, you must learn how to relate to it as an integral part of your body. No other organ, in fact, is so intimately involved in each human activity. Not only is your brain part of your body, it generates and regulates every bodily function.

But just as joints and muscles stiffen if we fail to move them, our brains lose their agility when neglected. It's vital to stretch and exercise in order to maintain our physical condition, and similarly, we must exercise our brains to keep them in optimal working order. Because your brain is directly connected to every other part of your body, vigorous physical exercise, good eating and sleeping habits, and healthy interactions with others all play important roles in keeping it fit. Intellectual activities such as reading, conversing with others, and playing strategic games are important brain exercises, but the Brain Education methods that you'll learn in this book stimulate the brain in a more direct and comprehensive way.

Inside the Human Brain

Before you can go very far toward mastering your brain, it's essential to grow comfortable with it and begin to get to know it like the friend it is. On the one hand, your brain is everything—it's been intimately involved with every breath, every thought, and every action you've ever undertaken. But on the other hand, it's a physical organ, unlike your heart, liver, or stomach only because of its phenomenal complexity. You don't need to know everything about your brain to bring more consciousness to every aspect of your life. But you do need to have a basic sense of how it works in order to take more control over it and improve your life in the ways you want.

Let's spend a few moments taking a brief brain tour. Place the palms of your hands on the sides of your skull and simply consider that beneath this bony protection is the mass of tissue that matters more than any other part of you—without which all the other parts are useless. As you hold your hands against your skull, note that your brain initiated and mediated the complex processes that moved your hands into position. And as you think about your brain, remember that the organ just an inch or so from your fingertips is what's doing the thinking. When your brain thinks, you think. Your brain is you in a literal and quite wonderful way.

FASCINATING BRAIN FACTS

Here are some interesting brain facts by the numbers. Do you find any of them surprising?

1. The typical brain is about two percent of a person's bodyweight, but uses about 20 to 25 percent of its energy and oxygen intake.
2. Each neuron connects with, on average, 40,000 synapses. And it takes one thousandth of a second for a message to travel between neurons.
3. Your brain contains about 100 billion neurons—so it might take you over 3,000 years to count them all.
4. A piece of brain tissue the size of a grain of sand contains 100,000 neurons and one billion synapses that all communicate with each other.
5. When you are awake, all your neurons together can generate about 10 to 20 watts of power. It's enough electricity to light up a room, though it would be very dim.
6. Teen brains are not fully developed until about the age of 25. Their decision-making can be overly influenced by emotions, because their rational neocortex is still a work in progress.
7. The average brain has around 70,000 thoughts per day, and 70 percent of them are believed to be negative.
8. If you lose blood flow to your brain, you'll last about 10 seconds before you pass out.

▶ Wrinkly, Squishy, and Pinkish-Gray

You've probably seen pictures of the brain and are familiar with its appearance. It's pinkish-gray and folded in on itself, creating a maze of meandering surface indentions. These folds create greater surface area for brain connections, making a highly efficient brain fit into a relatively small space; a piece of brain tissue the size of a grain of sand contains about 100,000 brain cells. The brain is protected by a skull and also by being suspended in a liquid environment.

The texture of the brain is said to be similar to soft tofu or gelatin, but with a network of web-like strands inside. The average human brain weighs three pounds, and it's a little smaller than you might think—about the size of a grapefruit.

Humans don't have the biggest brains among all animals. That honor belongs to sperm whales, whose brains weigh 17 pounds. But we have the highest ratio of brain weight to total body weight, about two percent. The brain of a sperm whale is more than five times heavier than a human brain, but in terms of body weight percentage, your brain is 100 times the size of a sperm whale's.

▶ Brain Cells and Neural Connections

At the microscopic level, the brain possesses a special kind of cell called a neuron. Neurons are the basic building blocks of our brains. All information in your brain is transmitted from a single neuron to a neighboring neuron, a process that's repeated neuron-to-neuron many thousands of times for even the simplest thought, recollection, or movement.

Neurons communicate with each other via synapses, tiny spaces between neurons across which electrochemical signals arc. Neurochemicals—chemical messengers produced in your brain—are released by each neuron for the express purpose of linking with a neighbor and activating it to "fire" in turn at other neurons. Billions of these connections have been created in our brains, and new connections are made every time we think a new thought or learn something new. Bioelectric signals travel at lightning speed through these connections, giving rise to our thoughts, emotions, and sensations. This happens at a speed 25,000 times faster than anything the fastest computers currently in existence could do.

Your brain performance depends not on the number of neurons but on the information network of neurons and synapses. The more synaptic connections that exist in your brain, the more intimately connected its neurons are, resulting in increased overall functioning of your brain, and therefore you.

When you were born, your brain possessed 100 billion cells. Every day, as many as 100,000 of these brain cells die. Neurochemical reactions, psychological stress, physical shock, and aging all contribute to cell loss, as do lack of sleep or exercise, poor diet, and certain drugs. Yet, even if you live to be 100 years old, about 96 percent of your brain will remain intact. And although all of us lose brain cells, brain mass can actually be increased. How can the brain become heavier when there are fewer brain cells? The more you use your brain, the more synapses form between existing brain cells, increasing brain density. This continual brain development and "growth" is both our responsibility and our divine gift.

Unlike a computer—in which changes in the information it receives, stores, or transmits have no structural effect—changes in information can alter the physiology of your brain, both subtly and dramatically. When you learned to speak as a child, your physical brain changed, growing ever more dense with new synaptic connections between neurons. The change in information when you learned a new word literally changed your physical brain forever. It's this lifelong interconnection that distinguishes your brain from machines—and that makes you capable of virtually limitless things.

Any kind of learning—whether it be the magic of language or the

NEURONS AND SYNAPSES

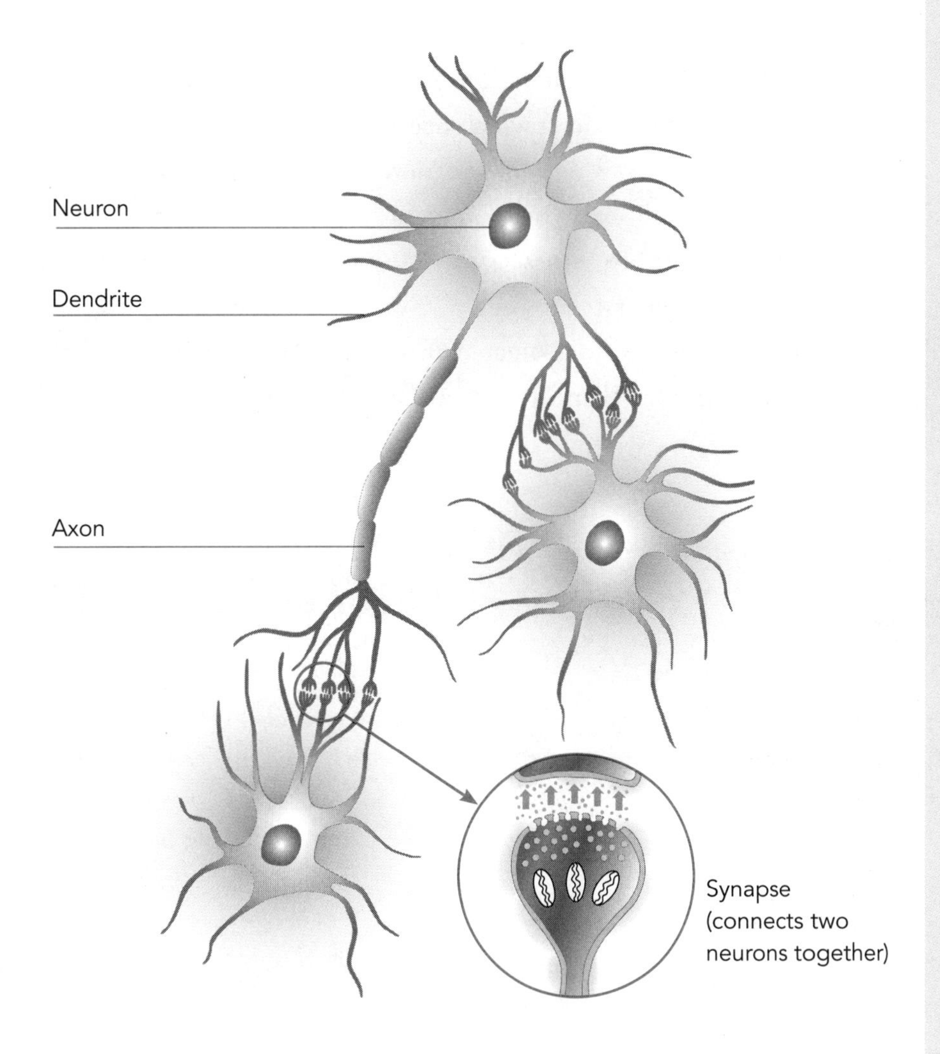

Typical Neural Network Maps During Early Growth Stages

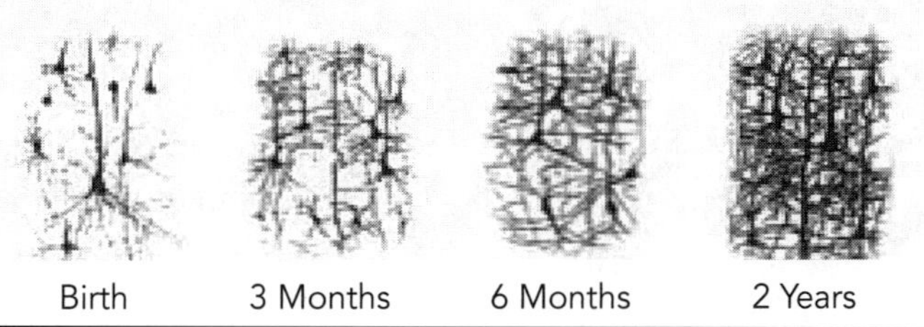

fine-motor skills involved in pitching a curve ball, the mastering of a yoga position or the accumulation of life lessons we call wisdom—represents the addition or alteration of neural pathways. These pathways are both the network along which neurochemical energy travels and the elaborate system by which information is processed. Your understanding of the world around you, your value system, personality, memories, skills, and even habits—these are the deeply ingrained physical patterns of well-traveled neural pathways.

Because your brain is capable of constant change, everything it controls—that is, every element of your life—is capable of change, too. You

YOUR BRAIN ON A MODERN LIFESTYLE

Our modern lifestyle is changing our brains. There's some evidence it's not all for the better.

1. Our attention spans are getting shorter. In 2000, the average attention span was 12 seconds. Now, it's 8 seconds. That's shorter than the attention span of the average goldfish, which is 9 seconds.
2. Surprisingly, millennials (aged 18 to 34) are more forgetful than baby boomers. They are more likely to forget what day it is or where they put their keys than their parents!
3. The chronic stress of daily life changes the structure and function of your brain. The part that retains memories (the hippocampus) shrinks, while the part where fear and anxiety reside (the amygdala) grows.
4. We evolved to live in nature. Sitting indoors all day is highly unnatural and stressful to the brain and body. The sensory deprivation from working in bland indoor environments takes a major toll on higher-order cognitive functioning like our ability to solve problems, create, and think.
5. When we don't eat, hunger-inducing neurons in the brain cannibalize themselves as a last ditch source of energy. So, in very real ways, dieting can force your brain to eat itself!
6. Electromagnetic frequencies emanating from your computer and mobile phone can rupture delicate brain cell membranes, causing them to leak. This means that harmful toxins can enter your brain cells and helpful chemicals in your brain cells can leave.

can learn new tricks every day—from a quicker route home from work to a new language, and from the functions of your new mobile phone to a lucid understanding of how the universe began. When you learn how to play golf or the piano, you forever alter your physical brain. Even when you seek to add new spirituality to your life, you literally change your brain. Because new information, experiences, and practices physically change our neural pathways, it turns out that even the deep transformation we call enlightenment is anchored in our neurons and the synapses that connect them.

Three Layers of the Brain

The brains of all animals, large and small, perform an astonishing array of activities. Even the brains of the smallest creatures constantly monitor and control life functions and natural healing processes. What, then, makes the human brain so special? That becomes much clearer when you look at your brain in light of the evolutionary process that created it. The three distinct brain layers that now co-inhabit the human head emerged successively over the course of evolution.

▶ The Basic Brain—the Brainstem

Cup one hand at the base of your skull, where it meets your neck. Underneath your palm, your hair and skin, your skull, and a thin layer of protective tissue called the dura is your brainstem—sometimes called the reptilian brain because it's the key component of all reptile brains. As humans have evolved, we've continued to possess this deep brain structure that's been with us from the very beginning. In evolutionary terms, your brainstem is the oldest part of your brain, and it is the guardian of your life.

Every bit of information that travels from your body to the higher centers of your brain must first pass through your brainstem. It's involved in cardiovascular system control, respiratory control, pain-sensitivity control, and alertness. Imagine having to think before you took a breath, or needing to remind your heart to pump, or having to consciously summon white blood cells to the site of an infection. The critical necessity of thinking through each moment of survival would leave you no time for anything else. But you don't have to pay incessant attention to the interaction of your brain and body because your brainstem does that for you, unconsciously and without interruption. The gift of the reptilian brain is relegating basic survival to the unconscious, allowing our conscious energies to be directed toward higher concerns.

▸ The Middle Brain—the Limbic System

Now, place your hands on both sides of the back of your head, with the base of your palms resting on the tops of your ears. Deep within this area and surrounding your brainstem are the several structures of the limbic system, sometimes referred to as the mammalian brain because all mammals have it. The small and cylindrical medulla oblongata, located where your spinal cord meets your brain, regulates respiration and blood pressure. The pons swells above the medulla and helps control balance and movement. The thalamus relays sensory information from nerve endings throughout your body to the higher centers of your brain, where it's recognized and acted on. Controlling your food intake, sex drive, endocrine levels, water retention, and autonomic nervous system is the adjacent hypothalamus.

It's your limbic system's autonomic nervous system that ensures your day-to-day survival. Its "sympathetic" system controls your "fight or flight" response to danger or stress, increasing your heart rate, blood pressure, and circulation, releasing food energy to your muscles and adrenaline and other neurochemicals in your brain to help you meet sudden challenges.

THREE-LAYER STRUCTURE OF THE BRAIN AND ITS FUNCTIONS

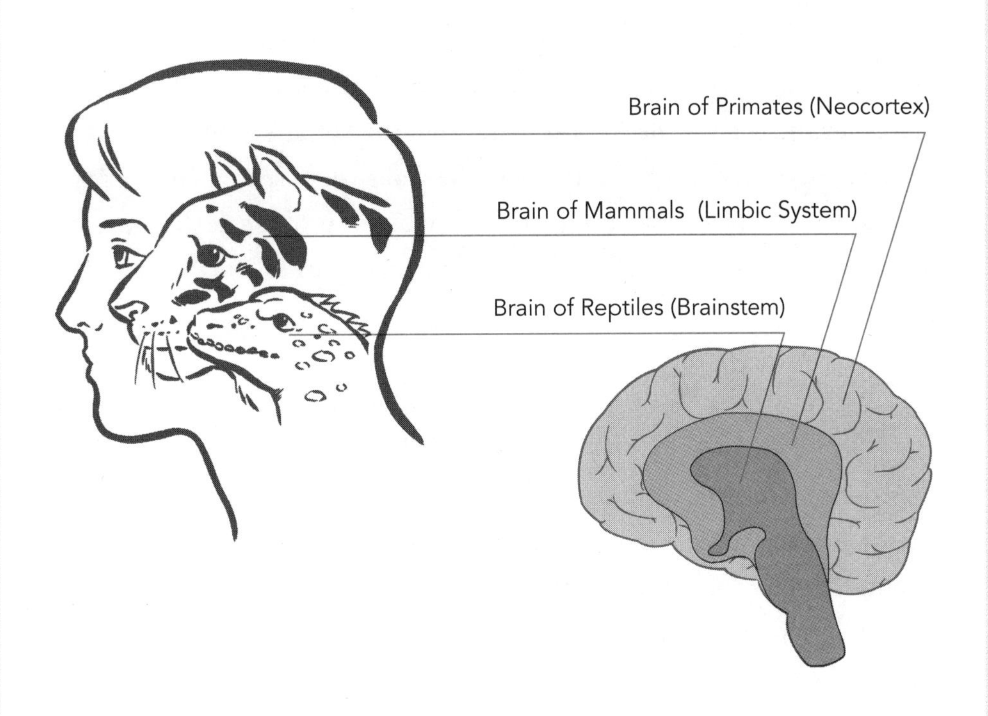

Brain Layer	Evolutionary Stage	Functions	Characteristics
Neocortex	Primates	Logic, Intelligence	Individual
Limbic System	Mammals	Emotions, Reactions	Group
Brainstem	Reptiles	Life Functions, Natural Healing	Universal

Your "parasympathetic" system, on the other hand, mediates "rest and digest" functions—calming your heart rate, stimulating digestion, storing food energy for later use, and inducing sleep.

Your limbic system plays a role in sexual arousal, sensations of pleasure and pain, and your varied and fluctuating emotions. It's also tightly linked to the thinking and consciousness centers higher in your brain, and contemporary scientists are increasingly convinced that skillful problem-solving involves the emotion centers in the limbic system as well. In spiritual terms, the gifts of this part of the brain can be seen as connecting us to others, offering us information about how to feel safe and secure, providing the pleasures of the body, and allowing us to truly appreciate the physical experience of our lives.

▶ The New Brain—the Neocortex

Spread the fingers and thumbs of both hands as widely as you can and rest them across the top of your skull, with your little fingers touching your eyebrows and your thumbs reaching as far to the back as possible. Beneath your palms is the 90 percent of your brain that makes up the cerebral cortex, often called the neocortex or "new brain" because its evolutionary development in humans makes it the youngest of animal brain structures. The many folds and undulations of the walnut-shaped cortex are what we commonly think of in visual terms as "the brain."

This is where all your higher-level functions are located, including language, memory, analysis, and the complex attribute we call consciousness. With the unique development of the neocortex, humans have been able to create incredibly sophisticated communication systems, organize societies, fashion ideologies and religions, investigate and explain the natural world, and create art and aesthetic beauty.

Your cortex is divided into right and left hemispheres. These, in turn, are made up of specific structural areas called lobes that are specialized for language, conceptual thinking, sensory perception, visual-spatial tasks, body orientation, attention, and the initiation of muscle movement. Although the two hemispheres are anatomically similar, there are key differences. If you're like most people, the role of your left hemisphere is more analytical than that of the right, controlling mathematical, linguistic, and analytical processes. The right hemisphere normally is the center of nonverbal thinking, visual-spatial orientation, and the holistic perception of relationships.

In every healthy human brain, however, both hemispheres are actively engaged in virtually every undertaking, and they constantly communicate and interact via a large bundle of nerve fibers known as the corpus callosum. Your cortex is resourceful and malleable enough that when trauma or disease disrupts function in one area, it often can "reprogram" itself in another—even in the opposite hemisphere.

Your neocortex mediates both your basic instincts and your highest ideals, and it is solely responsible for your conscious interaction with the contemporary world in which you live. Without the neocortex and its extraordinary ability to observe, contemplate, experiment, and act, you would never engage in meaningful work, drive a car, sing sweet lullabies to your child, or report your most profound experiences to your friends and loved ones. The great gift of this part of your brain is that it holds the keys to your most expansive potential, your ability to consciously transform your life and the world, and your capacity to connect with something much larger than yourself.

▶ Acting as One

The neural pathways in the reptilian brain, the mammalian brain, and the new "human brain" operate in constant harmony as you conduct your life. Each of these brain structures is essential to your well-being and your survival. Although it's the neocortex where you perform your fanciest stuff, without the complementary actions of the other areas of your brain, your most impressive work couldn't be accomplished.

It would be impossible for your neocortex to imagine and execute a painting, for example, without the emotional involvement of your limbic system and its critical role in controlling the arm muscles and mediating the visual feedback from your senses. And without the utterly unconscious operation of your brainstem, you wouldn't be able to paint at all because your heart wouldn't pump and your lungs wouldn't take in oxygen.

Each of us can be grateful, on the other hand, for the evolutionary

BRAIN-BOOSTING FOODS

A balanced, healthy diet benefits the brain immensely. Remember this simple rule of thumb: What's good for your body is good for your brain.

1. **Berries of all sorts,** including blueberries, strawberries, raspberries, and blackberries, help boost your brain's memory.
2. **Whole grains** release glucose—the brain's energy source—slowly into the bloodstream, keeping you mentally alert throughout the day. Opt for 'brown' cereals, wheat bran, granary bread, and brown pasta.
3. **Fish** contain plenty of omega-3 fatty acids, which promote a healthy brain, heart, joints, and general wellbeing. Focus on high-fat fish like salmon, sardines, and herring.
4. **Broccoli** is a great source of vitamin K, which is known to enhance cognitive function and improve brainpower.
5. **Tumeric,** usually used in curries, has powerful anti-inflammatory and antioxidant properties. It reduces plaques associated with Alzheimer's disease and dementia.
6. **Nuts** are a great source of vitamin E, along with leafy green vegetables, asparagus, olives, seeds, eggs, and whole grains. Vitamin E helps to prevent cognitive decline.
7. **Dark chocolate** is a deliciously decadent source of antioxidants. Due to the fat and sugar content of dark chocolate, limit yourself to about one ounce per day.
8. **Tea** assists healthy blood flow. Green tea is especially good for the brain, as it has been shown to regenerate brain cells.

benevolence that separates the brainstem and the neocortex. Without the ability of your lower brain structures to filter sensory input and direct it to the proper region of the brain, you'd experience life as a chaotic, confusing, even painful bombardment of stimuli—akin to the overload of sensory input that many people with autism suffer. Without that separation and filtering, fearful thoughts might suddenly stop your breathing, or a lover's kiss might so enthrall you that your heart would race uncontrollably, even dangerously.

I believe it's a mistake to consider only the neocortex as central to our human character. The emotions that rise in your limbic system have a profound influence on your relationships, decision-making, and sense of purpose—in both positive and negative ways. Learning to recognize and manage your emotions is a critical life task, and its importance can't be overstated. My many years of spiritual training have also convinced me that constant communication between the brainstem and the higher brain structures is the ultimate source of our brains' power and potential. If you can skillfully awaken your brainstem, you can harness primal life energy and tap into the limitless source of natural healing power.

Scientific evidence demonstrates that in a state of high concentration, activity in your neocortex and limbic system slows and your brainstem takes on a heightened—if still unconscious—role. Your greatest potential and truest creativity arise from the integration of the original life force that lies deep within your brainstem, the emotional breadth provided by your limbic system, and the experimental powers of your neocortex—the three structures working in beautifully coordinated and intricate balance.

Often, one part of the brain undermines another, as when rational thinking is overcome by emotion. Fear may motivate someone to make an irrational decision, or the rational mind may suppress the full expression of emotion. My Brain Education methods seek to educate all three layers of the brain, getting them to work together harmoniously rather than compete with each other.

Our current educational system usually focuses only on the top level of the brain by emphasizing rational thinking, language development, and mathematical skill. But my experience has led me to conclude that people's health and happiness are greatly compromised if they have busy heads full of facts and figures but no tools to help integrate their "thinking brains" with their emotional and subconscious brains. The basic principles and practical methods in this book will let you use your three-layered brain in an integrated way, developing it into a powerful whole brain.

CHAPTER 2

The Best Traits of Your Brain

The Brains Outside Your Brain

Although the brain is one of our body's organs, it's different from the others because it integrates and judges information and issues commands. The brain is connected to all the other organs and body parts through networks of nerves. In most cases, the brain issues orders, and the other organs receive instructions. However, two parts of the body are exceptions—the digestive tract and the heart, sometimes called the "gut brain" and the "heart brain."

The digestive tract and heart aren't simply connected with the brain; they also have their own neural networks. They communicate internally using the same types of neurotransmitters that the brain uses, and they also seem to be able to make non-intellectual "judgments." These are fed directly to the brain, and in many cases the brain's judgments and choices follow this feedback. You could say that the digestive tract and the heart are issuing orders to the brain. The intestines and heart also are special in that they have their own hotline for communicating directly through the endocrine system, immune system, and vagus nerve—unlike other organs, which exchange information only through the central nerves that pass through the spine.

▶ Gut Brain

We sometimes talk about having a "gut feeling" when we meet someone for the first time, or we're told to "trust our gut" when making a difficult decision. These euphemisms suggest that there's more going on in our digestive tract than the processing of food and elimination of waste.

As you may have experienced, our stress, anxiety, and emotions easily affect our digestive tract. Our gut brain, or enteric nervous system, receives input about stress and more from the central nervous system via the autonomic nervous system. These systems work together without our conscious awareness to produce our bodies' stress response, which involves changes in the digestive tract. As a result, we may feel "butterflies" in our stomach or get a stomach ache, diarrhea, or constipation when we're nervous, anxious, or fearful.

We can use these feelings to clue into our body's condition and some of the subconscious information our nervous system is taking in and processing about the world all the time. Is something making us nervous about a person or situation, even though we don't know why? Have we eaten something that doesn't agree with our body? By listening to our gut feelings, we can become more aware of this information and use it to make healthier decisions for our lives.

This process also goes in reverse. By caring for the health of our digestive tract, we can influence our stress response and emotions. This effect on the central nervous system is an important aspect of the extensive enteric nervous system, which includes hundreds of millions of neurons and can operate independently of the brain if the connections between them are cut. For example, people who suffer from imbalances such as depression, anxiety, and attention-deficit/hyperactivity disorder (ADHD) are more likely to have digestive issues such as irritable bowel syndrome (IBS) than people who do not. Doctors have found that treating the associated digestion problems alleviates the psychological ones. In addition, the enteric nervous system produces about 95 percent of the serotonin and 50 percent of the dopamine in the human body. These neurotransmitters are critical to our emotional well-being.

Our digestive health may also affect our cognitive ability. For example, eating foods that our digestive tract and enteric nervous system react to may make us feel tired and "fuzzy" in our heads.

Another major player in the gut-brain connection that influences digestion, mental health, and emotional balance is not part of our body at all. It was recently discovered that the bacteria that live in our gut also play an important role. They have a symbiotic relationship with our body, and have been found to influence anxiety, cognition, mood, pain, immunity, and neurotransmitter production, serotonin in particular. By making sure we have the right amount of the kinds of bacteria that are healthy for our gut, we can improve our overall health.

While many details about the gut-brain connection have yet to be discovered, it's clear that the health of our head brain is closely linked to the health of our gut brain. Brain Education stresses the importance of the abdomen with core-focused exercises that stimulate and improve its condition. It also teaches us how to listen to the condition of our gut better in order to reinforce the connection between our conscious and subconscious minds.

▶ Heart Brain

Thanks to cutting-edge technology enabling us to make scientific observations as never before, we know that the heart is a highly sophisticated organ—much more than a simple pump—that contributes in marvelous ways to our total human consciousness. Independent of the brain's cerebral cortex, the heart's neural center can learn, remember, and make functional decisions, at least on a subconscious level. And it influences the brain in our head by sending back messages that affect thinking patterns, perception, and emotions.

From the energy point of view, it could be said that the heart brain is often more powerful than the head brain. Although the heart brain contains fewer neurons, the electromagnetic field it produces is 60 times greater in amplitude than that of the head brain—and it penetrates every cell of the body. Moreover, the magnetic component is 5,000 times as

HEALTHY BRAIN HABITS

Incorporate these daily lifestyle choices to make your brain fit, focused, and recharged.

1. **Take a nap:** Even just 15 minutes of shut-eye time can boost your memory, cognitive skills, and energy level. But no more than 25 minutes. It may make you feel groggy.
2. **Focus on one task at a time:** No multitasking, please. By focusing on just one task at a time, you can keep your brain working at maximum capability and accomplish more than you imagined.
3. **Exercise regularly:** Find 15 to 30 minutes a day and get moving. Just a walk around the neighborhood can do wonders and benefit your brain.
4. **Have a good night's sleep:** Sleep deprivation is the number one cause of fuzzy, disjointed mental function. Get seven to nine hours of sleep per day. Sleeping less speeds up the aging process of your brain.
5. **Meditate daily:** Meditation benefits nearly every part of the brain. Spend time every day in meditation. You'll feel more relaxed and truly will be in a better state of mind.
6. **Be optimistic:** Being optimistic not only helps you enjoy life, it also does wonders for your brain. When you think positively, your brain can be a huge beneficiary.

strong and can be detected several feet away. For millennia, human beings have spoken of love as being centered in the heart and of people as having a magnetic attraction to one another. It appears that when we interact with others, we literally walk into their heart magnetic field, and a whole range of communication happens between hearts when we do.

The heart brain may be the source of our intuitive abilities, too. A study published in the *Journal of Alternative and Complementary Medicine* correlates the participants' heart-rate variability to a "pre-stimulus," a person's response to certain kinds of information split seconds before it is actually presented. For example, a person's heart might begin racing moments before terrifying photographs are seen. Thus, it appears that the heart brain, in a kind of "body premonition," can receive and respond to stimuli before the head brain processes them.

Rhythm is the language the heart uses to communicate its emotions, and the heart's rhythmic field has a powerful influence on the brain. The heart's beating patterns change significantly as we experience different emotions. Negative emotions such as anger or frustration are associated with an erratic, disordered, incoherent pattern of heart rhythms. In contrast, positive emotions such as love or appreciation correlate with a smooth, ordered, coherent pattern of rhythmic activity. This pattern is linked with a notable reduction in internal mental dialogue, reduced stress perceptions, increased emotional balance, and enhanced mental clarity, intuitive discernment, and cognitive performance. A happy heart makes your brain happier and stronger.

▶ Everything Is Connected

Brain Education doesn't ignore the dynamic relationship between the main processing center of the primary head brain and the secondary gut and heart brains. In a way, everything in the body can be seen as an extension of the brain, since everything is connected to the brain through the energy and nervous systems. New discoveries about the gut and heart brains make the importance of this even clearer. Even the other organs, such as the liver and kidneys, are seen as "little brains" that deserve proper attention for overall brain health.

Both gut brain and heart brain health are addressed specifically in various Brain Education exercises. The general emphasis on positive thinking and emotional well-being is important, since both gut and heart brains are clearly linked to emotional well-being and adversely affected by negative emotions and excessive stress. Intestinal Exercise, a foundational activity in the first step of Brain Education, is outstanding for releasing tension from the abdomen and restoring proper intestinal functioning in the intestines. Similarly, the emotional clearing exercises that make up the third step of Brain Education—Brain Refreshing—will strengthen and clarify the heart field that's so important to our relationships and sense of well-being.

Three Traits of Your Brain

Based on the scientific research so far, neuroscientists consider three things to be the human brain's most important characteristics: complexity, changeability (plasticity), and infinite potential. As a brain philosopher and brain educator, I'm glad that my personal experience with my own and other brains led me to the same discovery about the brain.

▶ The Brain Is Complex

The complexity of the connectivity between our brain cells is mind-boggling. The brain may be the most complex structure in the entire universe, not to mention the human body. Previously, I mentioned that our brains start out with 100 billion neurons. A single neuron creates 1,000 to 100,000 synapses, resulting in 125 trillion synapses in the cerebral cortex alone. That's at least 1,000 times the number of stars in our galaxy! And each of these synapses is like a minicomputer, ready to contain and process information.

The way this information is processed makes the brain even more complex. A particularly fascinating form of processing is commonly called "pattern recognition." Those studying this phenomenon ask how the brain, even when viewing an object for the first time, knows what kind of object it is. The brain has an uncanny ability to match information perceived by the senses with information stored in its memory, which helps us make sense of unfamiliar things.

For example, if we see the letter A in a fancy new font we've never seen before, we'll still be able to recognize it as an A because it matches information we hold in our brain about the letter. We're also able to read a handwritten letter A, even though everyone's handwriting is unique. The human brain perceives the letter A as an A regardless of how it's written. Thanks to this pattern-recognition capability, we're able to understand and use a variety of symbols—including language—and we can engage in the cognitive function of abstraction, which finds and universalizes the common elements of different objects. This allows us to interact well with each other, too, since we're able to read and react to the meanings of facial expressions, despite their great diversity in different individuals.

Understanding this brain characteristic is central to the development of artificial intelligence. Thanks to the application of pattern recognition principles, we now use phones that can understand commands spoken by humans and convert handwritten notes into text for storing or sending by email.

Where and in what form, then, does information on such patterns exist in the human brain? The answer to this question hasn't yet been precisely determined, but researchers are certain that it's not a one-to-one relationship, like information stored on a hard drive. Rather, it's believed to be a kind of multilevel structure that's still not fully understood. Stated simply, specific information isn't stored in a specific neuron or circuit. Rather, identical networks or neurons can participate simultaneously on many levels and carry different information, depending on the levels on which they're operating. In short, our brain is extremely complex, and the amount of information it can handle is virtually infinite.

▶ The Brain Is Always Changing

The brain likes change. Change is happening in your brain right now, in the very moment you're reading this book. If you feel fascination with the content of the book, if you're moved or even inspired by some part of it, then the changes taking place in your brain will be even greater.

Just a few decades ago, scientists generally agreed that a person's brain no longer changes after they reach a certain age. Even after the lifelong potential of the brain to change was recognized, it was commonly held that brain cells are continuously lost following birth and no new brain cells develop. It's now understood, however, that synapses and neural circuits definitely change throughout life, and that new brain cells are also created regardless of age. Neuroscientists call this property of the brain "plasticity."

There have been many cases of miraculous recovery from brain injury, thanks to the brain's plasticity. In one case, despite the fact that doctors had completely removed one hemisphere of a patient's brain, the other hemisphere fully adopted the missing hemisphere's functions. The patient's brain eventually functioned completely normally, as if it had both hemispheres. In another case, a patient showed cognitive abilities on a level that could be called "genius" even though he had only 10 percent of normal brain volume. Conversely, there have been cases where a specific area of the brain has been removed or the neural network in a certain part of the brain has been cut, resulting in a totally different personality or a great loss of cognitive ability.

The changeability of the brain is, in fact, a great hope to us all. It means that painful memories of the past can be forgotten or healed with time, and we can always have new experiences and accept new information. Thanks to this brain property, we can examine ourselves, alter our habits and thinking, and even change our personalities.

The principle most generally mentioned regarding brain plasticity is "use it or lose it." Although new networks between brain cells are easily created—forming a new synapse takes no more than a minute or two—maintaining synapses is another issue. The number of connections and synapses in the human brain actually reaches its zenith at about three years of age; then, through an incredible pruning process that eliminates unused connections, a stable network is formed. In this way, nature offers maximum potential to the brain and grants each individual the opportunity to accept and respond to environmental stimuli. By boldly removing unused circuits after a certain period of time, it ensures that frequently used circuits will receive plenty of nutrition and energy.

Quality or density of experience plays an important role—every bit as important as frequency and diversity of experience—in forming new circuits and reinforcing existing ones. The formation of new brain circuits can be quite different depending on a person's level of interest. Naturally, we learn much more quickly when we're focused and interested. New circuits can even be formed through experience gained from dreams and imagination, not just direct experience. For example, although taking a trip provides new stimulation and creates new neural circuits in the brain, you don't necessarily have to go anywhere to make this happen. Using your imagination to offer the brain vivid images of a place could provide even greater stimulation and cause more change in your brain than actually traveling there.

Many people think that varied and flashy colors or sensory stimuli help stimulate and change the brain. They often intentionally create such conditions as "an educational environment to stimulate the brain." This is only half true, however. Tranquil concentration and imagination can develop the brain more powerfully than any gaudy external stimuli.

▶ The Brain's Potential Is Infinite

According to a popular misconception, ordinary people use just five percent of their brain's capability, while geniuses use twice that. The source of this idea is unclear, but many people still consider it fact. It might be valid in the sense that we use only a fraction of the brain's incredible potential, but it's not literally true. In actual fact, we still don't know the true extent of the human brain's capabilities.

If we consider the number of possible connections within the brain, we could surmise that there's no limit to the brain's potential—that it's infinite. The brain's multilevel structure makes it possible for the same synapse to be used in many different ways. The brain's network isn't fixed but can constantly change in response to experience, so there's no definite limit to the potential capabilities of the human brain.

The limitless potential of the brain isn't confined to its cognitive aspects. Although they evolve very slowly, our physical abilities can also improve ceaselessly, as shown by changes in the world record for the 100-meter dash. Record times for this event, like many other athletic contests, have continued to get shorter and shorter for as long as they've been recorded. Only a couple of decades ago it was rare for a runner to complete the race in less than 10 seconds, but now that's common; and the current record holder, Jamaican sprinter Usain Bolt, ran the distance in 9.58 seconds. Why is this important in relation to the brain? It's significant because changes in this record don't signify an increase in muscle strength. Rather, most cases are the result of improvements in running technique—which means the brain is working better with the body.

That's why cognitive training is now used along with physical training in the development of athletes. Receiving feedback as they watch scenes of themselves running is commonplace. Other approaches include high-tech medical equipment for recognizing when an athlete's heart can output the most power. The burgeoning new field of sports science has one primary goal: enabling the body to use the brain's functions more effectively.

In this sense, changes in the world record for the 100-meter sprint are, in fact, a record of improvements in brain function. They indicate more than just an increase in speed; they show that people have gotten smarter. A few decades ago, it was thought that there was a physical limit to how fast humans could run. The records have already shown such assumptions to be incorrect. The error was in considering only physical and mechanical data—muscle strength, joint flexibility, bone strength—to determine the maximum speed humans could run. What wasn't recognized was the potential of the human brain.

Now, we merely watch in wonder as we see how quickly a person can run. We've begun to understand that even changes in sprinting records, which might seem unrelated to the brain, demonstrate the infinite potential of the human brain.

2

The Power Brain Basics

CHAPTER 3

The Background of Brain Education

The East Meets the West

My Brain Education methods are drawn from a variety of sources, and they address many aspects of the human experience. They also represent a blending of Eastern and Western approaches to well-being.

I began developing my Brain Education methods when I was studying martial arts and Asian medicine as a young man. They naturally include elements of Eastern philosophy, meditative practice, and traditional Asian healing arts—especially those associated with the Korean mind-body tradition of Tao. Some of these elements have been refined over thousands of years, and I've done my best to adapt them to our modern, technological society. I've also created training methods based on my own energy studies, which I've pursued for more than 40 years.

One of the central perspectives of the Korean Tao tradition is that the substance of the world is energy (known in Asia as ki, qi, or chi). Energy is the foundation of everything in existence. All life forms—including you and me—and also lifeless objects are fundamentally comprised of energy. Though they may differ in physical appearance, their basic substance is exactly the same.

The idea that energy is the source of the world isn't limited to the Korean Tao tradition, It's central to Eastern medicine and mind-body training traditions. Modern quantum physics also views energy as the building block of the universe. It's a well-known fact that physical properties such as color and brightness are the result of differences in energy frequency. Chemical characteristics like taste and smell are merely differences in how particles connect and interact through energy. More specifically, the differences we observe are merely differences in dynamic energy frequencies.

Energy is our most fundamental form and the root of existence. Therefore, to create positive changes in our personal lives and in society as a whole, we must properly understand and use the properties of energy. Detecting subtle feelings of energy and achieving energy balance in the body are important aspects of brain development through Brain Education.

Everything is interconnected, because energy is the substance of all creation. Through energy, we transcend our individuality and connect with all other people, all life, everything that exists. I'll explain in greater detail in the following chapters, but through Brain Education, instead of simply understanding this conceptually, you'll be led to feel and experience it.

When you actually feel energy, you're able to deeply and clearly experience a sense of oneness and connection with other lives and objects. Understanding, love, and respect follow naturally. Developing the heart that seeks to create good for all means that you've achieved what in the Korean Tao tradition we call Hongik. Someone with the Hongik spirit seeks to benefit all people and all life, and to contribute to society as an expression of the highest human virtues, not because of external information or intellectual understanding.

Such characteristics are innate to humanity's true nature, transcending differences in personality, disposition, and cultural environment; they aren't properties that have to be given or created from the outside. Energy and the Hongik spirit form the foundation of all the principles and methods taught in the Brain Education system.

The quickly expanding body of scientific knowledge about the brain is also valued and acknowledged by Brain Education. The last decade of the twentieth century was dubbed "The Decade of the Brain" because of the remarkable insights made possible by new research tools, such as magnetic resonance imaging (MRI) and nanotechnology. We're now able to observe the brains of living people to see how they respond to certain stimuli and how different parts of the brain interact. Discoveries in the twenty-first century have been even more exciting and inspirational, and I believe neuroscience has much to teach us about achieving our personal and collective potential. Along with others, I'm actively seeking to scientifically study the efficacy of Brain Education methods, and this has already yielded some exciting and informative results.

Positive psychology—the study of happiness—also contributes insights to Brain Education. Psychology has traditionally focused on dysfunction—mental illness or other psychological problems—and how to treat it. Positive psychology, on the other hand, examines how ordinary people can become happier and more fulfilled. It is based on the belief that people want to lead meaningful and fulfilling lives, to cultivate what's best within themselves, and to enhance their experiences of love, work, and play. This is consistent with the worldview and philosophical background of Brain Education.

Over the past few decades, trainers have gathered experience and knowledge by applying the Brain Education methods in a variety of environments. Hundreds of thousands of individuals around the world have used these methods, and they have been taught at schools, worksites, and rehab centers. This constant expansion has contributed a great deal to the ongoing improvement and optimization of Brain Education.

The Brain and Spirituality

Each of us has the bone-deep desire to understand the meaning of our lives. When you think about it, the desire to give your life meaning and a sense of purpose is what makes you most human.

I'd prefer that you not equate spirituality, as I speak of it in this book, with religion. As I'm defining it here, spirituality includes the belief that we are beings who transcend the finite individuality of the physical body; a belief in the existence of some kind of absolute power connecting all things; the feeling that we are connected with that power; and an understanding that unconditional love for other beings arises out of these beliefs and feelings. This invests our present lives with deeper meaning and helps us find direction and purpose. People may describe a spiritual experience as sacred or transcendent or simply as a deep sense of aliveness and interconnectedness.

One of the oldest scriptures of the Korean Tao tradition, the *Chun Bu Kyung*, beautifully summarizes the essence of human spirituality through its 81 characters. One of the key concepts of this ancient text is the triad of heaven, earth, and humanity. The essential message is that good and evil, life and death, heaven and earth are not opposites, but parts of the same cosmic harmony. The text places human beings between heaven and earth, suggesting that our essence is identical to the essence that makes up the universe, and that essence is oneness.

My own interpretation of this philosophy is that mankind's highest purpose is to bridge the earthly and heavenly realms. Although we're born into physical bodies with many attributes similar to those of other living creatures on the planet, we have an inborn drive to develop our divine aspect and to reconnect to both earthly and heavenly realms. As we realize our innate divine potential, we become one with the essence of the universe and one with creativity, peace, and love.

In the Western world, the word "brain" triggers medical and scientific images of brain anatomy, but in Korean, the word is full of nuance and metaphor. *Noe* is the Korean word for the brain, and it has connotations of "lightning, electricity, brightness." I'm fascinated that many millennia ago, my forbearers somehow understood that the brain operates electrically. In the words of the *Sam Il Shin Go,* another ancient Korean Tao scripture, "You must find your true nature. Your true nature (God) dwells in your brain."

As it is so beautifully stated in both the Chun Bu Kyung and the Sam Il Shin Go, the endless search for meaning is a universal human experience. We all yearn to live our lives in relation to something bigger than ourselves. The rendezvous point between the greater universe and our innermost being is the brain. Our search for meaning begins and ends with our brain. This is an image that has great appeal for me, and I hope it does for you as well—your miraculous, three-pound brain as the vital link between the essence of who you are and the great mysteries of the universe. When you wonder about your relationship to the whole of the universe, you very literally represent the universe becoming aware of itself. And when you consider the impact of all of the nearly seven billion people currently alive on Earth similarly considering their place in the great scheme of things, you realize the enormous power we collectively have to change our world for the better.

The Power Brain

Certain questions come up again and again when I teach people my Brain Education methods. One of them is this: "What does doing Brain Education improve?" When most people think about improving their brain, they're most interested in becoming smarter in an academic sense. Or they might wish to be healthier or more relaxed. Of course, Brain Education can bring such results, and specialized programs have been developed to target each of those goals. But as a comprehensive educational system, Brain Education's ultimate goal is to create what I call a Power Brain—a productive, creative, and peaceful brain.

A productive brain is realistic and responsible. It uses focus and drive to achieve worthy goals, and it uses time and resources efficiently. Through self-management and self-administration, it's able to complete the goals it has selected for itself.

How productive is *your* brain? You're probably hard-working and responsible. Yet most people complain that they have difficulty focusing, or maybe they procrastinate or spend too much time on the Internet. Can you imagine how much more productive you'd be if you mastered the art of concentration? It's not surprising that in today's world, we have a hard time focusing. We're inundated with information, so we constantly have distraction buzzing around us. The exercises of Brain Education are designed to help you get control of your brain so you can focus on moving toward whatever it is you want to be in the world.

Creativity is another attribute of a Power Brain. A creative brain can think flexibly and exhibit imagination freely. It can picture a bright future without collapsing under the burden of reality, even when life is extremely difficult in the moment. Creative people think of solutions when they confront obstacles on the journey toward their goals.

Creative brains aren't just important for artists and musicians. Everyone needs a creative brain, and everyone has this capacity. Growth and change are critical parts of life, but they aren't possible without creativity. Albert Einstein famously said, "We can't solve problems by using the same kind of thinking we used when we created them." In other words, we have to keep our thinking flexible or we'll be stuck in the same place forever. You must be able to imagine yourself as a better person before you can become a better person. We must first be able to imagine a better way of living before we can become a better world.

Peacefulness is the third characteristic of a Power Brain, reflecting how and for what the brain is used. This doesn't only mean being free of conflict and worry; it means using the brain for the good of the many—pursuing Hongik. If you use your brain to harm others, yours isn't a Power Brain, no matter how smart it may be.

The ability to use our brains peacefully often depends on the kind of information we store in them. A Power Brain contributes to realizing peace by producing bright, positive information. Unfortunately, many people hold on to information that does just the opposite. For example, many believe they must aggressively compete with and "beat" others in order to prove their worth. In reality, cooperation is often the better path. Or maybe you hold resentment about past events that are no longer relevant. This is information we can let go if we're determined to create a peaceful brain.

Developing a true Power Brain isn't just an accomplishment for a single individual; it is a gift to all people. We're living in times that demand that humanity step up and evolve to a higher, more workable way of being. Your determination to change your brain for the better is a big step in that direction.

CHAPTER 4

Exploring Energy

The Bridge Between the Body and Brain

I believe that we are energetic beings. By embracing this idea, we can open ourselves to greater health, happiness, and peace. Cultures all over the world hold this understanding and have given energy many names. Pacific Islanders call it *mana*; Australian Aborigines call it *joja*; Indian Hindus call it *prana*. In Asian cultures, it's *chi*, *qi*, or *ki*.

Especially in the East, people have long believed that life energy flows through everything in the universe. They've studied this energy over thousands of years and have deduced a set of principles by which it operates. Asian holistic healing modalities—including acupuncture, acupressure, qigong, tai chi, and yoga—are all based on understanding how energy works in the body. They view energetic health as the bedrock of physical health, emotional well-being, and spiritual growth.

My Brain Education system also views energy as a necessary element for developing a Power Brain. To get the most out of my methods, it's important to understand underlying universal energy principles and to learn how to feel and utilize energy on your own.

Energy is the bridge linking the body and mind. It is the essence of life, moving and flowing freely. When energy coalesces and becomes dense enough, it's transformed into a form of energy that we can see and touch. Energy's continuous joining together and drifting apart comprises the rhythm of life. Everything in existence undergoes constant energetic change. Ancient Asian texts teach us that the things that surround us—and even we human beings—are temporary manifestations of energy.

We're immersed in this grand flow of energy every moment of our lives, but we can't feel its currents unless our senses are properly attuned. Our busy minds and overdependence on rational thought have obscured our natural ability to sense the energy vibrations that define our existence—but it's possible to awaken this innate ability. By opening blockages in energy pathways, you can recover health and natural balance. When you develop energy sensitivity, you'll be able to utilize the potential of your body and brain more fully. And you'll be able to use the information transmitted on energy pathways.

Energy Pathways and Energy Points

We all know that our body has a circulatory system and a nervous system. Blood and oxygen flow through the circulatory system, while the nervous system carries information via chemical signals. If the circulatory system is analogous to plumbing, the nervous system is analogous to a telephone network. However, connecting two pipes doesn't mean that water will flow through them. In order for that to happen, you need power to drive the water. Likewise, just because two telephones are connected

THE RELATIONSHIP BETWEEN
THE BODY, MIND, AND ENERGY

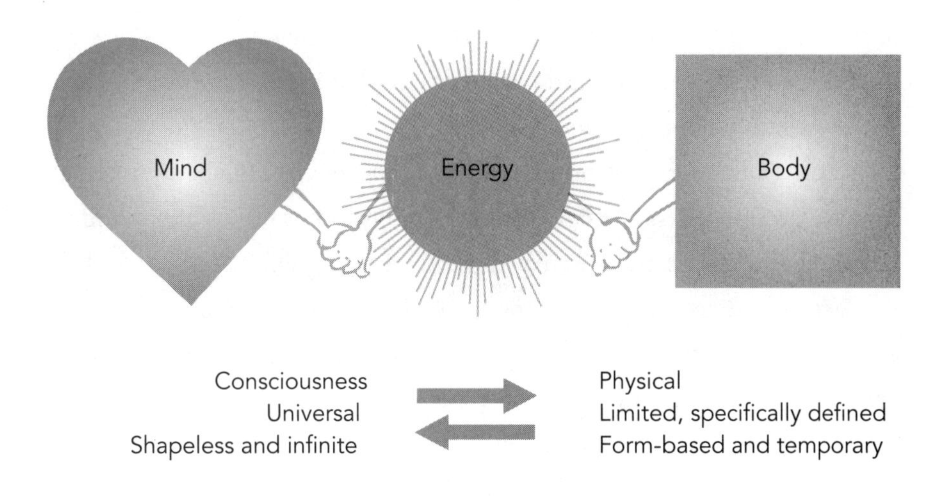

doesn't mean they can communicate. You also need electricity to power the lines and equipment. What, then, is the power that drives the human body? What moves the oxygen, blood, lymph, and neurotransmitters in the body? I believe it is ki energy.

Energy travels throughout the body along a system of pathways known as the meridians. It doesn't travel through a fixed, predetermined highway system, and its pathways aren't closed and specifically defined like the circulatory and nervous systems. Rather, meridians are pathways along which energy flows in its highest density, forming a network of "roads" through the process of continuous passing. According to Asian medicine, we have 20 major meridians in our body.

Principle energy points on these meridians are used in acupuncture and acupressure. If we think of meridians as the railroad tracks along which energy trains travel, then meridian points—or acupuncture points—are the stations where the trains stop. Just as people enter and exit trains at the stations, energy enters and exits the body at meridian points, which are also energy storage and distribution centers. The flow of energy pauses at a meridian point in order to provide life force directly to the organs and body parts associated with that particular point. About 365 meridian points are known to exist.

When our meridian points are open and energy flows unimpeded, we have optimal energy balance of body and mind. On the other hand, if our meridian points are closed and the meridian system is blocked, then the lack of energy supply will sooner or later be manifest as a physical or mental ailment. In Eastern medicine, the application of acupuncture, acupressure, moxibustion, or energy healing helps to restore balance and equilibrium in this energy system.

Sensors all over the body are connected to the brain, which manages the body's natural healing processes. When a signal is received from a particular place in the body, the brain initiates healing mechanisms, mostly triggered and controlled by hormones. The meridian/acupuncture points work as sensors in this process. When we stimulate these points, the effects are felt not only in the corresponding body parts, but also in the brain. Signals are sent to the brain telling it to begin repairing the body. Meridians, meridian/acupuncture points, and the body's endocrine system all play a role in this signaling process.

▶ Important Energy Points on the Head

Now, I want to introduce you to the meridian points that are most important for my Brain Education methods. As you learn the methods, it will be helpful to be familiar with these.

- BAEKHWE: Located on the crown of your head, this point is at the intersection of an imaginary line between the ears and a line connecting spine and nose. Baekhwe literally means "intersecting point of 100 meridians." Sometimes called "Great Heaven's Gate," this is where ambient energy flows into the body.
- JUNJUNG: About one-and-a-half to two inches in front of Baekhwe, this is another point where energy flows in. Junjung is called "Small Heaven's Gate."
- INDANG: Frequently called the "third eye" in the West, this is between your eyebrows. When this acupuncture point is activated, you might experience heightened sensory perception.
- MIGAN: Located at the top of your nose, this point is used for relieving headaches, insomnia, and dizziness.
- INJOONG: In the center of the valley between your nose and lips, this point is used for revival from fainting, shock, and weakness.
- TAEYANG: Located on the temples, between the eyes and the tops of the ears, these are important activation points related to the brain.
- AHMUN: This point between the first and second vertebrae is where the neck and head meet. It's said that a blockage here leads to language disabilities.
- OKCHIM: Okchim refers to two separate points an inch to each side of the slightly protruding point in the back of your head.

IMPORTANT ENERGY POINTS ON THE HEAD

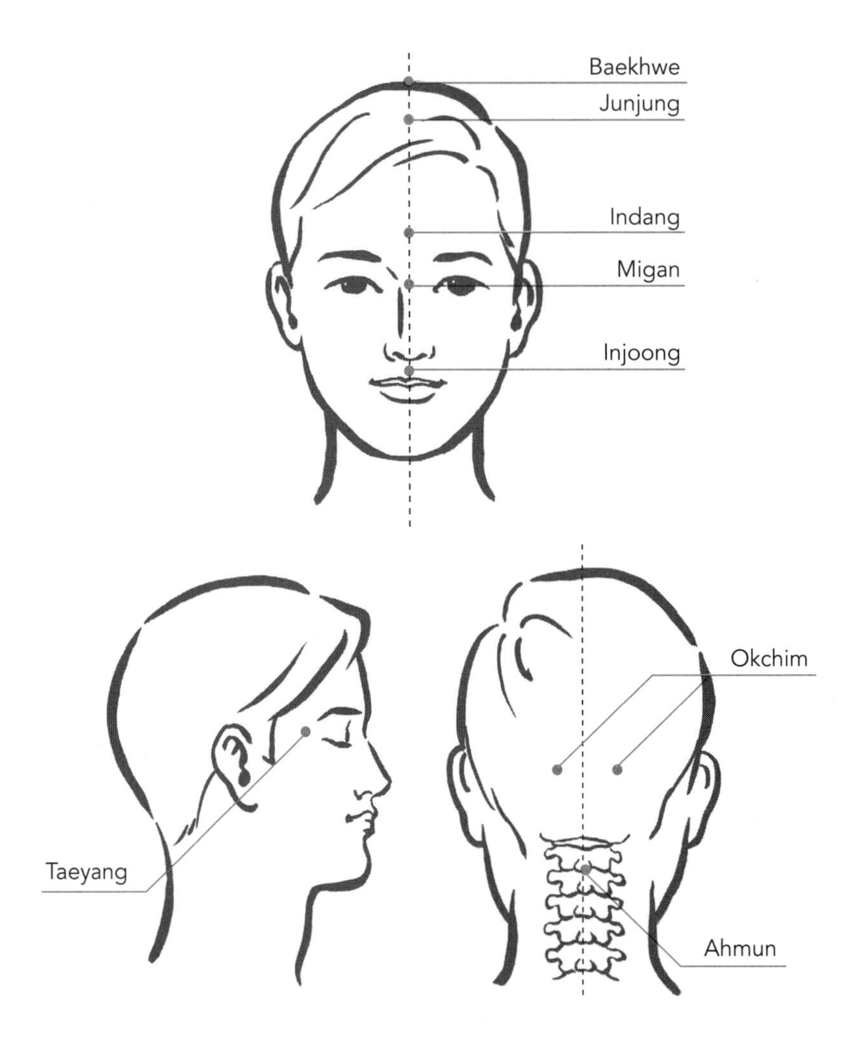

Key Energy Centers

Besides energy pathways and energy points, we have energy centers where energy is gathered and stored. Chinese healing traditions call these *dan tien*, and in my native Korean they're called *Dahnjons*. Directly translated, Dahnjon means "field of energy." Basically, Dahnjon has the same meaning as the word *chakra*, which means "wheel" or "circle" in Sanskrit, and is considered an energy bundle in the human body. The Dahnjon doesn't exist on a material level the way our internal organs do. Instead, it's part of a system existing only in the dimension of energy. With enough energy sensitivity training, you can tangibly feel the gathering of energy in the Dahnjon.

In my Brain Education system, we focus on three Dahnjons: in the lower abdomen about two inches from your navel (lower Dahnjon), in the middle of your chest (middle Dahnjon), and in the center of the forehead (upper Dahnjon). The three Dahnjons have their own unique properties and are defined by the roles they play.

The lower Dahnjon acts as the fuel tank in which energy is stored for circulation throughout the body. When your lower Dahnjon is strengthened, the overall energy balance of your body is restored, amplifying your natural healing power. You exhibit more patience and drive, and you develop a stronger sense of self-confidence. Red is the symbolic color of the lower Dahnjon.

The middle Dahnjon is associated with energy control. It's at the exact center of the chest, between the breasts. Because emotional energy is controlled here, strengthening of the middle Dahnjon imparts a peaceful and loving feeling. Blockage of the middle Dahnjon due to negative emotions and stress can have an undesirable effect on the nervous system, leading to many diseases. The color of the middle Dahnjon is gold.

The upper Dahnjon is linked to the intellectual and spiritual aspects of our existence. When the upper Dahnjon is strengthened, you develop clarity, creativity, and insight. You're able to see the big picture and feel a connection with the divine nature of the world. Blue-violet is the symbolic color of the upper Dahnjon. When you strengthen all three Dahnjons, you'll develop physical and emotional health, conscience, intellectual ability, and spirituality of a much higher caliber.

Key Energy Principles

You can develop your body's energy system by understanding the principles by which it operates and doing exercises to open and strengthen it. Since energy is the primary bridge between body and brain, this is also critical to brain development. Here are some key energy principles used in my Brain Education program.

▶ Energy Follows the Mind

This most basic of energy principles emphasizes the brain's focusing power. In Korea, we call this *Shim Ki Hyul Jung*. This literally means that where the mind goes, energy follows, bringing blood and transforming the body.

Try a simple exercise to experience the principle yourself. Breathe in and out a few times to relax your whole body. Focus intently on the center of your palms. Keep focusing and imagine that your palms are getting hotter than the rest of your body. After a while, if you measure with a thermometer, the temperature of your palms actually will have increased compared to the rest of your body. This happens because your conscious concentration sends energy to your palms, increasing circulation and warmth.

When you develop greater ability to focus energy with your brain, you gain the ability to send energy to any part of your body, or toward any goal you set. An amazing switch located in your brain makes it possible to draw on the infinite energy of the cosmos at will. With enhanced concentration comes an increased ability to control this access to energy.

When you've aligned consciousness, energy, and your body with a single intention and have developed the strength and maturity to maintain and protect that intention, you'll recognize your brain's amazing power. You'll see your intentions—which begin as thoughts in your mind—coming into being in the world. You'll have become a creator in the fullest sense of the word.

The principle of energy following where the mind goes can be compared to the process of concentrating light with a magnifying glass. If you move the glass around instead of leaving it in one place, then the sunlight will scatter. But if you fix the magnifying glass in place and focus it precisely, sunlight will collect and enough heat will build up to create fire. Our consciousness is like this. Like light through a magnifying glass, a diffused and scattered mind has weak energy, while a mind focused in one direction produces powerful energy.

This principle is fundamental for using your brain creatively. When consciousness is concentrated by your brain's ability to focus, energy starts to gather. This in turn starts to attract the material necessary to manifest the intention you've set.

The "law of attraction," discussed in many books, is based on the same principle: you'll attract what your energy and thoughts are focused on. Ultimately, the invisible creates the visible. It's crucial to be mindful about your choices, including your thoughts, words, and actions. You need to develop discipline and will, which align your words and actions with your intentions. The universe is filled with information and energy that you can draw on to manifest your innermost dreams, whatever they may be.

▶ Water Up, Fire Down

Cool water energy and hot fire energy flow simultaneously within our bodies. When the body is in balance, the cool water energy travels up toward the head while the hot fire energy flows down to the lower abdomen, where it's stored. The underlying principle behind this natural flow of energy is called "Water Up, Fire Down," or *Suseung Hwagang* in Korean.

We can readily observe examples of Water Up, Fire Down in the natural world. When the fire energy of the sun shines down, the water energy of rivers, lakes, and oceans rises to form clouds. Consider how

THE STATE OF WATER UP, FIRE DOWN

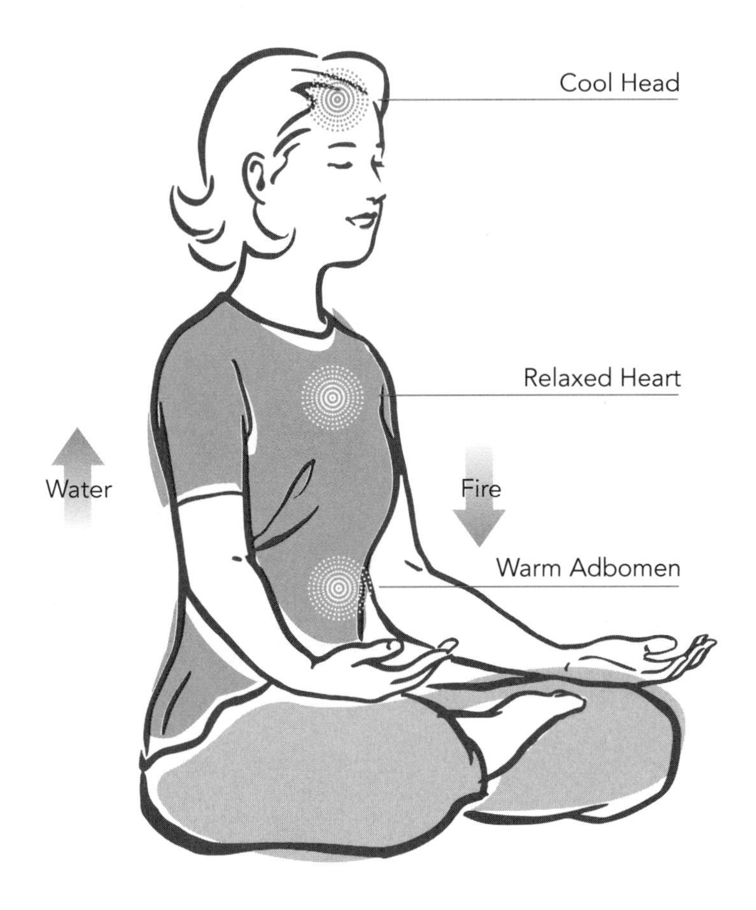

plants obtain energy; they receive fire energy from the sun shining down on their leaves, at the same time drawing water energy up from the ground through their roots. With this energy, plants grow and bear fruit. In winter, when the ground is too frozen to draw up water, leaves fall and no fruit is produced. Life goes into dormancy until the natural energy cycle is again possible.

Water Up, Fire Down is the core principle for human health. When the human body is in balance, cool water energy travels up along the back of the body toward the head, while hot fire energy flows down the front of the body to the lower abdomen. This constitutes a complete cycle of energy circulation. By repeating this, life maintains its balance and continuity. You've probably heard expressions that reflect this principle: "I have a fire in my belly," or "Keep a cool head."

The kidneys and the heart facilitate this natural circulation. The kidneys generate water energy while the heart generates fire energy. When the energy flow is smooth and balanced, the Dahnjon imparts heat to the kidneys and sends the water energy up. This cools the brain and brings down the heat from the heart so that fire energy moves downward. When water energy travels upward along the spine, the brain feels clear and refreshed. When the fire energy flows down from the chest, the lower abdomen and intestines become warm and flexible. The Dahnjon energy center in the lower abdomen performs the most crucial function in this energy cycle.

If the energy flow is reversed and fire energy moves upward, you'll become "hotheaded" and experience headaches, racing thoughts, lack of concentration, and insomnia. You may develop a stiff neck and shoulders and feel "weak at heart" or fatigued. And if cold energy gathers in your abdomen because fire energy doesn't sink, your intestines will become stiff and you'll develop digestive, reproductive, and endocrine abnormalities in the form of indigestion, constipation, or menstrual issues.

There are two common reasons for Water Up, Fire Down not to function properly. The first is that the Dahnjon, which acts to draw in and store energy, may be too weak or inefficient to do its job. In this case, the mind becomes cluttered with incessant thoughts as fire energy moves up to the brain. Stress can also interrupt Water Up, Fire Down by blocking the downward flow of energy through the chest. When this happens, energy backs up and returns to the head, resulting in anxiety and nervousness.

Water Up, Fire Down is an optimal energy balance that facilities the functions of all the organs and maximizes brain vitality. Occurring naturally in a healthy organism, this energy balance has gotten more and more difficult to maintain in modern times because chronic stress has become ubiquitous. Thus, stress relief is very important for your brain health.

▶ The Evolution of Energy

Your energy develops in phases. It starts in your lower Dahnjon, then moves to the middle Dahnjon, and finally goes to the upper Dahnjon. This correlates to the key functions of each Dahnjon—starting with physical strength, then moving on to emotional well-being and fully expressed spirituality. This is called *Jungchoong*, *Kijang*, and *Shinmyung* in Korean—"The body is filled with vital energy, the energy becomes mature, and spirituality is awakened."

This phrase refers to the whole process of energy development and maturation. The lower Dahnjon, the energy center in your belly, is the basis of the entire energy system. Think of it in terms of construction; without a stable and strong foundation, you can't build up to higher levels. You achieve physical health when enough energy gathers in your lower Dahnjon. Your adaptability to new surroundings and your resistance to disease increases. When your lower Dahnjon is filled with vital energy, you experience the truth of the statement, "My body is not me, but mine." You're grounded and able to enjoy the vitality and stamina of your physical body.

As your physical strength develops, the energy in your middle Dahnjon also matures. At this stage, your mental activities become clarified and your relationship with others and the world expands and deepens. Your heart is open to experiencing the natural wellspring of love and peace within. You get better at managing your emotions rather than being swayed by them. You realize that your emotions and your thoughts aren't you, but yours to command.

PHASES OF ENERGY DEVELOPMENT

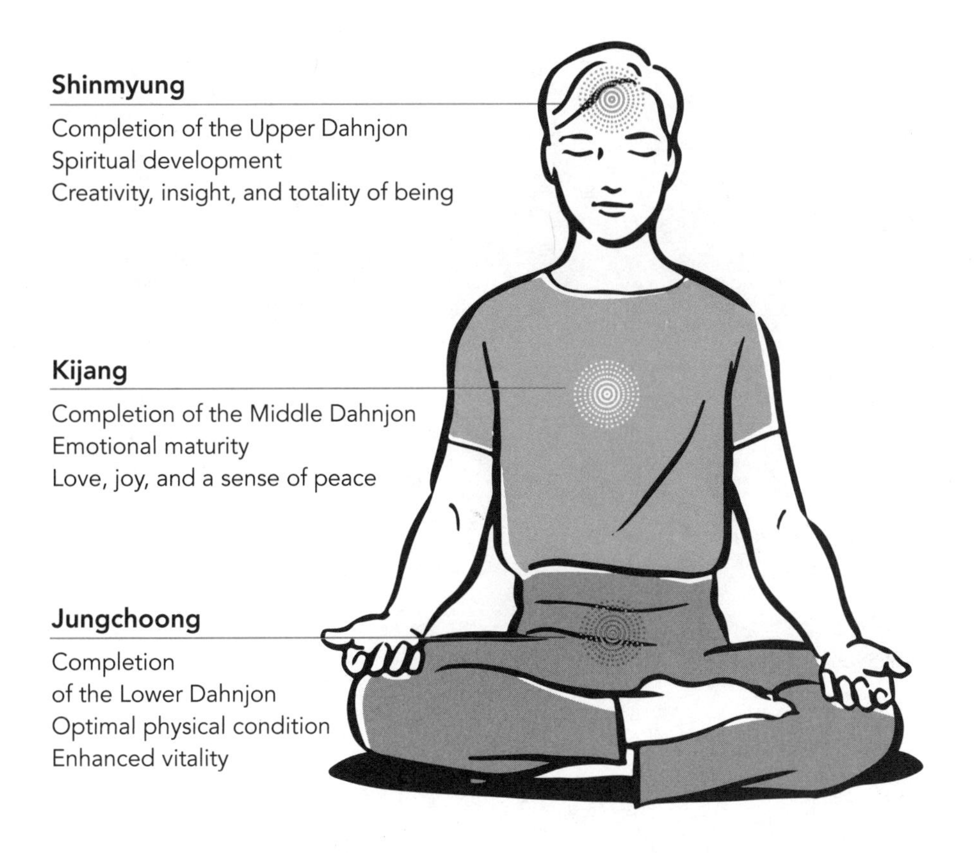

Physical and emotional well-being, in turn, allow you to awaken your spirituality, associated with your upper Dahnjon. Your consciousness develops an elevated awareness, integrating your physical, energetic, and spiritual aspects while imparting a sense of purpose to your life. You gain insight and intuition, frequently "knowing" the underlying principles of the world without a conscious learning process. You manifest consistent creativity and develop an overriding desire to create harmony and order in all that you see.

CHAPTER 5

Seven Tools of Brain Education

Brain Education uses various modalities for developing and training the brain. In this chapter, I'm introducing the seven basic tools that are most typically used. The concrete training methods explained in Part III, Five Steps to a Power Brain, are combinations of these basic components. You can use these seven elements selectively, depending on your specific purpose—managing stress, for example, or enhancing focus, changing habits, or developing personal character.

Breathing

For virtually everyone, what comes to mind when they think about breathing is the lungs. Most people accept as obvious the statement that the lungs breathe. But actually, all the cells in our bodies breathe, not just our lungs. Breathing is an exchange of gases that involves inhaling oxygen from the air with the lungs and then exhaling carbon dioxide into the air. In biology, this is called "external respiration." Breathing oxygenates our blood, which in turn delivers oxygen to all the parts of the body. The body's cells use this oxygen to obtain energy from nutrients, and the carbon dioxide generated in the process is released as a waste product. This gas exchange and energy production at the cellular level is called "internal respiration" or "cellular respiration."

In its most fundamental and substantial sense, respiration is this cellular process, not the mechanical movement of the lungs. Even if the lungs function as they should, our bodies don't breathe unless gas exchange and metabolism occur correctly at the cellular level. The lungs handle mechanical gas exchange, while actual respiration as a basic function of life takes place at the level of the cell.

Did you know that the brain's nerve cells are more sensitive to oxygen supply than any other cells? The brain suffers immediate damage when its oxygen supply is cut off, even for just five minutes. And although the brain makes up no more than about eight percent of the body's mass, it accounts for about a quarter of the body's calorie expenditure. Calories are used in bonding oxygen with nutrients, so breathing is a prerequisite for energy production.

To put it another way, the human organ that breathes the most is the brain. That's why expressions such as "The brain breathes" and "I breathe with my brain" are more than metaphorical.

▶ The Effects of Breathing

Breathing is the most basic and essential activity for maintaining life. We don't pay special attention to it, though, because it happens naturally, whether or not we try to control it. Breathing, pulse, blood pressure, body temperature—these are all vital functions controlled by the autonomic nervous system. In other words, our bodies take care of themselves, without our intentionally regulating them. Breathing is unique among these autonomic functions because it can be intentionally controlled the most effectively.

Purposely raising or lowering blood pressure, pulse, or body temperature isn't easy; only the most skilled people can do so. Intentionally speeding up or slowing down breathing, however, can be accomplished by anyone. And we can indirectly affect our other vital signs, such as blood pressure, pulse, and body temperature, through breath control. In fact, we can control more than the body's physiological functions through breathing. We can control our minds—our thoughts and emotions. This is why Brain Education considers breathing such an important tool for brain development.

Not all breathing is the same, however. There's rough, irregular breathing, and there's controlled, deep, and gentle breathing. You can bring great, positive change to your body, and especially your brain—if you learn to breathe well.

Count your breaths right now. How many times do you breathe in a minute? Is your breathing fast or slow? For an adult, the optimum rhythm when in a state of rest is one breath every 12 seconds, or five breaths per minute. Breathing at that rate maximizes cardiopulmonary efficiency. Seven to 10 breaths a minute indicates that you're slightly excited in a state of moderate stress. Going beyond 20 breaths a minute means you're under considerable stress. There are exceptions, of course, but generally the more relaxed your body and mind are, the more slowly you breathe.

The body's stress reactions are carried out by the autonomic nervous system. This is controlled by the brainstem, which is connected through the spinal cord to all major organs in the body. All vital functions—including respiration, sleep, digestion, heartbeat, and body temperature—are managed by the autonomic nervous system, which maintains homeostasis in the body. The autonomic nervous system is the key to internal stability and balance.

The body's autonomic nervous system includes two subsystems that are opposite and complementary in character. One is the sympathetic nervous system, and the other is the parasympathetic nervous system. The sympathetic nervous system excites us and causes fight-or-flight responses during crisis situations. The parasympathetic nervous system, on the other hand, brings our bodies back to a relaxed state, replenishing energy through digestion, discharging toxins, and repairing damage. The body is able to maintain vital activity safely over time thanks to the cooperation and balance between these two systems.

Exhaling slowly stimulates the parasympathetic nervous system, which initiates the body's relaxation response, reducing our everyday stress and bringing stability of mind. Conversely, if we habitually breathe rapidly, the concentration of carbon dioxide in our blood falls, causing our blood vessels to contract and reducing the amount of oxygen sent to body and brain—which ultimately damages our health.

Breath control is known to reduce anxiety and lower blood pressure, particularly by stimulating the vagus nerve. This nerve extends from the base of the brain to the lower abdomen, and one of its major functions is lowering the heart rate. When the vagus nerve is stimulated, the neurotransmitter acetylcholine is secreted, helping to increase focus and calmness. A direct benefit of more acetylcholine is a decrease in anxiety. Research suggests that consistently practicing breath control will lower blood pressure and heart rate—which in turn results in less wear and tear on blood vessels.

Researchers have found that it's actually possible to change the structure of the brain through breathing. Magnetic resonance imaging (MRI) has shown that the brains of people who've long practiced breathing meditation are different from those of nonpractitioners. Specifically, meditators experience growth in brain areas associated with attention and sensory input processing. Breath control doesn't just temporarily change feelings; it actually changes the brain for the better.

Brain Education uses Dahnjon Breathing (page 118), which encourages deep, light, and natural breaths while awareness is focused on the Dahnjon energy center in the lower abdomen. This facilitates full oxygen exchange to improve energy and blood circulation through the body and brain.

Meditation

What comes to mind when you hear the word "meditation"? "That's something Buddhist priests do," you might think. "I'm so busy. When am I going to find the time to sit with my legs crossed and eyes closed? I have better things to do." "I have so many distracting thoughts that I can't sit still." Or maybe you think meditation is just a New Age hobby that has nothing to do with your real life. Such thoughts all stem from a misunderstanding of meditation.

You may not have realized it, but everyone already meditates. Stereotypes suggest that you can only practice meditation with a candle or incense burning, and that you must adopt a special posture and sit in a special place. Such things, though, are simply used as aids; they're not requirements for meditation.

As you've lived your life, there have probably been a number of times when you've looked back on your thoughts or actions. Probably, at some point in your life, you've looked back on your choices and wondered whether they were right, and whether you might have made better choices. Stopping your immediate responses to stimuli for a moment in this way and turning your mind to look at yourself is the heart of meditation.

What's in your mind right now? Is your mind tranquil and peaceful? Or is it a tangle of busy thoughts and complicated emotions that are stressing you out? Don't you want to manage the things arising in your mind a little better? Don't you want your mind to be peaceful and your breathing to be more comfortable? Don't you want to empty your mind and look at things with a fresh perspective? Meditation makes all this possible.

The key to meditation is to remain completely in the here and now, in this moment. Meditation is not about thinking of the past or the future. Generally, our minds are filled with countless thoughts, both positive and negative. Our minds wander here and there, following the sensory stimulation around us or chasing after information, thoughts, and emotions. Meditation brings us to the present, taming a mind that wanders in the past and future or that immediately reacts to stimuli. Meditation keeps you in your body, letting you observe the subtle phenomena in your body and mind.

Any action that calms the mind and empties it of thoughts and emotions—anything that calls the wandering mind to the here and now—can be considered a form of meditation. You can meditate sitting down, walking, or drinking tea. When you do any of these things in a state of calm focus, the wandering thoughts and emotions that usually make a mess of your head have a chance to quiet down. You are able to see more clearly any situation that you're facing, and you can more easily determine what you need to do next. Wisdom and insights that help you make the right choices pour easily from a tranquil, lucid mind.

Brain Education uses breathing and energy meditations. By concentrating on the breath entering and leaving your body, and by feeling the sensations of life energy in your body, you bring your wandering mind to the here and now. We'll address concrete approaches to meditation in greater detail in the section on the Five Steps to a Power Brain.

▶ The Effects of Meditation

The effects of meditation on the body and mind have been studied thoroughly. One of the most directly observed effects is that meditation changes brain waves to a comfortable, stable pattern. "Brain waves" refers to the electrical current that develops when signals are transmitted between neurons. It's an important index for measuring the state of brain activity.

When you're normally awake and active, beta waves of 13 to 30 Hz (cycles per second) form the bulk of your brain waves. These are commonly called "stress waves" because they frequently appear when you're worried or thinking a lot. When you're resting physically and mentally, or when you have pleasant feelings and your mind is at ease, your brain emits alpha waves of 8 to 12 Hz. Right before you fall asleep, or when you're in a state of light sleep, theta waves of 4 to 7 Hz appear. When theta waves predominate, you experience deep insight; creative thoughts or ideas for solving problems pour from your mind. Delta waves of 1 to 3 Hz appear in deep sleep, deep meditative states, or unconscious states.

In the meditating brain, brain waves gradually change to alpha or theta waves. The slower your brain waves, the more relaxed you are, the more you feel a sense of carefree satisfaction, and the more your mind is at peace. What part of your brain is activated when you meditate? Dr. Richard Davidson of the University of Wisconsin, a pioneer in the study of mind-body medicine, used PET scans (positron emission tomography) to demonstrate that the left prefrontal cortices of a group of Tibetan Buddhist monks were activated when the monks were in deep meditation. This is particularly interesting, because the prefrontal cortex is responsible for feelings of contentment and joy. In addition, Dr. Davidson has identified interactions between the prefrontal cortex and the amygdala, a key center for processing memory and emotion.

Meditation helps recover balance in the brain's hormone secretions, too. It decreases the secretion of noradrenaline, dopamine, and cortisol, which can put you into an agitated, stressful state, while promoting the secretion of serotonin (the "happiness hormone") and beta endorphins, which reduce pain and create pleasant feelings.

Will physical changes take place in your brain if you meditate? A

BRAIN ACTIVITY AND BRAIN WAVES

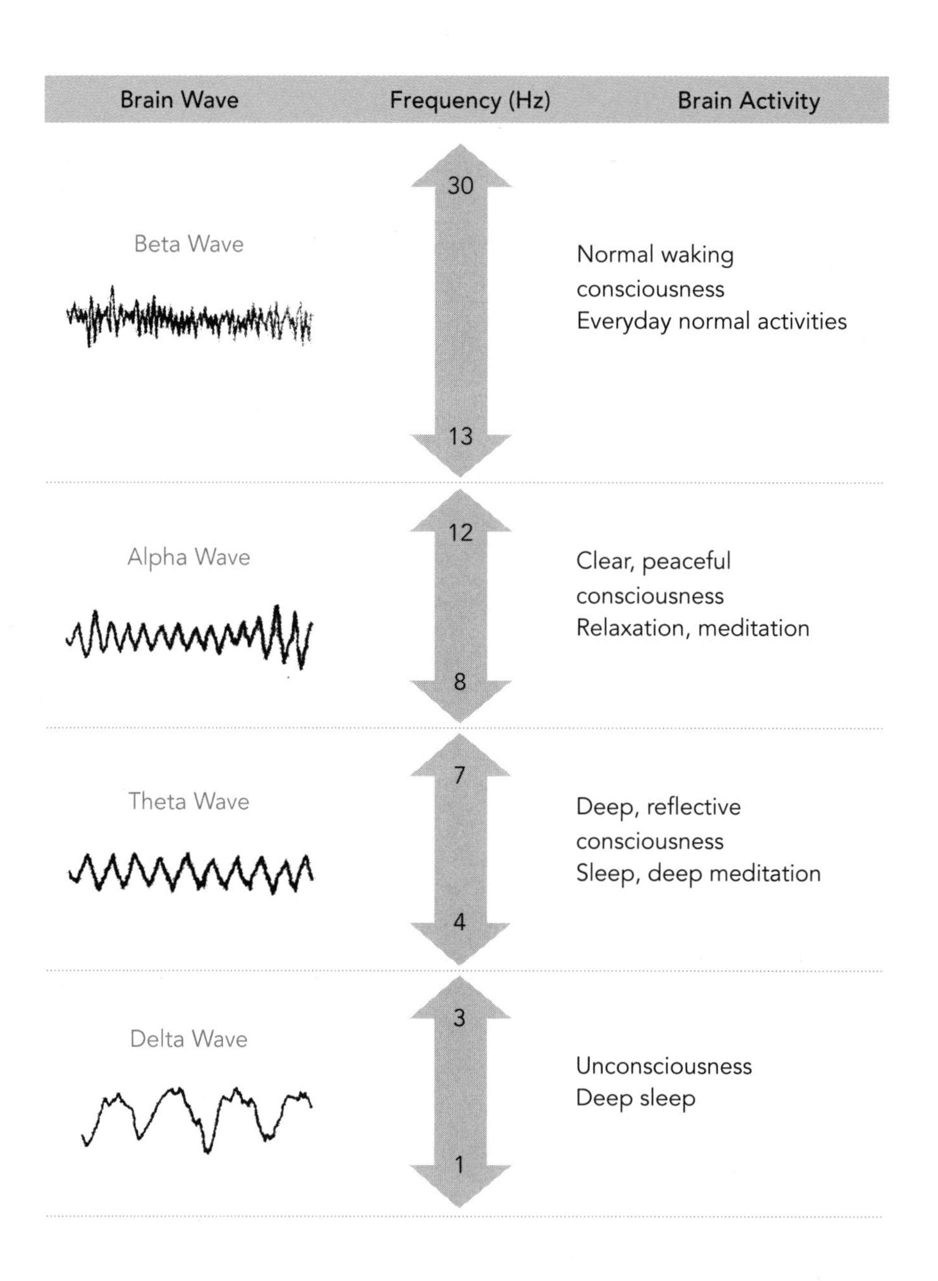

2009 research team at UCLA, led by Dr. Eileen Luders, discovered that the brains of longtime meditators are larger and function better than those of people who don't meditate. Dr. Luders found that the meditators had more gray matter in brain regions that are important for attention, emotion regulation, and mental flexibility. Increased gray matter typically makes a brain area more efficient and powerful for processing information. "We know that people who consistently meditate have a singular ability to cultivate positive emotions, retain emotional stability, and engage in mindful behavior," said Dr. Luders.

A 2011 study team headed by Dr. Sara Lazar of Harvard Medical School found that the thickness of certain parts of the brain increases, not only in those who meditate professionally—like Tibetan monks—but also in ordinary meditators. People from various professional occupations meditated for 40 minutes a day for as little as eight weeks, and then the researchers observed the results. They discovered that the subjects actually developed a thicker hippocampus (associated with memory, learning, and emotional regulation) and brain parts involved in self-awareness, compassion, and introspection. *Meditation actually changes the anatomy of the brain*, not just a person's mood, the study demonstrated.

Neuroscientists have also shown that meditation affects brain areas related to perception, body awareness, pain tolerance, complex thinking, and a sense of self. If you meditate, not only will you receive great mental and emotional benefits, but your body's immunity to disease will increase. You might even live longer.

Science suggests that regular meditation can help lower our stress levels, thus increasing the length of our telomeres, the protective endcaps on our chromosomes. Shortened telomeres make us more susceptible to age-related diseases such as cancer, diabetes, and heart disease. Some scientists think that telomere length may be the most important indicator of biological age and disease risk. It's thought that if you could stop telomere shrinkage, you could avoid age-related diseases.

In the past, meditation was considered the exclusive property of those who practiced spiritual and religious disciplines. Now it has become a mainstream relaxation technique. A National Health Interview Survey has revealed that some 20 million U.S. adults meditate for health reasons. If you really care about your brain, start meditating today.

Energy

Learning to feel energy is important for brain development, because it's a way to feel your brain more deeply and have deeper communication with it. There's no way to move or feel your brain the way you feel your hands and feet, because it has no muscles and no sensory nerves. The most direct way to commune with your brain is through energy and imagination.

We can make ourselves salivate, and we can make our bodies hot, through imagination. As has been verified through a visualization training experiment on athletes, it's even possible to train muscles using only the imagination. These are all actions of the brain. By focusing awareness on the imagined body part and allowing energy to flow there, you can initiate many changes you want to see.

If imagination can cause such changes in the body, isn't it obvious that it can do the same thing in the brain? The only difference is that the brain is affecting itself rather than some other part of the body. You might imagine that your brain is filled with bright, fresh energy, or even that your brain is smiling. Positive images have a positive effect on the functioning of the brain.

In Brain Education, we use energy as a means of communicating with our brains. After all, energy is the basis of everything that exists. Even objects that on the surface appear to be separate are ceaselessly communing with one another through energy. That's why we can perceive and feel things beyond the reach of our five senses. We can develop our brains much more powerfully when we combine imagination with the feeling of energy. More details are explained in Part III, Five Steps to a Power Brain.

Another significant aspect of energy related to the health of the brain is *balance*—or, to put it more concretely, the balance between hot and cold. If your head and belly are to function well, which should be hot and which should be cold? As we know through experience and intuition, your head should be cool and your belly warm. If you're stressed, this balance is broken and you develop symptoms such as headache, indigestion, constipation, and diarrhea. But if your head is cool and your belly is warm, energy is balanced and your organs will function optimally.

Brain Education uses a variety of exercises that help us recover this optimal energy balance. Most exercises that strengthen the lower body and the Dahnjon energy center in the lower belly will help promote this Water Up, Fire Down energy circulation.

Exercise

Perhaps nothing is more important to your overall health and well-being than exercise. It's a truth you already know but can't be reminded of too often. Exercise is essential for maintaining strong muscles and joints, and it's vitally important for your brain.

Numerous studies have demonstrated the positive effects of exercise on the brain. Exercise isn't only for losing weight and creating good-looking muscle. It's essential for a smart brain and a brain that feels happy. Exercising regularly will help you gain the strength and stamina to act on your creative ideas and plans, and you'll build the self-discipline and willpower you need to achieve your loftiest goals.

According to a study conducted at the University of British Columbia, the brain's information-processing capacity and memory improve with just 20 to 30 minutes of exercise a day. The hippocampus, a part of the brain closely related to memory and learning, gets bigger with regular aerobic exercise. It seems that aerobic exercise helps stem cells in the hippocampus divide and grow. Exercise also enhances the brain's plasticity, expanding and connecting its network of connections by increasing the blood flow to the brain. Even the simplest muscle movements spur new synaptic connections.

Another major effect of exercise is that it promotes production of neurotropins and neurotransmitters such as dopamine, serotonin, and norepinephrine, putting the brain into a pleasant, happy state. Exercise is a remarkable stress reducer—even the simplest movement neutralizes stress hormones and stimulates the parasympathetic nervous system. That, in turn, initiates a variety of calming and rejuvenating responses within your limbic system. Complex exercises involving coordination, balance, and diverse movements stimulate multiple brain areas simultaneously, reinforcing the connections between them. Your brain reaps instant benefits when you exercise in novel and unexpected ways. That makes cross-training far more productive than performing precisely the same exercises day after day.

The timeline of human evolution is thought to be about three million years. We've lived life as we do now—as modern humans—at most for 5,000 of those years. Before that, we had mostly nomadic lives, always on the move over mountains and fields. The structure of the human brain was formed long before we began leading "civilized" lives. This means that our brains developed to make active lives possible. In other words, exercise is essential for optimizing brain function.

What sort of exercise is good for the brain? In general, any exercise that's good for the heart is good for the brain. Aerobic exercise in particular improves brain function and helps restore damaged neurons. Experts say that moderate activity combining coordination with cardiovascular exercise—such as walking briskly or dancing—is especially good for the brain. Physical activity of moderate intensity yields the best results, according to scientists. Whenever the body is pushed to release stress hormones, the positive brain effects are eliminated. Brain Education mainly uses exercises of low to moderate intensity, such as yoga and tai chi, along with core-strengthening exercises, a variety of aerobic exercises, and exercises for enhancing left-right brain coordination.

One of the most effective and simple brain exercises is something that we do naturally—walking. Although stepping forward by placing one foot in front of the other may seem ordinary, it's actually a complex process that requires the harmonious coordination of all your joints, bones, muscles, and nerves. Normal walking becomes impossible if an abnormality develops in even one of these components. Taking a single step moves more than 200 bones and 600 muscles in the human body, and it requires multiple brain functions for all of this to happen simultaneously. Walking, in short, is an advanced brain exercise.

We walk virtually unconsciously, but with every step an incredible amount of information reaches the sensory area of the cerebral neocortex through the leg muscles—and all this happens at an incalculable speed. An incessant exchange of complex signals between our legs and our brains takes place while we're walking. Even if we take just one step, information about how we're walking—whether the road surface is safe, how steeply it's inclined, and so on—reaches the brain in an instant. On accepting that information, the brain sends instructions to the legs in real time, leading to the next movement.

In order to walk, we have to mobilize all our body's senses—watching with our eyes, moving our hands to maintain balance, feeling the temperature of the air with our skin, and smelling with our noses. All this information is delivered to the cerebral neocortex. These diverse stimuli help activate the brain.

While we control the movement of stretching out a hand according to our own intentions, the regulation of our breathing, digestion, heartbeat, and body temperature occurs all on its own. The muscles of the internal organs and blood vessels are controlled by the body's autonomic nervous system. This system is subject to less control from the brain because information-integration functions take place primarily in collections of nerve cells called nerve ganglia. That's why brain researchers have given the name "little brains" to nerve ganglia, and why they say that the brain isn't only in the head but is also in the body. To train your nerve ganglia, you have to move your whole body.

Freehand exercises that are done gently and raise only a slight sweat are better for this than exercises requiring intense, concentrated exertion. Gentle, full-body exercise gives the brain pleasant stimulation by repeatedly tensing and relaxing the muscles; in response, the brain increases ganglia functioning by releasing hormones. That, in turn, maximizes brain capabilities. Energy Sensing Exercise (which involves feeling energy) and Meridian Exercises (which sensitize the body through stretching) are among the best for strengthening the ganglia. The most autonomic nerves are gathered in the abdomen and lower back, so Dahnjon–strengthening exercises and Dahnjon Breathing are wonderful for improving brain function and sensitizing the brain. All these exercises are included in Part III of this book.

Our Senses

Through our senses, we can accept signals coming from the world around us, recognize them as information, and respond appropriately. Without the senses, the brain could make no judgments at all. The development of our senses is particularly significant for maintaining a healthy brain and enhancing brain function.

The brain's highest cognitive function is concentration, when it focuses its attention in one place. Concentration is what makes all of our high-level actions possible, from language acquisition to creative work to performance. In the cerebrum, the prefrontal lobe handles concentration. This spot has to be as empty of extraneous thoughts as possible for someone to be able to respond appropriately to changes or stimuli in a new environment. It's easy to make mistakes when this area is filled with the noise of random thoughts; distracted people often make mistakes—breaking a dish, missing a ball thrown at them, taking a false step, giving an off-the-wall answer.

The brain has limited capacity for short-term memory. A common example is failing to remember a telephone number we've just heard unless we quickly write it down. Superficially, this characteristic seems inconvenient and unhelpful, but in fact, that isn't the case at all. Such short-term memories aren't retained unless we hold on to them through concentration; if we try to hold on to them, we can't perform other work requiring concentration. It's like having too many applications loaded on your computer when you're using it—the system crashes. You've probably experienced a computer slowing down in such a situation, just as you've probably experienced your brain being overwhelmed with too much information.

So the brain doesn't permit information to remain in the prefrontal lobes any longer than necessary. But if your brain is constantly exposed to external sensory stimuli, you'll have that much less concentration ability available for high-level mental activities. To make proper use of your brain, you need to be able to cut yourself off from outside sensations. You need to create a free space in your brain's prefrontal lobes.

The first sensory training of Brain Education teaches participants how to reduce the inflow of sensations. It's a simple exercise that anyone can do. Simply take a moment during the day and find a quiet space for meditation, close your eyes, and feel your breath. Like freeing up memory on a computer, this easy meditation cleans the residue of previous information from the prefrontal lobes.

The second form of sensory training is developing the sensitivity of your five senses. Sensitivity of this sort increases with focus, and new senses also develop. We think that we see with our eyes, hear with our ears, taste with our tongue, and feel texture with our fingers. But all of these senses actually arise in the brain; the eyes, ears, tongue, and fingers simply gather information for the brain to process. We can see, hear, and feel because our brains interpret the information delivered through our sensory nerves. When we've felt something new, it means that both domains—our five sensory organs and our brains—are awake. That's why sensitizing the body also awakens and activates the brain.

It's possible to further develop our five senses through concentration. The "energy sense," however, involves developing a completely new kind of sense—what you could call a "sixth sense." New parts of the brain awaken when we feel energy flowing in our bodies. In images taken of the brain, the parts activated during energy sensitivity exercises are quite different from those activated during normal concentration. Virtually the entire brain is activated when we concentrate awareness and feel the sense of energy throughout our bodies. By concentrating on the feeling of energy, we make it possible for our brains to perceive and process information from beyond the five senses.

Information

Information is the brain's food. That's why the brain is always hungry and thirsty for new information. You might think this is just a literary metaphor. Actually, it's a factual description.

Information plays the same role for our brains that food does for our bodies. But while we need food to live, it can also cause problems: indigestion, food poisoning, food addiction, and weight gain or loss. Likewise, information can make our brains sick as our minds become contaminated by information. Yet most of us don't worry about the information entering our brains—we're far more concerned about the food that enters our bodies. Our brains function as well as they do only because they're able to digest and purify information. Imagine what would happen if, from the time you were born, your stomach had been supplied with negative (toxic and hazardous) food to the same extent that your brain has been exposed to negative information. Would you be alive right now?

Develop a habit of examining the bits of information you ingest, thinking of them as food for your body. For your brain's sake, try to refrain from accessing negative information, just as you refrain from eating harmful food. If necessary, try to quit using the negative information you habitually seek, just as you might quit using tobacco or alcohol. It helps to occasionally go on an information fast, just as you might stop consuming food for a short time for the sake of purification.

If you begin to deal with information the way you deal with food, you'll probably be shocked by two facts. One is that the relationship between information and the brain is surprisingly similar to the relationship between food and the body. The other is that once you've managed your brain this way, its condition will improve rapidly—faster than your body improves with a healthy diet.

The brain is the most flexible organ in the body. It changes ceaselessly, likes change, and will change really quickly if we so choose. Two people who've been enemies can one morning apologize, forgive each other, and become like brothers. Although their bodies before and after the reconciliation probably aren't much different, their minds—that is, their brains—are totally different. If you consider and treat the information entering your brain like food entering your body, your brain will change in no time.

Tens of thousands of units of information enter and exit our brains each day. Certain things benefit us; others do not. And although we may recognize and control access to our brains, some kinds of information enter and exit without our being aware of it. We can't live apart from information. Whether we want it or not, we come across it, and we can't help but choose, judge, and act in accordance with information. However, we can either control or be helplessly controlled by information, depending on how we handle it.

Much of the information in our brains was input from the outside; we didn't choose it. We unconsciously accept information input by parents, by teachers, and by society—such as ethics, morals, and religious beliefs. Many people live their lives believing that this is a necessary part of who they are. But all the information in our brains is just that—information. We can assess it, and we can revise or delete it.

All of us should strive to become masters of information instead of being led by it. You should be able to say, "I'm the master of my brain." This signifies a new realization about the "self," the one who sees itself as the user of the brain—and this realization transcends all emotions, thoughts, and information. You are not your thoughts. You are not your emotions, either. And you are not your body. You are not a bundle of information stored in your brain. You're something that transcends all these things.

Your brain is like a high-performance notebook computer. What to do with that computer is up to the user. It can be used to help people or to harm them. Your thoughts, emotions, body, and brain, as well as all the information you hold, are tools that have been given to you. It's up to you what you'll create with them.

Imagination

Imagination is the brain's ability to picture what doesn't exist just as if it did. We can forget our boredom and endure loneliness because we have imagination. If you have an excellent imagination, to some extent you can even resolve physical discomforts such as thirst and hunger, as well as mental needs like boredom and loneliness.

According to studies on the brain's visualization mechanism, anything we look at is broken down through the optical nerve into data, like a digital signal, and then reconstructed as a picture in the brain. Everything we experience—not just what we see—basically follows this same mechanism. Physical stimuli accepted by our sensory organs are converted into code and sent to the brain through its neural network. These signals are then reconfigured in the brain. What's delivered to the brain isn't the physical stimulus itself, but information and data about that stimulus.

Whereas visual perceptions are reconstitutions in the brain of information entering from the outside, the images we imagine are created directly in our brains. In this sense, the only difference between the two is the input pathways; both exist as images in the brain. If the images we imagine are realistic enough, our brains can't tell the difference and experience them as if they *are* real. As we know, imagination is capable of filling our mouths with saliva, bringing tears to our eyes, causing our hearts to throb, and raising goosebumps on our arms.

The brain loves imagination. Linguistic information is best understood and communicated when it's combined with imagination. Sound in particular stimulates the imagination. Long ago, minstrels in the West and folk singers in Korea used a variety of musical rhythms and sound effects when they told their stories. This was probably an effective way to communicate information, ideal for the mechanisms of the brain, especially back when today's imaging technologies didn't exist.

Intuition is often the source of imagination, but intuition doesn't apply only to images created by sculptors and artists. Even the formulas handled by physicists and mathematicians are often first understood intuitively as images. Creation of all kinds begins with the imagination. When we can picture what we want, we can establish goals, and we can then identify the actions we need to take. Because of this, imagination occupies an important place in the Brain Education system, especially in the development of latent abilities.

One fascinating and important fact about imagination is that it contains no negatives. What would pop into your head right now if I told you *not* to imagine fire? You already know the answer. You're already picturing it in your imagination, and what you're imagining is fire. In our imaginations, there are no elements that are "not something" or "something that doesn't exist." "Not" or "nonexistent" are purely intellectual constructs; they can't be visualized.

This fact is important when we form our intentions. For example, the picture drawn in your head when you think "eradication of poverty" is an image of poverty. The picture in your head when you think "the end of war" is an image of war. And when you think "no more violence," you see an image of violence. The creative power of your imagination ends up being used not for what you want, but for something you *don't* want.

To make good use of the creative power of imagination, we have to practice expressing what we want through positive language. We should examine our habits of thinking and speaking, and we should consciously change our thoughts and our words. When you do this, you'll be able confirm that the content of your imagination changes dramatically along with your thoughts and words. Your imagination gains power. Concrete, completely positive imagining makes possible powerful action that has a clear direction.

Fulfilling Your Potential

My intention is to help bring greater health, happiness, and peace to as many people as possible—working with the best insights currently available and with the expectation that all of us will continue to experiment and grow, adopting and expanding new ideas. Our lives are short, and we owe it to ourselves to make the most of them. This book will help you reach the fulfillment that you desire by employing your Power Brain.

Hundreds of thousands of people around the world can already attest to the wonderful benefits to their physical, emotional, and spiritual health that this system has brought. I'll share my five-step system in great detail in the following chapters, including practical exercises that engage the brain in exciting and important new ways. And I'll explore with you how you can use these steps to achieve mastery of your life.

I believe strongly in the usefulness of these methods, and in the essential truth that your brain and our collective brains can indeed create the kind of world we all seek. I encourage you to dive in with an open heart and mind—and, of course, with your remarkable brain.

3

Five Steps to a Power Brain

CHAPTER 6

Experiencing Your Power Brain

Am I My Brain?

The January 29, 2007 issue of *Time* magazine declared bluntly, "You are your brain." In many ways, I agree with this statement, but it is not the end of the story. We cannot think or act without our brain. We do not know how our mind is created, but we can be certain that the brain is the mind's stage for action. But I do not agree that we can completely equate the mind with the brain, as though it were simply a product of a biological machine.

I think that the mind exists not only within the brain, but it is also a phenomenon affected by the interaction of brain, body, and world. Ultimately, you cannot separate the mind from the brain. However, through studying the brain as a distinct organ, I believe that we will be able to understand the principle of how the mind works.

In 1848, the brain of a person named Phineas Gage was injured when a steel rod punctured his skull and passed through his frontal lobe. Amazingly, he survived the accident and appeared to be as healthy as ever. However, his life never really returned to normal. Before the accident, Phineas Gage had been emotionally well-balanced and an excellent construction site superintendent. But after the accident, he became erratic, rude, impatient, and indecisive. His family and friends all said that he did not seem like the same person anymore. The brain damage completely changed his personality.

Cases like this show that personality and character have an intimate relationship with the structural features of the brain. Personality is not something fixed that you cannot change for the rest of your life, but rather it stems from the current traits of the brain, and if there is a change in the brain, then personality may change as well.

On the other hand, if the brain keeps being stimulated by new information, it will change, just as your muscles develop if you exercise. To know this is important because it shows that the self you think you are can change at any time, and that you are not stuck in a limited conception of self. Through this kind of realization, you can avoid the trap of equating your thoughts and emotions with self.

You have to realize that there is an unlimited self in your brain whom you may know nothing about. The brain knows both the self you know and the self you are not aware of. All life experiences are stored in the brain, but these are not all you are. The existence of self is not limited to your memories, experiences, or information.

Strictly speaking, you cannot separate yourself from the brain. But I would like to suggest trying to think of the brain and self as separate entities in order to utilize the brain even better. Let's try to think, "I am the owner of my brain," instead of, "I am my brain." I believe that such recognition will make your life more abundant and exuberant. When you say that you are the owner of your brain, you will be awakened. The awakened self automatically knows the wise way to approach any situation, whereas your brain tries to process information based on primal survival instinct and habits, and you end up making poor choices after all.

Let's say that you feel a huge desire to smoke in a highly stressful situation. One part of your brain will say, "I want to smoke," but another "you" in the brain will observe such a desire and the thoughts surrounding it. And that self may decide, "No! I've already decided to stop smoking this year no matter what! Instead, I'll go for a walk or meditate." This is how the real you starts to take control of the brain.

When you observe the emotions and information arising in your brain and actively intervene in the processes, you can finally make more positive choices in your life. And that's when you can say, "I am the owner of my brain."

The Brain, Not Just the Mind

In my Brain Education methods, I choose to focus on the brain rather than on the concept of "mind" because working at this level lets us identify practical ways to be more aware of the brain and to train it. This can lead you to more permanent and meaningful solutions to problems and a richer and deeper experience of your life and your potential.

As you might already know, the brain is more difficult to master than the mind. Put simply, if you want to stop eating too much, your mind can quickly grasp the idea and articulate it clearly: "I want to stop this—I'm going to stop this." But it's your brain that tends to slip into the well-worn track of doing what's familiar—even if that goes against what your mind states as its goal. This explains why so many people understand the problems they have with their health, relationships, spirituality, and careers, yet fail to act effectively to change their lives.

Your mind must change first, but after that initial intellectual shift, your brain itself requires deliberate and prolonged training to truly change. When you feel the difference between changing your mind and actually changing your brain, you'll be on the way to self-mastery. And you'll make the great discovery that when you work with your brain, you can resolve problems at their root. You'll be able to make changes that free you from things as small as a bad habit or as big as the self-limiting ideas and behaviors that have kept you from achieving your greatest potential.

Shifting Perceptions to Reshape Your Life

As you embark on this exploration, you'll recognize how intimately related outer consciousness and inner consciousness are, and the differences between the thoughts of your mind and the deep workings of your brain. You'll become aware, as well, of the remarkable degree to which you can manage the whole of your life, even if you face enormous challenges.

I hope one day it will be otherwise, but unfortunately, many people throughout the world still suffer incredibly as children. The patterns and habits that arise to cope with the pain of childhood often continue to negatively shape adult lives for many decades. When many people talk about the wounds that go the deepest, they rarely include an event that happened at the age of thirty in this litany. It seems that for many people, what happens from birth to young adulthood is what becomes so locked into the brain that it dictates thinking and behavior throughout adult life, until those patterns are challenged. I know it's possible for people who have suffered greatly to live in the present moment more fully and to redirect their energy and consciousness to healing the past and creating a better future. I've seen the transformation many times.

Neuroscientists have demonstrated that emotional memories are stored in deep brain areas. The amygdala, in particular, holds our conditioned fears, and tests show that its stimulation can cause us to act on the basis of old and no-longer-valid fears. Worse, everyday stress amplifies those mechanisms. But by removing old traumas and managing stress, Brain Education training minimizes negative reaction patterns and empowers better and freer choices.

Managing consciousness is not easy when your life is limited by old and unconscious patterns. But with practice, that relationship reverses. You take control and become so comfortable with directing your thinking and actions that your old unconscious way of being becomes impossible, and you naturally gravitate toward better living.

The Body-Brain Connection

Your brain mediates everything that happens in your body, and although your body will break down eventually and your life will come to an end, you can delay that deterioration and improve the way your body functions by working skillfully with your brain. We all age, but we can stimulate the brain to stay as vital as possible for as long as possible. The natural neuroplasticity of your brain gives you the daily potential to make new connections and to learn, grow, and change throughout your entire lifetime.

If you relinquish control of your life to undisciplined and subconscious tendencies—unhealthy thinking, unrelieved stress, lack of attention to your physical body, and neglect of the psyche and spirit—you are certain to have these things play out in negative ways in your body. And the opposite is also true. You create a strong platform for physical health when you nurture the connections between spirit, brain, and body.

We can be proactive about our health even when forced to cope with the realities of a significant injury or illness. If you are dealing with an injury, illness, or disease, know that your brain can be enlisted in the work of improving your life. It's a matter of choosing happiness—not just when you experience what you think are exactly the right circumstances, but peace and contentment in this moment and in your present situation.

If you're presently in good health, brain empowerment can help you maintain and expand your potential for excellent health throughout your life. Numerous studies demonstrate that reducing stress is one of the most important things we can do to improve and safeguard our health. We all know that reducing stress is a good idea. We're clear about that. So how can stress reduction be accomplished regularly, completely, and as a deeply ingrained habit? This is one of those instances where changing your mind is only the first step. As you now understand, the big challenge is to change your brain.

You've been dealt certain genetic cards in your life. The time and place and family into which you were born are factors, but so are the responses you've made to the opportunities and difficulties you've faced. Examine your life as it is right now and know that how you're living and what you're experiencing are continually being created by your patterns of belief and your behavior.

If you've become comfortable with the discomfort in your life, I invite you to take on the challenge of examining your assumptions and changing what can be changed. Take time to assess your physical and emotional health. What have you come to accept as your normal state of health? Do you hold patterns of belief and behavior that have locked in limitations—and can you consciously challenge them? As you educate your brain, a stronger brain-body connection will improve your health and every other aspect of your life.

Chattering Brain Vs. Composed Brain

An untrained brain often behaves like an overindulged child who lacks focus and easily becomes discontented. Like a spoiled child, the brain of an undisciplined person is afraid to be bored and seeks constant company, music, or visual stimulation. Immersion in the world around you can be a wonderful thing, but balance is essential. If both your free time and your work are saturated with stimulation and you're always talking to people, on your computer, in meetings, solving problems—thinking, thinking, thinking—you can miss the profound ideas and enlightenment that enter the quiet mind. You and your brain need some open space—time that isn't tightly scheduled, a chance to drift and enjoy a lack of stimulation.

When we don't bring balance and conscious intention to our lives, we may spin out of control and get lost in neurotic tendencies. But with new purpose and regular practice, you can create healthful ways of thinking and acting. You can make new brain connections and experience a wonderful sense of self-mastery, with the peace and contentment that brings. You can give up being flighty and become newly focused. What was once overwhelming now can stimulate clear action. The frantic and stressful energy you may have exhibited in the past can become poised and relaxed effort that generates great results.

Living too much in your "head" but without conscious control of your brain is a common problem in modern life. But when people experience the difference between a chattering brain and a composed brain, they quickly prefer the latter. Living with mental peace is the way to thoroughly enjoy your days and nights, and to experience life fully.

Invite Change and Transformation

Change comes whether we seek it or not. The seasons of life impose change, the imperative to provide for ourselves brings us change as we work in the world, society changes, and personal relationships change. Our experiences change us, and things change around us. Some people are naturally attracted to change, while others will do almost anything to avoid it, but the truth is that change can't be avoided. Change is as certain as the reality of death. Coming to terms with this reality, deep within your brain, can free you to live more fully.

I encourage you to flow with the natural energy of life and invite change and transformation by giving them a place of honor in your life. What we resist with inflexibility and rigidity wears us down, but what we explore with grace and conscious attention works to pull our best life toward us. What we envision and how we use our brain to create it make all the difference in what we experience. It's not always easy to begin life anew in a quick, dramatic way. In many cases, your brain will simply lead you to make a series of subtle choices to change your life for the better. Yet I'm sure that once your life is in order, you will connect with the world in wonderful new ways.

Life is meant to be lived with passionate engagement, and your brain is happiest when it is used well. If you think small, you end up living a small life. When you expand your vision to include your greatest potential, you engage your brain in meeting expansive priorities and your largest expectations.

WHERE YOU STAND NOW

Before beginning the five steps of Brain Education, let's find out what you think about some important questions. There will be plenty of time for deeper exploration later. For now, simply write your answers as quickly as you can, "off the top of your head," as they say.

- My physical health is . . . .
- My relationships with others tend to . . . .
- Spiritually, I'd say I'm . . . .
- I'm happiest when . . . .
- I think of change as being . . . .
- I think my body is . . . .
- The thing I worry most about is . . . .
- I'm afraid I won't be able to . . . .
- The worst experience of my life was . . . .
- I'm miserable when . . . .
- My worst habit is . . . .
- My best habit is . . . .
- I know I limit myself when . . . .
- I'd most like to change . . . .
- To fulfill my life's purpose, I must . . . .
- Right now, my life is . . . .
- I will feel I have lived well if . . . .
- Self-mastery will allow me to . . . .

These very preliminary answers will give you a baseline for what your mind thinks about a few important things at this moment in time. As you become the master of your brain, you'll be able to probe your thinking and change your perspectives, your habits of thought and behavior, and your life for the better. If you're willing to play some interesting "brain games" that I'm about to introduce, you can explore these and other questions and have fun in the process. It's fine to keep a healthy sense of skepticism, but also relax into the spirit of exploring new ways of thinking. Your brain will love you for it.

Five Steps to a Big Breakthrough

The five steps of my Brain Education system are a linked series of exercises that are practical, easy to learn, and fun. I've drawn many of them from time-honored Eastern meditative practices, others from contemporary Western understanding of brain physiology and psychology. If you study and practice them faithfully—agreeing that there's no harm in occasionally looking a little silly—you can transform your brain, and even your life. I promise you.

The five steps are organized to match the structure and functions of the brain as well as its physiological characteristics. Each step is functionally linked to the next, so you can easily and effectively move from one to another. Viewed in terms of the brain's anatomical structure and functions, this system begins in the body and activates the three-tiered structure of the brain.

- *Step One, Brain Sensitizing,* is designed to raise overall awareness of the brain and wake up your senses. This step addresses the whole body and brain.

- *Step Two, Brain Versatilizing,* helps make the brain more flexible so that it can easily accept change. This step generally activates the functions of the neocortex.
- *Step Three, Brain Refreshing,* deals with the fixed concepts of the neocortex and the emotional memories stored in the limbic system. The focus is on learning how to free your brain from unhelpful negative patterns of emotion or thought.
- *Step Four, Brain Integrating,* helps you integrate the brain functions of the different layers of your brain and unleash your potential by revisiting core information affecting your life. This is meant to awaken the brainstem and access the original life force that lies deep within it.
- *Step Five, Brain Mastering,* addresses the entire brain. This final step is for learning how to intentionally employ the brain's core functions.

As you go through these five steps, you'll awaken the infinite potential of your brain. You'll become able to use the functions of all parts of your brain in an integrated way. Generally, these steps are done in order, but they all require continuous practice. Many Brain Education training programs use different steps simultaneously.

▶ Brain Sensitizing

In this first step, you'll become very aware of your brain and its importance in your life. Much of the work is done on the physical level, since the connection between body and brain is strengthened at this point. Many mind-body exercises that have a long and honored history in the East are used to awaken your body's multiple senses. As each muscle is moved and each nerve stimulated, corresponding areas of the brain are awakened. As a result, balance and coordination in your body are improved. Breath work helps restore energetic balance while releasing stress and restoring mental clarity.

Basic energy meditation techniques are also used, helping you to develop better concentration and energy awareness. By learning to view ki energy as the source of communication between body and brain, you'll be empowered to begin changing habits that negatively affect your body and mind. Once you've developed basic energy awareness, you can awaken the senses of your brain more effectively.

▶ Brain Versatilizing

Just as the muscles of the body need to be moved and stretched to become flexible, so does the brain. This step seeks to take full advantage of "neuroplasticity," the brain's ability to adjust to new environments and to rewire itself. By challenging your brain to master new tasks, you help it create new connections and develop greater capacity to recognize new patterns of thought and action. Essentially, the goal is to create a highly adaptable brain that can learn quickly and easily.

This step is likely to have a profound effect on your life, because you'll learn to break destructive mental and physical patterns and create new, life-affirming habits. "Bad" habits can be difficult to break because they become, to some degree, hardwired into the brain through repetition. Fortunately, the brain never loses the ability to restructure itself, so new connections and habits can always be created. At the most advanced level of training, this includes changing deeply ingrained prejudices and preconceptions in order to create a better, more satisfying life.

▶ Brain Refreshing

In some ways, this step represents a rebirth for the brain. Throughout your life, you've experienced things that have had a lasting effect on your brain. These have lingered on as a kind of emotional residue that has affected your life, leading to preconceptions and thought patterns that have kept you from reaching your full potential. The intention of Brain Refreshing is to release and clear away burdensome memories and negative information for deep healing and renewal.

Through expressing and releasing emotions rooted in traumatic past experiences, you'll learn to control the contents of your mind rather than be controlled by the whims of emotion. You'll learn to use the energy of your mind in a more concentrated, uninterrupted way.

▶ Brain Integrating

When you've learned to empty yourself of emotional baggage and unhelpful information, you'll be ready to expand your awareness and transcend fixed ideas about yourself and what you're capable of. You'll be ready to answer essential questions about life with honesty and sincerity. You'll empower your brain with new, positive information and be able to create a personal identity based on your newly discovered core values and life purpose. Once you've fully integrated this new identity, your potential for creativity is practically unlimited.

This stage is called "Brain Integrating" because all the layers of your brain work together toward the creation of your ideal life. The left and right hemispheres begin to communicate better, and disparate parts of the brain start to work together in full cooperation. Through this deep exploration, you can discover the part of you that is truly meant to be in charge of your brain.

▶ Brain Mastering

Now that you've discovered the life you truly want to live, you're ready to create a lifestyle based on the goals you develop through understanding that purpose. In this step, you'll maximize your brain's potential by ceaselessly applying the principles and methods learned in the previous steps. In particular, you'll implement in your daily life the self-identity and core values obtained through Brain Integrating. By minimizing the gaps between what you want and your actual life, you'll be able to pour your energy completely into action without internal conflict, creating the results and life you want.

Through the process of Brain Mastering, your brain will continue to transform and solidify neural connections that support the creation of a truly happy life. Increasingly, your brain will be able to find creative, workable solutions to life's basic problems. You'll become more decisive, and your mind will develop the habit of forming more peaceful relationships with other people and the world as a whole.

Keep Your Mind Open

Remember that your life is determined by the choices you make. As you explore the following ideas, practices, and exercises, be aware that your attitude will shape your experience. If you bring sincerity, passion, and earnestness to the journey we're about to take together, you will make wonderful improvements in your life.

I ask that you suspend judgment for a while, keep your mind open, and focus on your experience rather than your thoughts. Your brain needs to experience in order to fully integrate understanding. If your mind is full of chattering thoughts and goes on intellectual side trips as you read, you won't understand things as deeply as if you just relax and experience the powerful dynamics at work within you.

CHAPTER 7

Step One: Brain Sensitizing

Let us consider for a moment what it is about our bodies that we're most interested in: weight, height, waist size, skin complexion, cholesterol level, blood pressure, blood sugar level? We define our health, and to a great extent ourselves, by such measurements. Yet how familiar are you, really, with your own body? How close are you to it—not just to the human body in general, but to your own body? How deeply do you know yourself? How well do you know your own brain?

In order to fully experience your body and brain, it's necessary to fully awaken all their senses. The most important factor in doing this is the communication between the mind and the body. No matter how sensitive you may be, if your mind is somewhere else and you're not paying attention, you'll never feel the subtle sensations of your body. Our consciousness is often lost in the past and the future. In order to fully experience our own bodies, we need to remain in the present.

Our understanding of the brain is generally conceptual rather than experiential. We're aware of the fact that we have a brain, but we're not normally conscious of its existence. To become closer to our brain and to use its functions well, we first have to have a *feeling* of our brain. This is what it means to "sensitize the brain." To put it a little more precisely, it's about awakening the brain's senses. This process enables us to feel our brains in a sensory way, and it opens a channel for communing with our brains.

In this vital first step to assuming mastery of your life, you'll learn how to become more acutely aware of your brain, your whole body, and the remarkable way in which all your senses communicate the reality of the world around you to your brain. Before you can achieve the specific goals you set for yourself, it's critically important for your brain to become sensitive—as aware as possible of the physical, emotional, and energetic being you are, and of every nuance your senses can convey.

In the same way that a painter can't create the seascape she imagines if she can't distinguish the colors blue and green—or even more specifically, aquamarine and turquoise—your senses must be acute if you're to succeed in reaching the goals you set for yourself. Awakening your senses is the key to achieving your Power Brain—one that's creative, focused, productive, and peaceful.

What a Sensitized Brain Feels Like

Having a physical sense of the brain is the first meaning of "sensitizing your brain." Sensing feelings in the head area—the weight and temperature of the head, the major energy points, pain, and so on—is important. But sensitizing isn't limited to the head. It's important to sensitize your whole body as you move and adopt various postures and feel different body parts, because the senses of your entire body are connected to your brain through your nerves. Awakening the body is the quickest and most effective way to awaken the brain. This process includes understanding the basic structure and functions of your brain as you connect it with your everyday experiences, reactions, and habits.

Brain Sensitizing means feeling your brain's energy, too. It means examining how your brain feels with different thoughts and emotions—light, clear, heavy, refreshed, hot. Concentrating on these different feelings will awaken a sense for how your brain energy changes depending on your emotions, and you'll be able to recognize major patterns. Such emotional reactions are accompanied by certain signals in different parts of the body, including your brain. Being aware of these signals makes it much easier for us to regulate our thoughts and emotions.

On a deeper level, Brain Sensitizing means being aware of the information entering and leaving your brain. All the bits of information coming into the brain compete fiercely for the attention of our consciousness. Restless thoughts arising in our minds are like children raising their hands in class, struggling to be picked by the teacher. Of these restlessly arising thoughts, those that get the attention of our consciousness are processed in the brain and then expressed through the body. This happens almost automatically in many people. Once you're able to monitor this process, you'll be able to use your brain's functions and power—and your precious time—much more effectively.

Healing Begins in Self-Awareness

Through the Brain Sensitizing process, we develop the attention to carefully observe all the phenomena that arise within us, beginning with our bodies and going as far as our thoughts, emotions, and ideas. We learn to identify where and how our bodies are uncomfortable and when we easily get stuck in what kinds of emotions and thoughts. In this way, healing begins and habits start to change.

Healing starts with awareness of what parts need healing. You'll start to change when you become aware of discomfort and unnaturalness—in your body, your emotions, and your thoughts—that you weren't aware of previously. Being aware of—and paying attention to—such discomforts means that your energy will flow to those areas. Energy flows where you focus your consciousness. This is, in fact, one of the important functions of pain. You focus your awareness on painful areas because you have pain, and your energy flows to them.

Changing habits is a similar process. Though they may be obvious to others, our own habits are hard for us to see. They seem natural because we're used to them. Such habits end up feeling unnatural and uncomfortable once our brains are sensitized. Habits aren't easily changed simply by understanding them. They change when they feel uncomfortable. This applies to all sorts of things, from our posture to our use of tobacco and alcohol.

When our senses awaken and we feel ourselves more deeply and mindfully, we're able to see ourselves objectively. And as we come to have a feeling for energy, we realize that what we see with our eyes and feel with our hands isn't all there is to the world. We have a new view on life.

Stress Awareness

A brain under chronic stress is almost never at its best. Before you can begin to sensitize your brain, it's vital to learn how to manage your stress. Virtually every attempt to develop your brain and utilize it better will fail if you don't first gain some control over your stress response—stress that's initiated exclusively in your brain, though its effects are felt throughout your body.

But we shouldn't get too stressed about stress itself. Stress is what allows us to respond quickly and decisively to situations that demand immediate action. When it's under control, stress helps stimulate the brain, bringing your attention to bear on important issues at hand and stimulating the problem-solving mechanisms in the brain. Controlled amounts of stress, research has shown, lift your mood, improve your immune system, and keep your brain agile.

On the other hand, prolonged stress that's seldom relieved is destructive—to your brain and to your whole body. Prolonged exposure to cortisol, one of the hormones released during stress, kills brain cells in the hippocampus, the part of your brain that mediates learning and memory. This impairs learning and inhibits recall. And many neurological diseases and disorders—including Parkinson's disease, ADHD, and even Alzheimer's disease—have been linked to long-term exposure to stress hormones.

In its healthiest state, your brain creates a balance, or "homeostasis," between the limbic system's sympathetic and parasympathetic functions, creating a constantly shifting equilibrium between your "fight or flight" and "rest and digest" responses. But with too much stress, the sympathetic system remains in a kind of constant overdrive, keeping your body in a state of chronic tension and stimulation and putting you at risk for both physical and psychological problems.

HANDLE STRESS IN THE MOMENT

1. **Don't wait to release your stress:** The best way to manage stress is to deal with it the very moment you feel it come up. Don't wait until you have time for a long soak in a hot bath, an evening yoga class, or the weekend off. Unfortunately, when we put off regaining our own inner balance, our bodies have already activated the stress response, and it's our health that suffers. With practice, you can learn to identify your stress signals as they are happening in the moment and stay in control when the pressure builds.
2. **Learn relaxation techniques:** Learn and try many relaxation techniques introduced in this book, and check what works best for you. The quickest and simplest remedy is to take deep breaths. Deep breathing is a real savior for a stressed body and mind in any situation.

Nature's original intention was for the stress response to operate only when absolutely necessary—helping us escape from crisis situations—and otherwise for body function to be centered on digestion, rest, and healing. Nature's intention functions well for most animals in their natural state. For humans, however, problems develop because mental activities constantly instigate the stress response, even in the absence of physical stressors.

How can you determine whether your normal amount of stress is too much? And how can you purposely reduce your stress response when it's desirable to do so? Stress becomes a problem when, even though your body and mind are experiencing it, you fail to recognize it—or if you do, your stress level has already grown so high that destructive results are inevitable. Self-awareness through Brain Sensitizing has great power in this respect.

We usually feel we're under stress when we recognize responses such as a pounding heart, intense emotions, or a hot head. But by then, it's already too late. The body and brain have been fully exposed to the stress response, and they have to carry the resulting burden. So one of the most effective ways to handle stress is to detect it before it reaches that level.

In Brain Sensitizing, we do training to feel energy. We can discern our body's more subtle responses through this energy sense, which greatly helps us detect the stress response. An early stress response is usually felt in the gut, chest, shoulders, and neck. You may get a feeling of something wriggling and rising up in the gut, a constriction in the chest, stiffness in the neck and shoulders, or heat. When you recognize such signs, you can alleviate the stress response by doing some deep breathing, moving your shoulders up and down to relieve tension, rubbing your palms together and sweeping them over your face, or going for a short walk.

If you recognize the stress response rising within you and use simple means to disperse or change the direction of the stress energy, you'll be able to prevent yourself from saying, doing, and deciding things you might regret later. Internally, you'll be able to reduce the destructive burden placed on your heart, cerebral blood vessels, and stomach.

Brain Sensitizing Methods

Brain Sensitizing exercises can be grouped into the following four categories. Among them, feeling the body and feeling energy are the most essential because they build a foundation for the rest of the exercises in the whole Brain Education system.

- Feeling the Body is for awakening parts of the brain connected with the body by moving seldom-used joints and muscles. As your energy and blood circulation improve while you do this, you achieve optimum energy balance, your body and mind relax, and you recover balance of body and peace of mind. While all exercise helps sensitize the body, the program introduced in this book centers on Meridian Exercises for opening and strengthening the body's energy pathways along with exercises for strengthening the body's energy center.
- Feeling the Breath involves checking whether your breathing is comfortable or uncomfortable, fast or slow—and, as you do that, communing with your body through breathing. When you pay attention to your breathing, it naturally becomes slower, deeper, and more comfortable. Your awareness of body and mind increases as you feel and control your breathing.
- Feeling Energy is for experiencing ki energy in the body by stopping your thoughts and emotions and concentrating your awareness in one part of your body. During this process your brain waves slow to alpha waves, and a new energy sense awakens and develops.
- Feeling the Brain uses visualization techniques and the sense you developed in Feeling Energy to increase your brain awareness. As you pass through this step, your body and mind grow more relaxed, your stress is relieved, and your concentration is enhanced.

Feeling the Body 1: Meridian Exercises

Meridian Exercises are carefully chosen movements designed to relax the body and mind by releasing tension in muscles and joints. The pulling and stretching motions of these exercises stimulate the meridian system of the body and facilitate the free flow of energy.

With careful and concentrated breath work, you can assist in a dynamic exchange of energy. When exhaling, imagine that you're releasing all the accumulated stagnant energy in your body. When inhaling, imagine that you're breathing in fresh, clean energy. This conscious concentration on the exchange of energy is what sets Meridian Exercises apart from other stretching exercises.

To maximize the benefits of Meridian Exercise, breathe in before the start of a movement, then pause and hold your breath during the movement itself. Breathe out as you release the movement and return to an at-ease position. Imagine that you're having a conversation with the part of the body that's being worked on, concentrating fully on the sensation of the moment. Develop a deliberate rhythm and pace for your movements and breathing.

Although there are more than 300 different movements in Meridian Exercises in the Brain Education system, we can divide them into six basic categories. It's best to choose one exercise from each category and learn it well, rather than trying to do as many exercises as you can.

BOUNCING

Bouncing is used to release stagnant energy from the body. Ki energy can be simplified into clear or positive energy and unclear or negative energy. Clear energy tends to be dynamic, while unclear energy is static, blocking the flow of clear energy through your body. Bouncing lets you literally shake loose the unclear energy trapped within you. It feels surprisingly good, and it's quite easy. As you bounce, visualize the negative energy being released through your fingers and toes. Bouncing is more effective when you actually imagine the flow of energy while you move.

1. Stand with your feet shoulder-width apart. Make loose fists with your hands and tuck them under your armpits. Straighten your back and release the tension and tightness from your body.
2. Let your hands drop down along your sides as you bend your knees and lightly bounce downward. Release your fists as you drop your hands so that energy escapes from your fingertips.
3. As you bounce back up, bring your hands back up under your armpits, making loose fists again.
4. Repeat this down and up motion at least 50 times. After the first set of 50 bounces, lower your hands and feel the stream of energy being released through your fingers and toes.
5. After you're comfortable doing 50 repetitions, increase to 100 or 200 bounces.

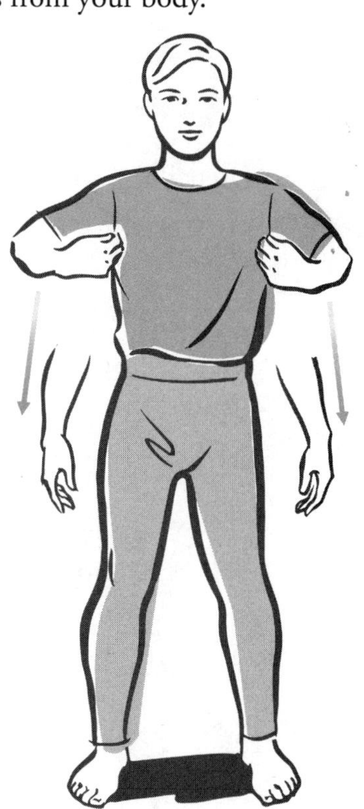

TAPPING

Tapping is designed to open up the energy points distributed throughout your body—the same sites that acupuncture and acupressure focus on. With concentrated light tapping, every part of your body will come alive. You'll feel a relaxing and refreshing sensation, as if you're breathing through your skin. The movements in this exercise follow the energy pathways—known as meridians—along which ki energy naturally flows through your body.

1. Form your fingers into stiff claws and lightly tap your fingertips all around your head.

2. Stretch out your left arm in front of you with your palm facing up and fingers relaxed. With the palm of your right hand, start at the left shoulder and rhythmically tap down your left arm all the way to the hand.
3. Turn your left palm downward. Still using your right hand, tap your way back up to the left shoulder.
4. Switch arms and repeat Steps 2 and 3.

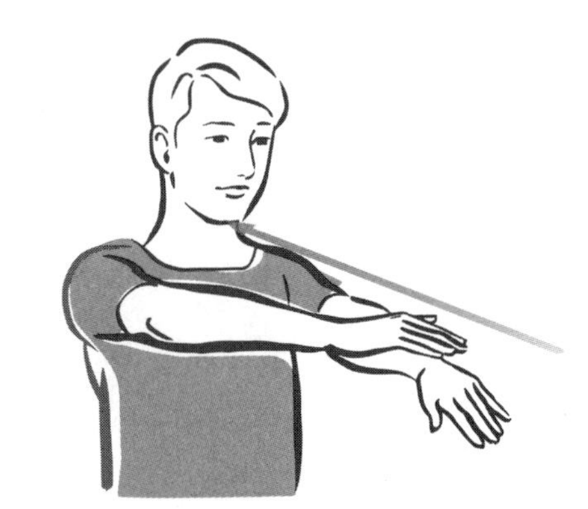

5. Now, tap your chest with both hands. Starting from your chest, tap your ribs, abdomen, and sides.

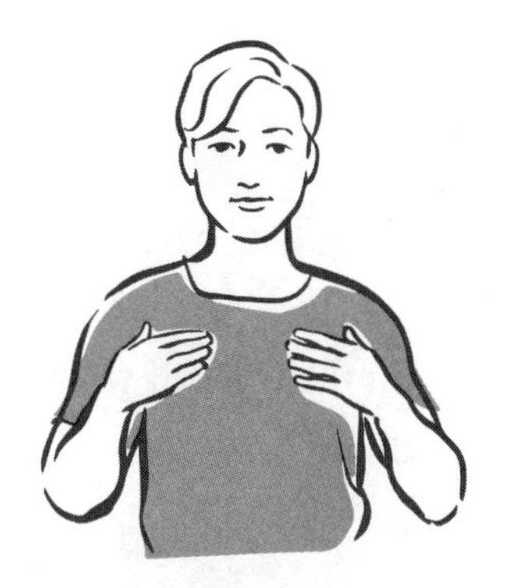

6. Using both palms, tap the liver area just below the right rib cage. Concentrate on radiating positive, clear energy to the liver.

7. With both hands, tap the stomach area just below the left ribcage. Concentrate on radiating positive, clear energy to your stomach.

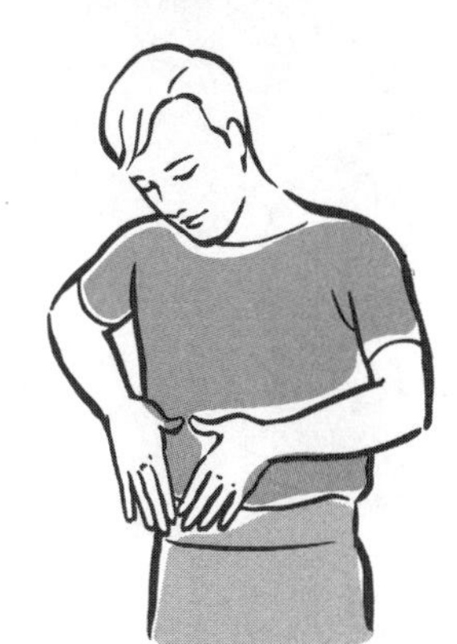

8. Bending forward slightly from the waist, tap the kidney area on both sides of your lower back. Tap as far up as you can reach, then tap down to your buttocks.

9. Starting from your buttocks, tap your way down the back of your legs to your ankles.

10. Tap your way down the back of your legs to your ankles. Then, tap up the front of your legs to your thighs.

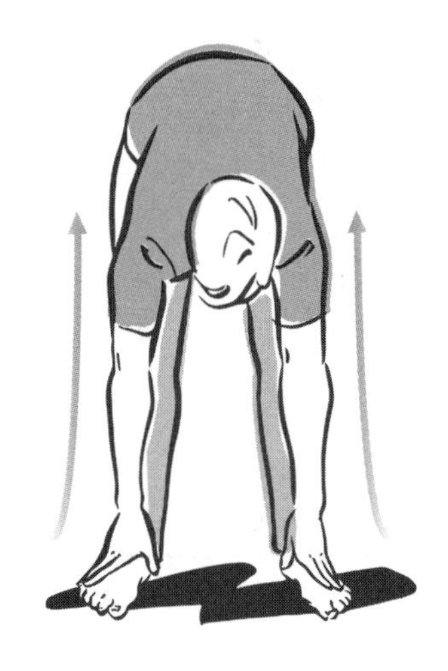

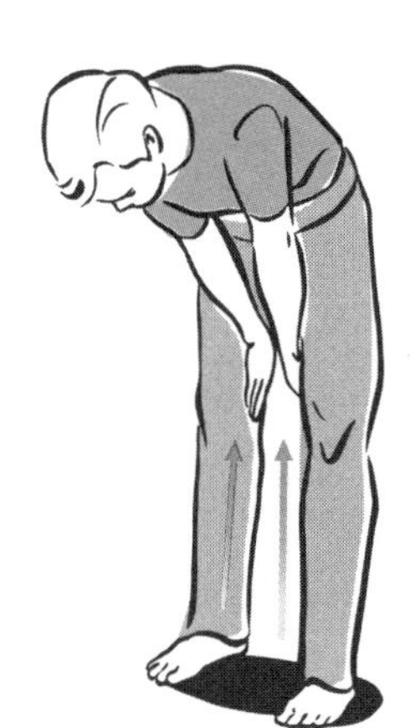

11. From your upper thighs, tap down the outsides of your legs all the way to your ankles. Now, tap your way up the insides of your legs to your upper thighs.

12. Finish by striking your lower Dahnjon about 20 times. Dahnjon Tapping is most effective when done with the legs shoulder-width apart, knees slightly bent, and feet parallel to each other.

STRETCHING

If you exercise regularly, you know the importance of stretching before you begin. But are you aware that stretching itself is excellent exercise? Besides helping you avoid muscle injuries, stretching readies your brain for action and gives you new energy. Focus on stretching as many muscle groups as you can, in as many directions as possible. Enjoy the stimulating sensation that stretching brings to every part of your body. The stretching exercises described here are designed not only to stretch and make supple your muscles, joints, and ligaments, but also to power the flow of ki energy throughout your body.

1. Stand with your legs shoulder-width apart, and clasp your hands together in front of you.
2. Breathing in, lift your clasped hands and straighten your arms overhead, palms facing the sky, until your arms touch your ears.
3. At the same time, lift your heels, tilt your head backward, and look up at your hands.
4. Lower your hands slowly as you breathe out.

5. Repeat the motion, but this time, with arms raised and palms up, tilt your body to the right as far you can go without losing your balance. Feel your left side being stretched. Return to an upright position and lower your hands as you exhale.

6. Repeat the motion, now moving to the left. Feel the entire right side of your body being stretched.

7. Breathe in as you bend forward from the waist, and try to touch the ground with your palms without bending your knees. Try to touch your knees with your forehead, or come as close as you can. Return to your starting position as you breathe out.

8. Repeat the whole cycle four times. As you stretch your limits, imagine yourself becoming the person you can be.

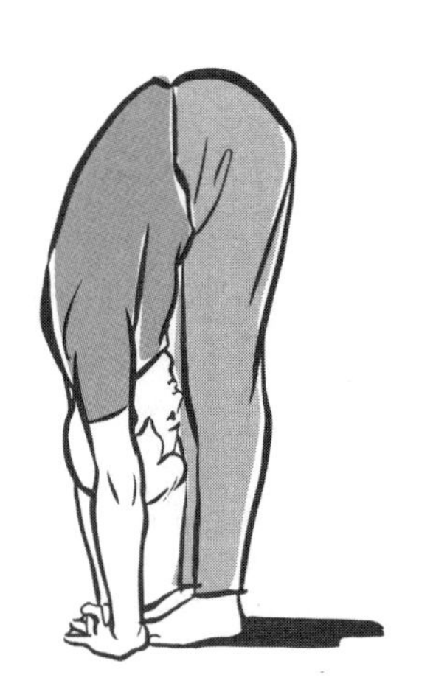

ROTATING

Rotating is exactly what the name suggests. This exercise is used to loosen the rotating joints in the body with a slow and deliberate circular motion. Do the movements slowly and carefully.

1. Slowly rotate your neck counterclockwise four times, then clockwise four times.

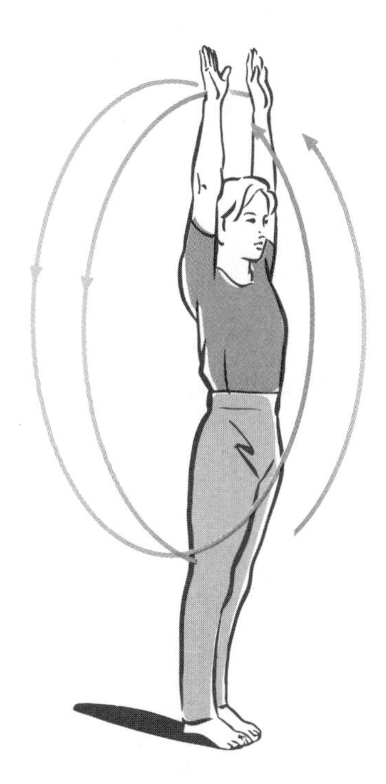

2. Next, rotate your arms in large circles, four times forward and four times backward.

3. Raise your arms to shoulder level and rotate your wrists four times forward and four times backward.

4. Place your hands on your waist, and rotate your waist counterclockwise, and then clockwise, four times each way.

5. Place your feet together and bend slightly, placing your hands on your knees. Turn your knees counterclockwise and clockwise, four times each.

6. Sit with your legs straight in front of you, and turn your ankles counterclockwise and clockwise, four times each. Imagine what it feels like to move more freely in every aspect of your life.

TWIST

This motion is a little like wringing the water out of a towel. To facilitate the flow of energy, you're trying to loosen your muscles and joints by putting your body through a "wringer," so to speak.

1. Stand with your feet shoulder-width apart. Raise your arms out to your sides, level with your shoulders, palms down.
2. Breathing in, twist both arms forward as far as they will go. Breathe out as you return to your starting position, arms level with your shoulders and palms down.
3. Breathing in, twist both arms backward as far as they will go. Breathe out as you return to your starting position.

4. Breathing in, twist both arms in a clockwise direction as far as they will go, keeping your eyes on the right arm. Your right arm twists back; your left arm twists forward. Relax while breathing out and returning to the starting position.

5. Breathing in, twist both arms in a counterclockwise direction as far as they'll go, keeping your eyes on the left arm. Your left arm twists back; your right arm twists forward. Relax while breathing out and returning to the starting position.

BURST

A sudden burst of strength pumps stagnant energy out of the body and brings up the energy stored in the lower abdomen. During this exercise, hold your breath as you concentrate on your lower abdomen and tighten your fingers and toes as much as you can, feeling the energy flow through your body. Then, breathe out as you release them.

1. Stand with your feet more than shoulder-width apart; bend your knees at a 45-degree angle. Breathing in, raise your hands to chest level in front of you. Hold your breath as you extend your arms out to the sides. Tighten the muscles of your arms, fingers, and toes as you hold the position for three to five seconds.

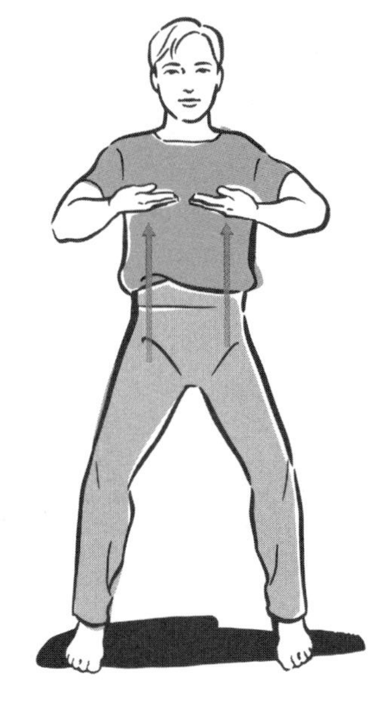

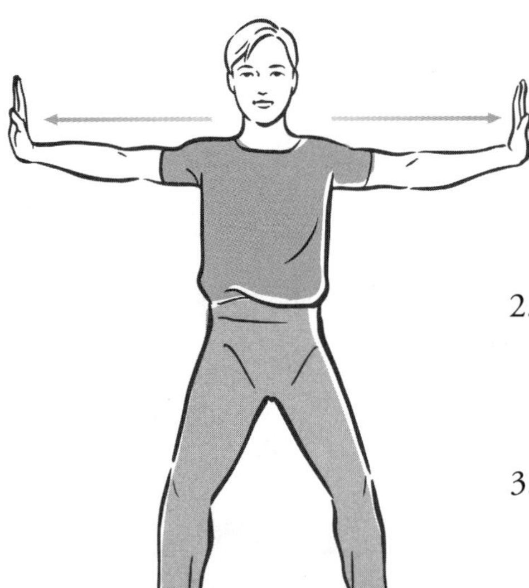

2. Breathe out as you relax your muscles and return to your starting position.
3. Repeat three times.

Feeling the Body 2: Dahnjon Strengthening Exercises

The Dahnjon in the lower abdomen acts like an energy pump for the body, receiving universal energy and releasing it to the meridians in the body. Its strength is essential in maintaining the natural flow of energy in the human body. A strong Dahnjon and an ability to create Water Up, Fire Down energy balance are important physical prerequisites for getting the most out of a Brain Education training..

The lower abdomen, the location of the lower Dahnjon, is filled with the small and large intestines, which together hold about a third of the body's total blood volume at any given time. A smooth and unimpeded flow of blood through the intestines is crucial to the circulatory efficiency of the whole body—including, of course, the gut brain and head brain.

But modern life doesn't promote intestinal health. Long hours spent sitting often lead to hardening of the intestines, which can result in inefficient absorption of nutrients and chronic constipation. When the intestines regain a supple condition, the energy and blood that have pooled in that area will circulate more efficiently throughout the body, resulting in an increased feeling of lightness and mobility.

There are two basic mechanisms for strengthening the lower Dahnjon. The first is an exercise called Dahnjon Tapping, which calls for rhythmic striking of the lower abdomen with the hands. The second, simply called Intestinal Exercise, consists of pushing out and pulling in the abdominal muscles.

DAHNJON TAPPING

Dahnjon Tapping is a simple but effective method for strengthening the lower Dahnjon by rhythmically striking (patting) the lower abdomen with the palms or fists of both hands. This facilitates the circulation of both blood and energy throughout the body. You'll also begin to feel increased warmth in the area, and this exercise will assist in the prompt removal of excess gases and waste from the body. For a beginner with a weak lower Dahnjon, or for someone having trouble feeling heat in the lower Dahnjon, this basic exercise will help.

1. Stand with your feet placed shoulder-width apart and your knees slightly bent.
2. Point your toes slightly inward and feel a slight tightening of the lower abdomen.

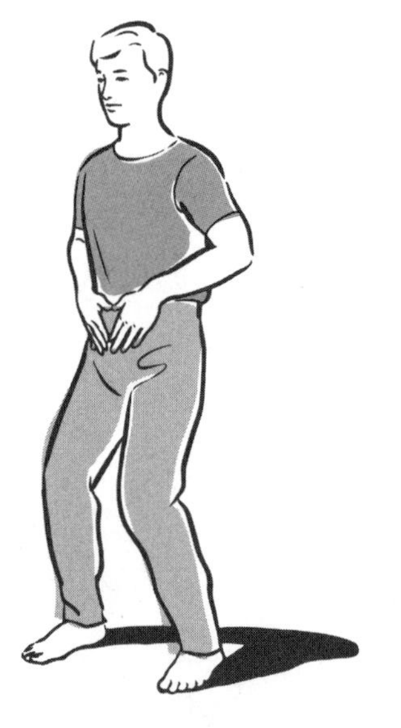

3. Pat or tap the lower Dahnjon area rhythmically with both palms or fists, lightly bouncing your knees with each strike.
4. Start with just 50 taps at a time and work up to 300 to 500 as the lower Dahnjon is strengthened. You may increase the force and number of strikes with more practice—up to 1,000 or more if your health is good.

INTESTINAL EXERCISE

Intestinal Exercise refers to the rhythmic pulling in and pushing out of the abdominal wall, stimulating the intestines. This will increase the flexibility of the intestines and facilitate efficient circulation of energy and blood. Intestinal Exercise can also be used to improve the condition of the major internal organs. Though we don't have muscles that we can use to exercise our internal organs, we can indirectly work on them by moving the intestines. If you tighten your rectal muscles during each repetition, you'll be able to gather energy and feel warmth much more quickly. Don't overdo this exercise in the beginning, as it may cause discomfort. Start with a few repetitions, and work your way up.

1. You can do this exercise either standing up or lying down. When standing, assume the same position as for Dahnjon Tapping . When lying down, lie on your back with your feet shoulder-width apart. Form a triangle by touching your thumbs and forefingers together; place lightly on the lower Dahnjon.
2. Pull in your abdominal muscles as if you were trying to touch your back with the front wall of your abdomen. If you wish, tighten your perineal muscles at the same time.

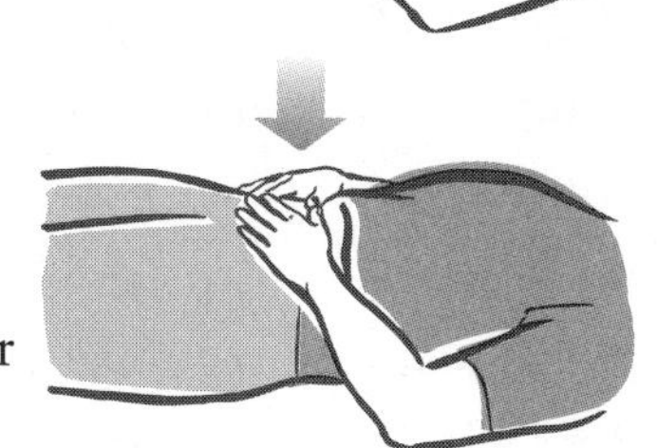

3. As if breathing into a balloon, push your lower abdomen out slightly until you feel outward pressure in your lower Dahnjon area.
4. Start by doing 50 repetitions at a time, and work your way up to 300 to 500. As with Dahnjon Tapping, more experienced practitioners can work up to 1,000 or more repetitions for optimal benefits.

Feeling the Breath

Perhaps nothing is more important to brain health and vitality than proper breathing—and that's certainly true for your overall health as well. Without the essential oxygen that breathing supplies, your brain couldn't live for more than a few minutes. And your brain consumes oxygen voraciously. While it accounts for only about two percent of your body weight, your brain demands about 25 percent of all the oxygen you consume.

What's your breathing like right now? Placing one hand on your chest and the other on your lower abdomen, try to breathe naturally. Which moves more, your chest or your lower abdomen? If the hand on your chest moves more and your shoulders rise and fall, that's evidence that your breathing isn't deep. If you're like many people, you breathe poorly—shallowly, incompletely, and inconsistently. And that's a shame, because it wasn't always that way. As a baby, you breathed remarkably well and deeply, and no one had to train you. Your entire chest and abdomen swelled with each breath, and you effortlessly consumed the nutrients in the air. You were a natural-born breather, as it turns out.

But as each of us ages, our breathing becomes compromised as improper posture, bad habits, and stress take their toll. Does this sound familiar—your chest is tight, your abdomen stiff, and (when you take time to notice) you find yourself taking rapid and shallow breaths most of the time? It's a natural reaction to prolonged stress, but it's harmful to virtually all your body's organs and systems—and especially your brain.

However, even if you've been breathing poorly for decades—and you probably have—you can breathe like a baby again if you set your mind to it. You'll need to bring a great deal of daily attention to your breathing, something you're probably not accustomed to doing. As a basic principle, healthy breathing should be deep, light, and natural. Deep breathing occurs naturally if we breathe with our awareness focused on our lower abdomen or Dahnjon, the body's energy center.

Breathing is closely related to the movement of the diaphragm, the dome-shaped structure that acts as a natural partition separating the heart and lungs from the stomach, spleen, pancreas, liver, kidneys, bladder, and intestines. When we breathe deeply, the diaphragm moves downward as we inhale and upward as we exhale. The more the diaphragm moves, the more our lungs are able to expand—which means that more oxygen can be taken in and more carbon dioxide released with each breath.

You may find it difficult at first, but practice until your exhalations are a bit longer than your inhalations. Intentionally slow the cycle of your breathing as much as you can. Even in the midst of a hectic day, try taking long, slow, deep breaths, focusing on the out-breath and consciously releasing tensions as you exhale.

You'll almost certainly notice immediate benefits from better breathing. Sophisticated brain imaging systems now demonstrate that in addition to simply oxygenating the blood, conscious deep breathing stimulates regions of your brain that are often dormant otherwise. As a daily part of your Brain Education practice, be mindful of how you breathe, and modify your breathing habits for your optimal health.

WHY DEEP BREATHING?

Here are five more reasons you should practice deep breathing besides that it's free and automatic.

1. **Detoxification:** Deep breathing gives your lymphatic system a chance to become fully charged with lots of oxygen. This naturally leads to detoxification.
2. **Weight loss:** When the body gets enough oxygen, the cells and tissues are nourished. The extra oxygen in the body helps you burn off more fat.
3. **Relaxation:** Deep breathing helps return your body to a state of equilibrium by deactivating your stress response.
4. **Pain relief:** Deep breathing helps your brain release endorphins—your body's natural pain-killing hormones.
5. **Mental clarity:** Deep breathing stimulates the vagus nerve to release a neurotransmitter called acetylcholine. This signal brings you increased focus and calmness.

BODY SCANNING

This exercise will help you relax your whole body effectively before you start any breathing exercise.

1. Sit or lie in a comfortable position. Close your eyes. Breathe deeply but comfortably.

2. Bring your attention to the top of your head. Slowly begin to scan down the body, checking for areas of tension. As you exhale, release tension from those areas.

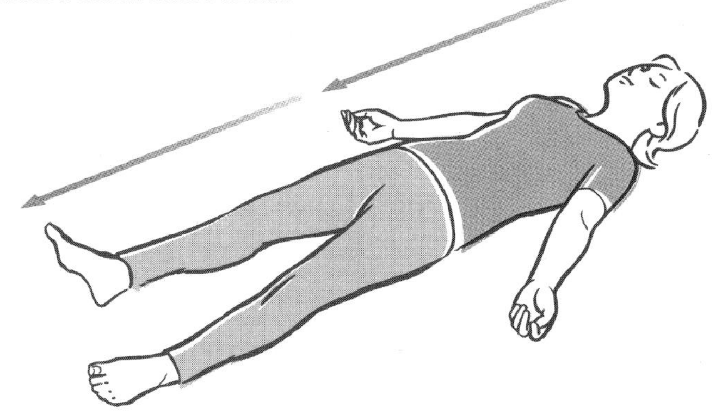

3. Feel you face, checking first the forehead, then the eyes, mouth, and cheeks. Release tension each time you exhale.

4. Check your neck and release tension from that area. Rock your head gently from side to side to help release tension.

5. Move on to your chest, imagining all stagnant energy and stress exiting with each breath.

6. Feel your abdomen as you extend it with each inhalation. Release tension as you exhale.

7. Relax your arms and legs completely. Feel energy releasing from your hands and feet as you relax further.

CHEST BREATHING

For deep and natural breathing, the blockage around the chest caused by stress has to be opened. Chest Breathing can be very effective at helping to release stagnant energy from inside the chest. If you haven't yet tried an abdominal breathing exercise or if your chest feels tight, do this exercise before you proceed to Dahnjon Breathing.

1. Lie on your back in a comfortable place that's not too hard or too soft. Extend your arms out from your sides at a 45-degree angle, palms facing up. Spread your legs so your feet are shoulder-width apart.

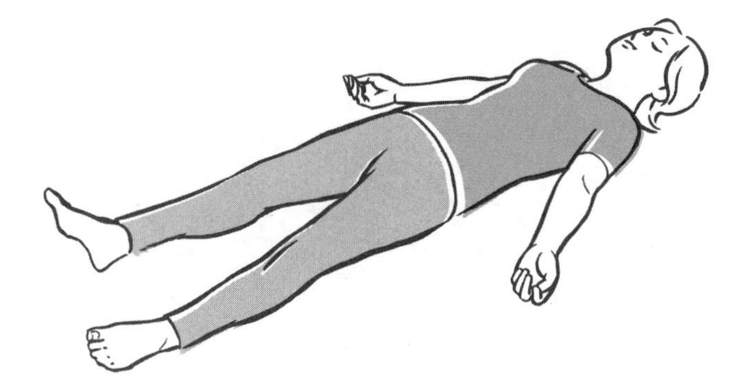

2. Relax the muscles of your face and jaw, and let your mouth open slightly.
3. Concentrating on your chest, inhale slowly as you count one, two, three, four.
4. Concentrating on the tips of your fingers, exhale slowly as you count one, two, three, four, five, six. As you exhale, imagine the stagnant energy in your chest leaving your body through your fingertips.
5. Do this breathing exercise for about five to ten minutes.

DAHNJON BREATHING

Dahnjon Breathing can allow your breathing to become natural and deep. Take time to do this daily. With constant practice, it will become part of how you breathe. Whether or not you give yourself a chance to "consciously breathe" every day can greatly influence your health.

1. Lie on your back in a comfortable place that's not too hard or too soft. Spread your legs so that both feet are shoulder-width apart. Put both hands on your Dahnjon.
2. Concentrating your awareness in your lower abdomen, inhale slowly as you push your belly outward.

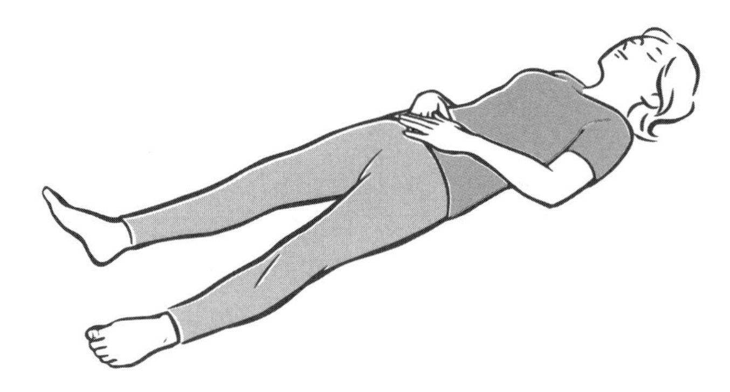

3. Exhale slowly, pulling in your lower abdomen toward your back.
4. Continue to inhale and exhale with your lower abdomen, rhythmically repeating the movement of pushing and pulling your lower abdomen. Do this at a rate that's comfortable for you, but be sure to use a steady rhythm as you push and pull your belly.
5. When your body and mind are in a comfortable state, inhalations and exhalations will continue naturally. When you've inhaled suffi-

ciently, you'll exhale automatically, and once you've exhaled enough, you'll automatically take another breath. Practice this regularly, and you'll feel your breathing growing deeper as it gradually sinks from your chest to your lower abdomen.

6. With practice, the warmth of the energy moving inside the abdomen will become apparent. When there's a feeling of heat in the abdomen, the Dahnjon has been identified. Concentrate on that area. As your awareness of the Dahnjon increases, you'll feel more energy and heat. The sense of heat may change into a magnetic or electric sensation.

7. Do this exercise for five to ten minutes.

Helpful Hint: Better Posture, Better Breathing

Make sure to relax your neck, shoulders, chest, and abdominal muscles. Try to touch the floor with your lower back. If you curl your tailbone gently up, it will help your lower back touch the floor naturally. Find the angle of your body that helps you breathe most naturally and comfortably.

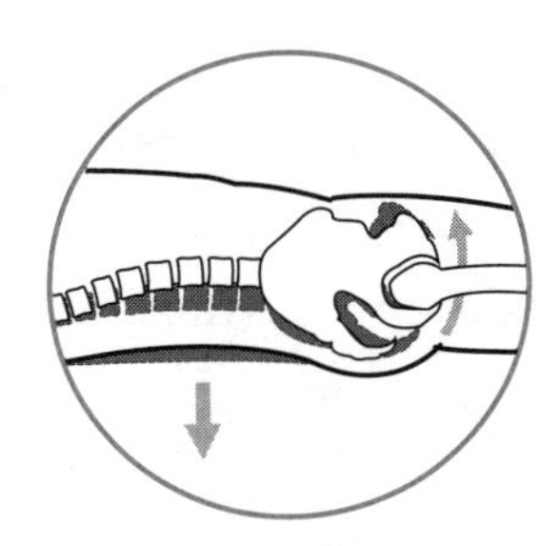

Feeling Energy

Once you've awakened your senses and discovered how to limit brain-inhibiting stress by feeling your body and breath, you're ready to tune in to ways in which you can feel energy flow through your body.

▶ Your Sixth Sense

To experience this energy flow, we need to awaken a new sense, one we haven't been consciously aware of before now. You can't experience ki energy with any of your five senses. Instead, it requires the development of your sixth sense—the inner consciousness—with relaxed concentration. And the best way I know to reach this state of inner consciousness is with a form of meditation I've developed, which I call Energy Sensing Exercise or Jigam.

Relaxed concentration is an absolute prerequisite to being able to feel the flow of energy. We usually tense up when we concentrate, and we let our thoughts wander when we stop concentrating. Relaxed concentration may sound like an oxymoron. But only when we can direct our consciousness while maintaining a relaxed state of body and mind can we feel the flow of energy.

Brain wave frequencies were discussed in Chapter Five (page 62). The lower the frequency of the brain-wave cycle, the more relaxed, peaceful, and focused you feel. Brain-wave rhythms in the range of five to ten cycles per minute, or alpha brain waves, accompany the most profound and effective meditation practices. When your brain reaches this quiet state of relaxed concentration, the flow of energy becomes remarkably perceptible by your sixth sense.

Jigam introduces energy awareness with a meditative exercise that both develops and strengthens relaxed concentration. To begin, it's essential to turn the focus of your consciousness inward. During the meditation, turn away from distractions that stimulate your five senses. Neither thoughts nor emotions play a role in Jigam; it's their *absence* that allows you to become deeply quiet and entirely focused on the non-sensory, non-cognitive realm of energy.

The Energy Sensing Exercise I've devised begins by paying particular attention to your hands. Your hands are remarkably sensitive and can readily sense the flow of energy when you allow them to do so. And once you've awakened your hands to the reality of energy while in deep meditation, it becomes far easier to experience it in other parts of your body—including your brain. The time it takes initially to experience energy varies significantly from person to person. You might feel it powerfully on your first Jigam exercise, or you might need to practice many times before you experience the flow of energy. But I can assure you that you *will* feel it powerfully at some point.

When you're accustomed to feeling energy in your hands, you'll be amazed at how you can maintain that sensitivity without having to initiate a Jigam meditation. In turn, you'll begin to experience energy—in your body and in your environment—in your daily life, and you'll be able to direct that energy toward whatever goals you choose.

YOUR HANDS AND ENERGY SENSITIVITY

1. **Why are hands more senstive?:** The part of your brain that receives information from your sensory neurons doesn't treat all parts of the body equally. The reason your hands are more sensitive than your back or legs is that there are many more sensory neurons on your hands. When an area has more sensory neurons, there is a larger brain area devoted to receiving their signals, resulting in more sensitivity. About one-fourth of the motor cortex in the human brain, which controls all movements of the body, is devoted to the muscles of the hands.

2. **Boost your hands' energy sensitivity:** Before you start the Energy Sensing Exercise on the next page, tap your fingertips together, shake your hands, rub your palms briskly, or clap your hands for two to three minutes. These exercises will give an extra energy boost to your hands and will help you sense energy more easily.

ENERGY SENSING EXERCISE (JIGAM)

1. Sit on a chair or in half lotus position and straighten your back.

2. Place your hands on your knees, palms facing up, and close your eyes. Relax your body, especially your neck and shoulders. Relax your mind. Inhale deeply, and let go of any remaining tension while you exhale (soft, meditative background music may be helpful).

3. Raise your hands slowly to chest level, palms facing each other. Concentrate on any sensation you may feel between your palms. At first, you may feel warmth in your hands, but soon, you may feel your own pulse.

4. Now, place your hands two to four inches apart and concentrate fully on the space between them. Imagine that your shoulders, arms, wrists, and hands are floating in a vacuum, weightless.

5. Pull your hands apart, and then push them close in again as you keep concentrating. You might feel a tingling sensation of electricity, a magnetic attraction pulling your hands toward each other or pushing them apart. You might even feel as if you're holding a cotton ball between your hands, or moving slowly through warm water. All these feelings are manifestations of your energy flow.

6. When the sensation becomes more pronounced, pull your hands farther apart or push them closer together. The sensation won't go away, but will expand and grow stronger.

7. Breathe in and out slowly and deeply three times.

8. Rub your hands together briskly until they're warm, then gently caress your eyes, face, neck, and chest.

Helpful Hint: Sensation Expands with Relaxation

The sensation of energy expands with increased relaxation. Since there's no exact standard of relaxation for feeling energy, you simply have to relax to the best of your ability and enjoy the journey into your inner world. Though the sensation might be too subtle to notice at first, nurture it carefully until it becomes palpable.

EXPANDING ENERGY SENSING EXERCISE

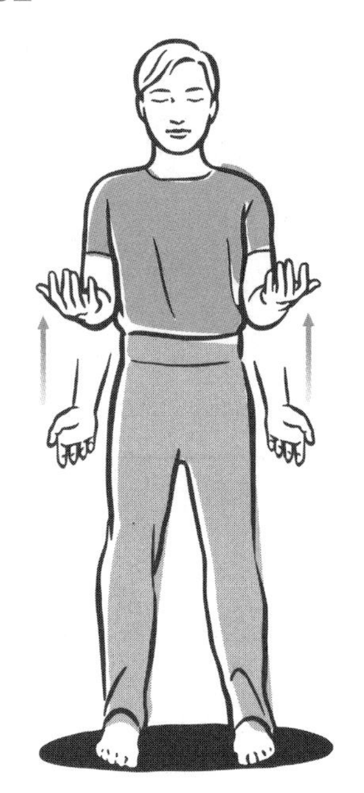

1. With your eyes open and your body relaxed, stand with your feet shoulder-width apart. Push your chest and shoulders out; let your hands fall to your sides, palms facing up. Lift up your hands by bending your arms at the elbows; concentrate on any sensation in your hands. (When you're used to the flow of energy, you can maintain this sensation even standing up with your eyes open.)

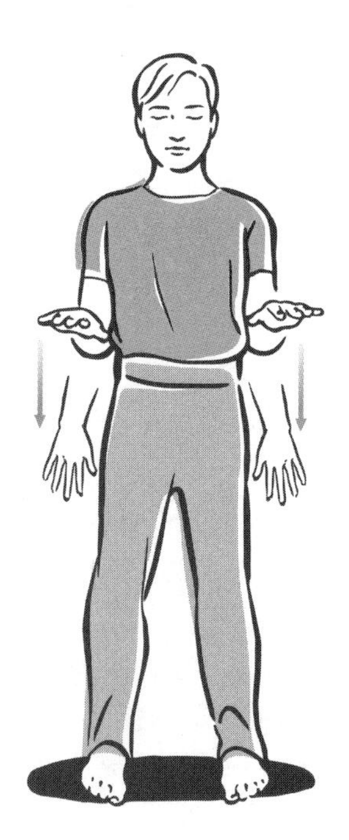

2. Turn your palms over and lift your hands to shoulder level. Then push your hands down toward the ground, feeling the weight of your fingers as if you were moving underwater.

3. Combine Steps 1 and 2 into one motion and repeat. When you lift your arms, lift the heels of your feet at the same time. When you push your arms downward, lower your heels.

4. Now, slowly walk around. Take one step while raising your hands and another while lowering them. When you get used to the motion, take two steps while raising your hands, and so on.

Feeling the Brain

Now, you are ready to explore some exercises for taking your brain into your own hands to see how it feels.

You're accustomed to thinking—and thinking about your thoughts. But what about feeling the energy of your brain, and different parts of your brain? You really can, though the sensations people experience vary widely. Some people aren't able to feel these without long practice, while others feel them quite easily.

You may feel something dramatic as you complete the following exercises, or it may be very subtle. People commonly report tingling, prickling, tickling, buzzing, or pulsing sensations. No matter what the sensation is or how small the feeling, focus on it and let it expand. The first goal here is to meet and become familiar with the energy of your brain, and then to be able to work with it more consciously.

Don't feel hurried if you can't easily visualize the shape of your brain. The energy of your consciousness is communicated to your brain even if you only think about the specific parts without creating visual forms in your mind. The purpose of this exercise is to link your consciousness with your actual brain through the flow of energy. If you have trouble visualizing the specific brain areas, try to visualize the general shape of the whole brain; if even that is difficult, just focus quietly on the brain without attempting to visualize it. You can also try drawing a rough outline of the brain on a piece of paper and imagine energy being communicated as you draw.

BRAIN AWARENESS VISUALIZATION

Brain Awareness Visualization is the first step in becoming familiar with your brain. This exercise asks you to imagine the brain as if you're actually looking at it, and to concentrate and expand the sensation you experience as you gaze carefully at the various parts of your own brain. You might feel a prickling, a tingling akin to a slight electrical current, or even a refreshing dissolving sensation. Studying a color-coded diagram of the brain, or drawing one yourself, will help you imagine your own brain and increase the effectiveness of this exercise.

1. If you're sitting on a chair, rest your hands lightly on your thighs. If you're sitting on the ground in a half lotus position, rest your hands lightly on your knees.
2. Breathe in and out three times and relax. Close your eyes. As you breathe out, imagine tension melting away through your fingertips and toes.
3. Bring up a mental image of your brain, first imagining the skull that protects it.

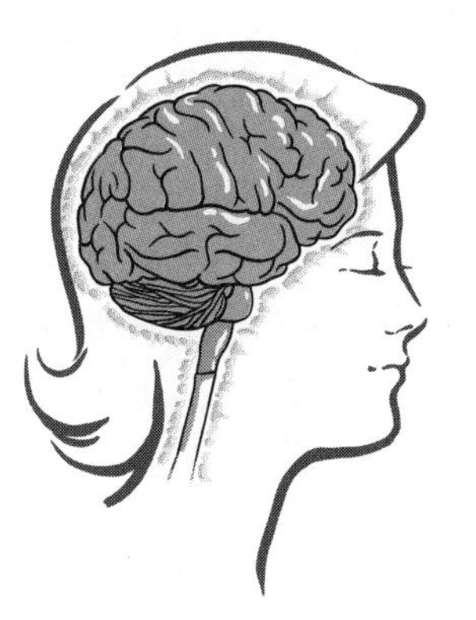

4. Now, imagine the neocortex, with its many folds and crevices. Look in all directions—front, back, right, and left.

5. Now, look at the left and right hemispheres, slowly shifting your gaze from one side to the other. Now, gaze at the corpus callosum, the bridge that links the two hemispheres, imagining the flow of information between the hemispheres.

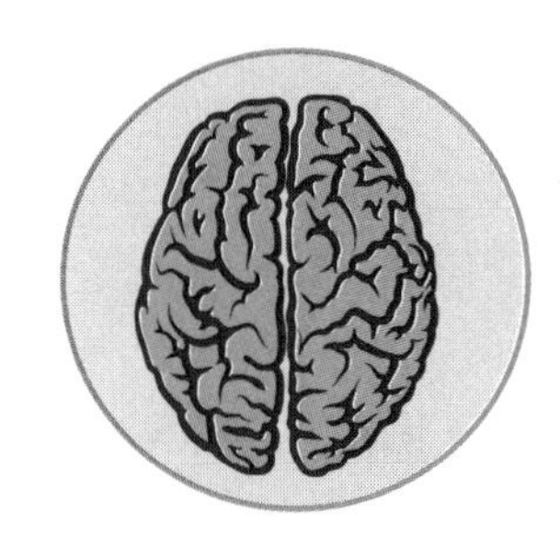

6. Next, go below into the sub-cortical region and look at the amygdala, which controls emotion.

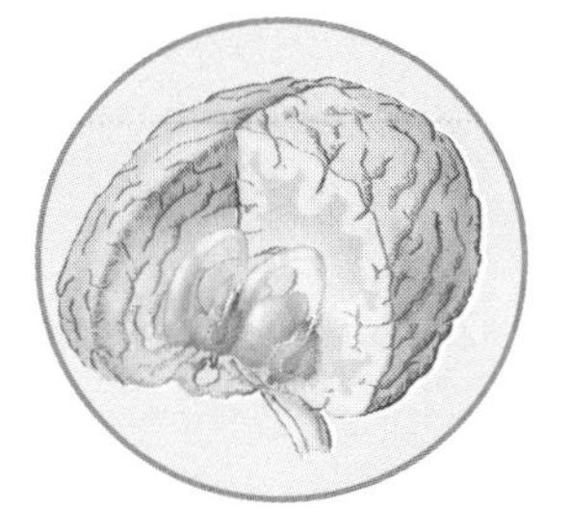

7. Then, move your gaze toward the back and look at the cerebellum, which controls motion and balance.

8. Now, go further below to see the thalamus, which gathers sensory inputs and sends them to the cerebral cortex.

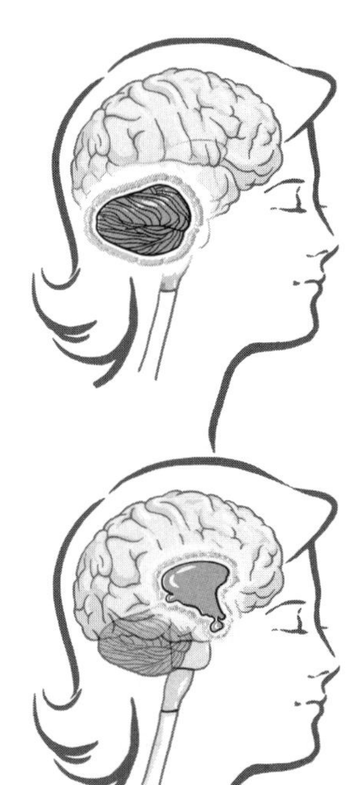

9. Let your eyes drift lower, and find the hypothalamus under your thalamus, which is responsible for the production of many essential hormones that maintain the body's homeostasis.

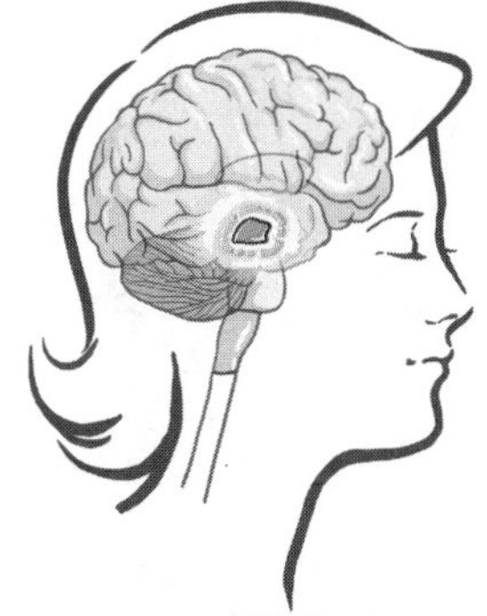

10. Now, go even lower, and find the medulla oblongata, which controls our most basic life functions.

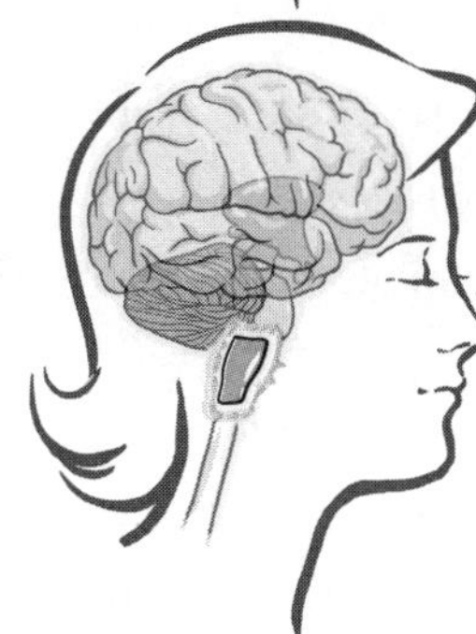

11. Move your gaze to the spnial cord, which is the link between the brain and the nerves in the rest of your body.

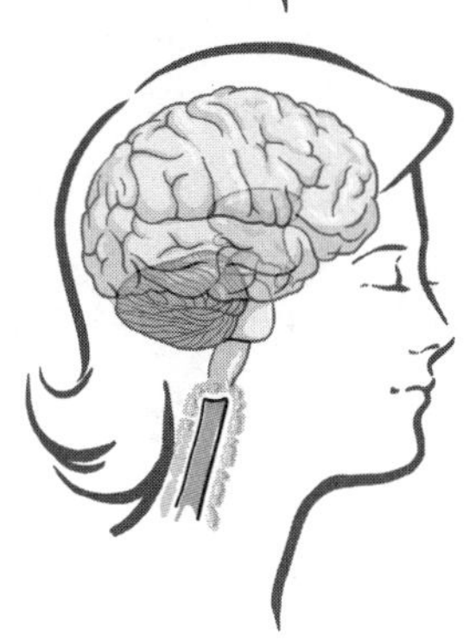

12. Pull your gaze back, and observe your whole brain floating in space, rotating slowly in front of you. Briefly observe the various brain areas that you've seen, from the neocortex to the limbic system to the essential parts of the brainstem.
13. Breathe deeply in and out three times, and then open your eyes. As you breathe out, imagine the stagnant energy in your brain escaping through your breath.

BRAIN ENERGY AWARENESS EXERCISE

The Brain Energy Awareness Exercise trains you to feel your brain through the energy in your hands. The sensations from your brain may feel similar to what you felt during the Energy Sensing Exercise (page 122). Let yourself enjoy the sensations for now—just explore and experiment. Don't be nervous about what you will or won't feel. When your personal brain awareness becomes finely tuned, you'll notice when you're overworking one part of your brain and need to shift to a different activity. You'll be able to feel rigidity and underutilization in parts of your brain, and you'll be able to direct nourishing energy to areas that need stimulation.

1. If you're sitting on a chair, rest your hands lightly on your thighs. If you're sitting on the ground in a half lotus position, rest your hands on your knees.

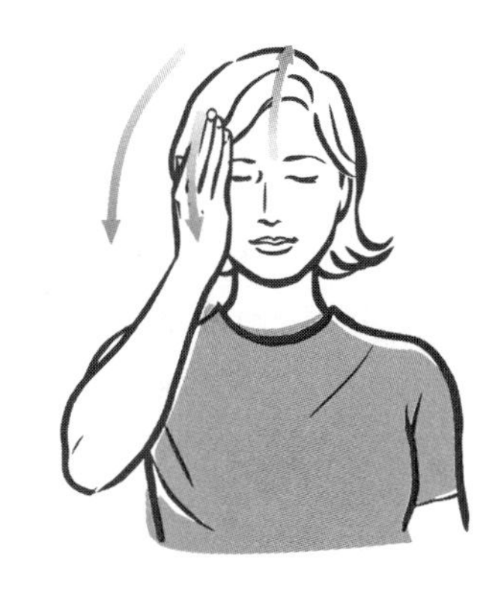

2. Lift your right hand so your palm is facing the right side of your face, about one to two inches from your face.

3. Feeling the sensation of the energy in your hand (keeping your hand one to two inches from your face), sweep your hand down the right side of your face with a slow, deliberate motion. Move your right hand up from your forehead over the top of your head and then down to where your head and neck meet.

Then, circle your hand around the right side of your head and feel your brain's energy radiate out toward your hand. Once you've felt the energy, slowly lower your hand.

4. Repeat Steps 2 and 3 with your left hand. When you've felt the energy from the left side of your brain, slowly lower your hand.

5. Now, raise both hands and feel the energy from both hemispheres at the same time. If one side is less responsive than the other, place both hands on the less-responsive side and mentally whisper positive messages of support.

6. Rub your hands briskly together until warmed, then gently massage your face, neck, and head.

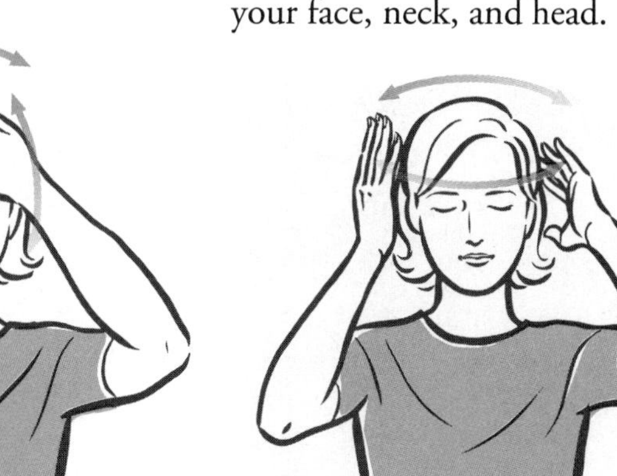

Further Brain Sensitizing Activities

Every waking hour of each day, you're bombarded with sensory information. Whether you're at the office, driving home, gardening, cooking, watching television, or reading, your five senses assault your brain with information gleaned from the world around you.

Your brain, however, pays conscious attention to only a fraction of the stimuli it receives. It "decides" what images it consciously sees, what sounds it hears, and what aromas it smells. It consciously recognizes only some of the information about heat and humidity sent from the nerve-endings in your skin, and it "tastes" and "smells" tuna sandwiches and diesel exhaust only when it chooses to do so. If you could consciously monitor and influence this process, you'd gain far greater control over the way you experience your life—and, in fact, you can do just that.

As you sensitize your brain, you'll find that it increasingly pays attention to stimuli from all or most of your senses rather than just the visual stimuli that, for most people, completely dominate other sensory input. When you describe an object that catches your attention, you'll learn to note not just its appearance, but also its texture, its sound or absence of sound, and even its smell.

WIDE-AWAKE WALKING

Here's an excellent way to train your brain to recognize the stimuli that all your senses offer. At walking speed, whether on a nature trail or a city street, you have time to observe closely both what's very close at hand and what's far in the distance. Even if you take precisely the same walk every day, practice experiencing your environment with new eyes and ears every time you go out.

1. Go for a walk. Note the "feel" of each foot striking the ground; feel the rhythm of your steps.
2. Experience the temperature of the air and whether it's humid or dry. Does the air carry any aromas, perhaps a hint of rain or dust blown by the wind?
3. Hear every sound as you walk—from the chirps of birds to the rumble of a distant freeway—and see what surrounds you in new ways.

SENSITIZED TO YOUR EMOTIONS

As I help people with problems of many kinds, often they are challenged when I ask them to become sensitive to their brains—as I've done in this chapter. They understand that the brain itself has no sensory receptors—that's why certain types of brain surgery can be performed when the patient is awake and free of anesthesia. Yet with practice and great focus, the truth is that you can physically experience your brain, just as you can experience your heightened senses.

Neuroscientists often assert that we experience emotion solely via the changes it induces in our bodies. When we experience fear, for example, our heart rate and blood pressure tend to increase. When we're joyful, muscles in our face respond and we reflect our happiness with broad smiles and sparkling eyes.

Our bodies do reflect our emotions in many ways, but I reject the belief that this is the sole manner in which we experience the feelings engendered in the brain. I believe it's possible to experience an emotion directly in your brain before it's manifested in your body, much as you directly experience input from your senses.

Try this experiment to see for yourself: the next time you experience a significant emotion—whether joy, anger, sadness, or something else—focus for a moment on your brain itself. If you're experiencing joy, notice whether your brain feels particularly light. If you're angry, does it feel hot? If you're sad, your brain may feel heavy when you bring your attention to it.

As you pay careful attention, I suspect that you'll begin to notice that your brain does feel—in a physical sense—something that correlates closely to the emotion you're currently experiencing. You may begin to notice body signals—an increased heart rate, a rise in body temperature, perspiration, or other physical signs of an emotion you haven't yet begun to "feel." Over the course of a few weeks, pay as much attention as you can to your emotions, your brain, and your body. What you'll discover is that, as you become comfortable with this process, you can dramatically change the emotion itself. With sensitivity and practice, you'll begin to recognize your own unique, emotionally reactive patterns. With further practice, you'll be able to "head off" or redirect and process your emotions.

Teach yourself to "feel" your brain and watch the rest of your body for signs that your brain is about to produce a certain emotion. And if what's emerging is an unwanted emotion, you can literally tell your brain to stop and produce a more desirable emotion instead. It sounds challenging, but I can assure you that when you've mastered your brain, your emotions will be yours to control—helping you to cope with your daily experience in the best ways possible and present yourself to the world as you choose.

Once your brain is sensitized—once you've learned how to rid yourself of stress, heighten the brain's experience of your senses, and support your brain with stretching, exercise, meditation, and deep breathing—a wide array of creative possibilities is laid before you.

In the next chapter, you'll discover how very versatile your brain is—a subject that's at the forefront of contemporary brain research. Your brain is extraordinarily powerful, yet also readily accessible. And as you'll see, it's capable of almost infinite change. Are you ready to discover the whole range of possibilities for you and your brain?

CHAPTER 8

Step Two: Brain Versatilizing

Becoming flexible is one of the keys to living well, staying healthy, and experiencing joy. The blocks between you and your greatest potential are probably much the same as they are for others—rigidity, fear, weakness, insecurity, imbalance. These represent the opposite of flexibility. Such unhelpful living patterns can become so deeply ingrained that it's hard to set yourself free from them. But when you successfully let go of old conditioning, you reap the benefits of flexibility, calmness, security, courage, strength, and balance. And you become more receptive to the opportunities life brings. The key to living a better life is to open yourself up enough to establish new patterns of thought and behavior, and to form new pathways in your brain.

Just as it's desirable to create flexibility in the body, it's desirable to create flexibility in the brain. Though our brains have the ability to rewire themselves throughout life, they often become "stiff" as time goes by. That's because we tend to become entrenched in certain behavior and thought patterns. The second step of Brain Education aims to reestablish and enhance the brain's ability to adapt to new environments, to approach problems in novel ways, and to transcend negative habits. I've coined a word to describe this process—"versatilizing."

Versatilizing relies on the brain ability known to neuroscience as "neuroplasticity." Not long ago, common wisdom held that once we passed our early years, our brain capabilities became fixed and brain cells died off at an alarming rate, never to be replaced. Everything brain-related was thought to be one long downhill slide from adolescence to old age. If you remember hearing those old—and incorrect—ideas, you can now replace them with more sophisticated, accurate, and exciting information.

An explosion in brain science has revealed that the nerve cells of your brain and nervous system are proficient at rewiring themselves. They are flexible and capable of regeneration. We now understand that the brain can redistribute functions from one anatomical area to another. It can increase the territory devoted to a particular function, and it can become more efficient at performing tasks—and it can do these things to the end of your days.

What can you achieve with your wonderfully changeable brain? Perhaps a better question would be, what *can't* you achieve? The goal of versatilizing your brain is to increase the flexibility of your thinking and enhance your ability to use your malleable brain to make positive changes in your behavior.

The Benefits of a Versatile Brain

Have you had the experience of looking at an object that you've always seen in a certain way and suddenly having it appear completely different to you? Or being deep in thought over some issue and coming up with a solution that's totally different from what you'd been considering? This happens as the brain circuit processing the information changes.

Viewed from the perspective of the brain, "information" signifies a certain mode of connecting neurons, and "learning" means creating new connecting networks. "Fixed ideas" are neural circuits that have been standardized by repetition of the same mode of information processing.

Fixed ideas feel natural because they're familiar to us, and that's why we have trouble recognizing them. The biggest reason it's hard for us to view something differently is that we have trouble even recognizing that we have a certain way of looking at things, since our usual perspective feels so natural. Even if we acknowledge this, we fail to accept new ideas because of the hardwired resistance created by fixed neural networks.

When our thinking is freed from fixed ideas, however, communication between neurons grows more active and brain function becomes more flexible. Then, the brain is able to accept new information more readily. A versatile brain can view things in new ways and be more creative. With a versatile brain, it's easier to find novel, interesting, and effective solutions to the problems, big and small, that you face in your daily life. Your stress decreases, and life becomes richer and more enjoyable.

The power to see things differently brings us greater composure and breadth of understanding. It becomes easier to see things from a different perspective, or to consider the possibility of different interpretations for a situation. A versatile brain lets us easily resolve problems in our relationships with other people and form more harmonious, amicable personal connections.

Flexible brains also make us more capable, for handling many things simultaneously becomes possible. Actually, the brain *cannot* do many things at once. Various experiments have revealed that so-called multitasking significantly lowers attention, which reduces quality of performance and can cause serious safety problems. What seems like doing many things at once is actually rapidly shifting attention between different objects.

Quality of performance in this state depends on how gently and rapidly the mode-switching can occur. Such switching is much easier when the brain is flexible. If you can't switch easily, it takes extra time and effort to move from task to task. Unless the switching is efficient, the mode of the previous situation affects the mode of the next, making it impossible to handle each one appropriately.

New office machines, new business processes, new institutions, fashions, culture, inventions—all of these things are rapidly changing our living, work, and social environments. Always having to experience and learn new things does make our lives fascinating, but it also poses a burdensome challenge. How well we adapt to the changes depends on the flexibility of our brains, not on our ability to learn. People with versatile brains aren't stubborn; they accept the fact that everything changes. That's why they aren't burdened by change, and why they easily adapt to it.

Research shows that the five senses—as well as language, intellect, logic, and so on—have their own respective areas in the brain. But in many cases, if one part of the brain is damaged, other parts take up at least a portion of the activity lost by the damaged area, displaying amazing adaptability. Furthermore, the brain enhances a specific sense when deprived of information from another sense. For example, a blind pianist may be able to memorize a whole song by listening to it just once. And experience tells us that our hearing becomes sharper at night. This is because the brain has assigned higher priority to hearing to compensate for lack of visual information. By taking advantage of this innate ability of the brain, we can learn to see, hear, and taste better. We can experience life in a livelier, richer way.

Brain Versatilizing lets us have an open mind and a broader perspective by maximizing the coordination between neurons. In the process, we feel our consciousness expanding and come to see ourselves and the world through a larger, deeper vision. Brain Versatilizing also opens up a world of a higher consciousness, through which we can integrate contradictory and conflicting life modes and interests, and thus understand paradox.

Actually, anything that challenges the brain to learn new skills and to rewire itself can be considered a Brain Versalitizing exercise. It might be a game that challenges the brain to work in new ways or a mind-body coordination exercise that's difficult to master. It might also mean examining our biases and preconceptions, including those that keep us from becoming our best selves. Most importantly, Brain Versatilizing gives us the power to transcend our old ways of being so that we create the life we really want. We can examine old preconceptions that limit us and finally break free of them. At last, we can feel empowered to overcome our negative habits.

Body-Brain Coordination Exercises

Every one of our movements, from a twitch of the eye to the subtle movement of a smile, is connected to a specific part of the brain. The brain controls every single motion that we consciously make. Therefore, working on specific parts of the body translates into stimulating the associated areas of the brain.

Most of us have well-established patterns of movement and thought. Our range of physical motions and the sorts of intellectual tasks we engage in tend to repeat themselves day after day. As comforting as routines can be, however, repeating the same patterns without extending beyond them can result in our body and brain becoming fixed and stagnant. Even when it comes to exercise, we tend to repeat the same motions over and over, needlessly neglecting parts of our body and brain. New exercises made up of novel rhythms and patterns will help you engage more of your brain, improving its plasticity.

According to a 2015 study done by University of Pisa researchers, moderate levels of physical exercise can increase the brain's flexibility. People who exercised showed enhanced plasticity in the visual cortex, the part of the brain that processes visual information, compared to those who were sedentary. The visual cortex is thought to lose plasticity as we age, making it more difficult for adults to recover from injuries and illness. The benefits of exercise on your brain can't be overemphasized. Intentionally adding novelty and variety to your exercise will make your brain even more malleable.

When you do Body-Brain Coordination exercises, you'll find that you have a dominant side of the body—just as you have a dominant hand. Use this to help reawaken the nondominant parts of your body and improve the coordination between your body and your brain.

A successful change in one area tends to loosen you up in wonderful ways and makes it easier to make positive change in another area. Practice Brain Flexibility exercises with as much variety as you can. Listen to unfamiliar music while doing them—or try silence if you usually play music when you exercise. Stand outside if you normally exercise indoors. Switch things up as much as you can, and enjoy tuning into your brain.

TAP AND SWEEP

This is a little like the old children's game of patting your head and rubbing your stomach at the same time.

1. Tap your right fist on the right side of your chest while your left hand sweeps up and down the left side.

2. Now, switch sides, so your right hand is sweeping and your left fist is tapping.

3. See how fast you can switch back and forth.

Helpful Hint: Start with One Hand First

Performing two different activities with each hand can confuse your brain when you first try it. Start with one hand first instead, and get into the rhythm of tapping or sweeping, whichever you find easier to do. Then add the other hand, matching the rhythm of the first hand. Do the exercise slowly in the beginning until you become more comfortable.

THUMB AND PINKY

Follow this movement with your eyes for a good eye workout and a fun brain challenge.

1. Make your hands into fists and extend your arms out in front of your chest. Look at your fists.
2. Point your left thumb and right pinky to the left. Then, point your right thumb and left pinky to the right.
3. Keep switching left and right. See how fast you can switch back and forth.

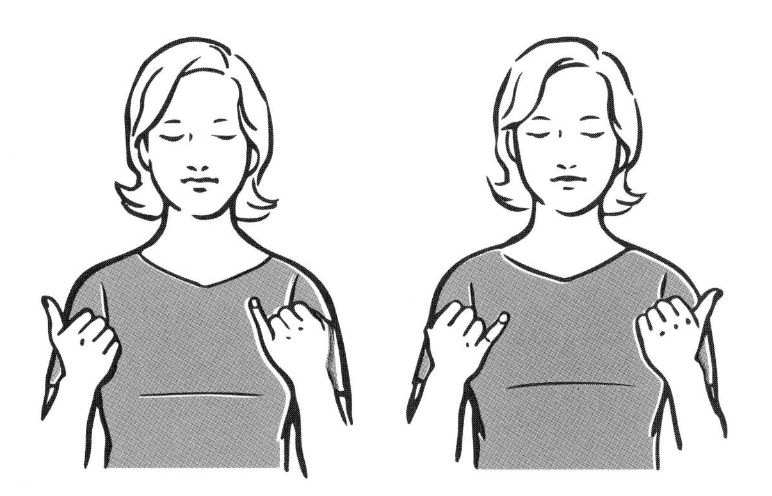

TRIANGLE CIRCLE SQUARE

Doing two tasks simultaneously challenges different parts of the brain to work together.

1. In the air, draw a circle with your left hand and a triangle with your right, drawing the shapes continuously with both hands at the same time.
2. Now, switch hands. Draw a triangle with your left hand and a circle in the opposite direction with your right.
3. Keep alternating hands and repeating the motions. When you become proficient at drawing the circle and triangle, try drawing a square and a triangle instead.

ROCK, PAPER, SCISSORS, BRAIN

When you try anything new, you make new connections in your brain. For this fun and stimulating exercise, you're going to play that familiar childhood game, "Rock, Paper, Scissors"—with a grown-up difference.

1. Practice playing "Rock, Paper, Scissors" with yourself. Make a symbol with your nondominant hand and then use your dominant hand to slap the winning symbol over it. Remember how it's done? Rock smashes scissors, scissors cut paper, and paper wraps rock.

2. Next, switch hands and use your nondominant hand to slap rock, papers, and scissors onto your dominant hand against an imaginary opponent.

3. Now, play the game against yourself as quickly as you can, with each of your hands playing against the other, making sure that each hand makes a different symbol and that one cancels the other out. Start by slapping down each symbol on the count of three, but then begin making a change with each beat. Continue practicing until you can do this quickly and fluidly.

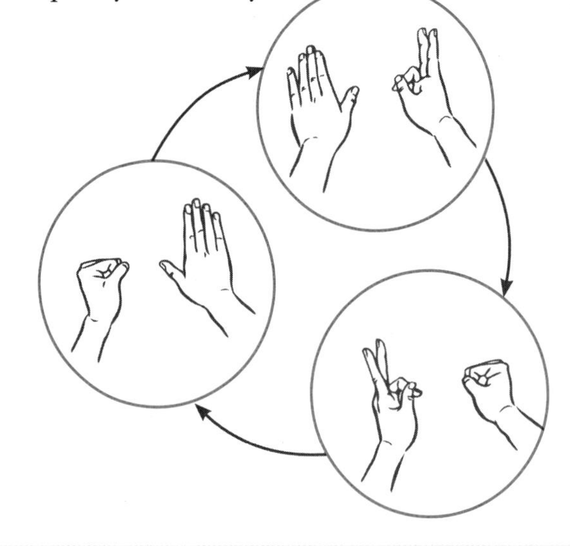

OPPOSITE SHOULDER ROTATION

Besides being a challenge for the brain, this exercise helps to open the shoulder joints.

1. Stretch your arms straight ahead with your palms facing each other.

2. Rotate one arm clockwise, at the same time rotating the other arm counterclockwise. Do about five to ten repetitions.

3. Alternate directions and repeat.

EYE-HAND INFINITY

If you work at a desk for long periods and often feel shoulder and neck stiffness, this is a good exercise for relieving some of the tension.

1. Raise one thumb (pointing upward) to eye level, holding it at a point between your eyes and away from your face. Gently bend your elbow so that your arm isn't stiff. In the air, draw the shape of the infinity sign (a sideways figure eight) with your thumb. Move slowly and deliberately, concentrating on the movement of your thumb. Hold your head still and follow your thumb with just your eyes. Repeat at least three times.

2. Repeat using your other hand.

3. Try using both hands together. Clasp your hands together with your thumbs crossing on top. Focusing on the intersection of your thumbs, draw the shape of the infinity sign.

BODY-AND-MIND INFINITY

1. Raise both arms in front of you and trace a large infinity sign in the air with your hands, one hand following the other.
2. Move your neck along with your hands and arms.

3. Now, move your arms, neck, waist, and hips. Trace the infinity sign using your whole body as you simultaneously imagine the sign being drawn in your head.

4. Now, rest your hands by placing them behind your waist. Imagine an infinity symbol on the ground in front of you. Trace the symbol by skipping and hopping your way around its edge.

5. Stop and sit in a half lotus position. Using your imagination, trace the infinity symbol in your mind.

Helpful Hint: Infinity of Your Mind

You've drawn the infinity symbol on a small and a large scale, with your body and in your mind. You can also meditate on infinity as a concept. Allow your mind to be opened by a visit to a planetarium or observatory. Look through a telescope and connect with something outside yourself that offers your brain a feeling for the infinite. Look at the stars, or read something from theoretical physics or astronomy—even something that's a bit "over your head." Let your brain chew on something more complex than you're accustomed to and feel the pleasure of being out of your depth yet in touch with something larger or perhaps more mystical. You'll be amazed at what an invigorating experience this can be.

Brain Energy Exploration

While we can't move our brains on a physical level, we can do so on an energy level. Brain Energy Sensing Exercise uses the power of imagination to stretch and pull the brain to stimulate fixed neural pathways and increase activity. With practice, you'll be able to match the brain's expansion-contraction cycle to the rhythm of your breathing.

For this exercise, you'll use the energy sensitivity of your hands that you experienced in the Energy Sensing Exercise or Jigam exercise (page 122). In fact, this exercise is often called "brain Jigam exercise."

As you breathe, your hands and brain will become attuned to a single rhythm. You'll feel your whole body expand as you breathe in, then contract as you breathe out. With enough concentration, your body will seem to expand to infinity when you inhale and contract to a dot on a page as you exhale. With even deeper immersion, your body itself will seem to disappear and your consciousness expand to infinity, then contract to nothingness with the rhythm of your breath. You'll feel your body filled with fresh energy, every part of it purified and rejuvenated.

Brain Massage is an exercise designed to use the power of energy to restore the brain to balance. In our complex and stressful world, we develop imbalance in body and brain on a daily basis. By utilizing the principle of Shim Ki Hyul Jung—where your mind goes, energy flows—Brain Massage directs the flow of energy to the brain through relaxation and gentle stimulation.

BRAIN ENERGY SENSING EXERCISE

1. Sitting in a comfortable position raise your hands to chest level, palms facing each other. Begin Energy Sensing Exercise by pushing your hands close together and then pulling them apart.
2. Now, move your hands toward each other and apart again as you breathe in and breathe out.

3. As you continue, picture your lungs. Let your lungs inflate as you breathe in and deflate as you breathe out, while your hands move outward and inward. Feel the fresh air enter your lungs as you inhale and the spent energy and gases flow outward as you exhale.

4. Cup your hands on either side of your head, without touching it, and feel energy flowing from your brain.

5. Spread your fingers apart, and then bring them in again to expand the feeling of energy from your brain.

6. Bring your hands closer to your head, and then push them farther out as you feel energy manifest as magnetic attraction and repulsion.

7. Let the movement of your hands, your breath, and your brain synchronize into a single rhythm. Let your body inflate and deflate with the rhythm of your breath, like a large balloon.

8. Release the tension in your shoulders and rest your hands on your knees. Concentrating on your lower Dahnjon, breathe in and out deeply three times.

9. Clap quickly 10 times. Briskly rub your hands together and gently massage your face, neck, and chest.

BRAIN MASSAGE

1. Raise your hands in a prayer position, but without the hands touching each other. Connect with the sensation of energy by practicing Energy Sensing Exercise.

2. Feel bright energy gather in your hands, and feel your own pulse. Visualize the energy swimming around your hands.

3. Observe your brain as you become acutely conscious of your breathing. Feel for areas of your brain where energy is blocked.

4. Now, imagine gently taking hold of the brain and lowering it to chest level in front of you, surrounded and protected by the healing light of your hands as you freely but carefully caress it. Try to correct any deficiencies or imbalance you feel in your brain as you knead, massage, and smooth it.

5. Now, imagine stretching the brain in all directions—up, down, and diagonally. Depending on the individual, one direction will feel more comfortable than the others.

6. As if you're playing with a soccer ball, roll the brain to one side and then the other.
7. Gently place your brain back into your head.
8. Move your concentration to your lower Dahnjon, and breathe in and out three times. Open your eyes.
9. Rub your hands together briskly, making them warm. Gently massage your face, neck, and chest.

Helpful Hint: Sounds in the Brain

As you practice this exercise with full concentration, you may hear sounds that seem to come from your brain—as if your brain is "stretching." Don't be alarmed—this is a natural phenomenon that may occur when the energy inside your brain begins to circulate and expand more.

Brain Flexibility Exercises

Your brain will gain a great deal of flexibility if you get in the habit of changing your point of view quickly. This is critical for creative problem-solving, and it will help you manage human relationships as well.

This process involves techniques that force your brain away from the ordinary into the realm of the extraordinary. It may take the form of moving or doing things in an unusual way. Or you may have contact with an unusual object or a new place so that many senses and associations are engaged simultaneously. This surprises the brain, getting it out of its rut.

Always seek new experiences. Novelty is one of the secrets to the versatile brain. When you engage in the same activities day after day, your neural pathways become solid. There's no reason for new connections to form—why should they? Your brain has all the connections it needs to handle the demands you put on it.

But when you demand more of your brain—when you start reading books in genres you've never tried before, or learning how to cook a new dish for dinner—you surprise it with new information. It's like adding a new element to a workout. The brain doesn't have the wiring to process these new demands, so it's forced to forge new connections. Out come the neurological road crews to lay new electrical cables from one area of the cerebral cortex to another. Fresh nerve connections spark with electrochemical messages. Your brain activity increases. This is the secret to having a more agile, creative mind.

Try activities that open up your brain to new ways of thinking. Take the brain outside its normal routine to encourage original thought patterns. The brain loves to try new things and thrives on a challenge! It hates tasks that are boring. Give your brain fresh physical, intellectual, and emotional stimulation. Challenge it in new ways every day.

The following exercises are designed to help you learn to shift perspective easily and quickly. Normally, we have a lot of preconceptions attached to just about anything we look at. Try these games, and you'll start to think "outside the box."

Some of the exercises in this chapter may feel silly. But try them anyway. Your brain benefits greatly when you play hand and word games, jump rope, solve puzzles, learn new physical skills, and read material that challenges your thinking and comprehension. Try new things with exuberance—be willing to fail and look silly as you attempt something unfamiliar. Don't let the last textbook you read be the one you studied in your final class in school. Life is an infinite university, and as a happy and willing student you can continue to learn and grow until the very end of your life.

MORE TIPS FOR A FLEXIBLE BRAIN

Here are more things you can do to make your brain more malleable.

1. **Pay attention to detail:** Look closer at the subtleties in things and people—the shadings and brushwork in paintings, the fruit flavors in fine wine, or the body language of two people speaking on the other side of the room. Paying attention to minute detail is a spectacular workout for the brain.
2. **Plan to be spontaneous:** Change up your regular routine. If you have been following a daily schedule for ten years, break it. If you take an evening walk, occasionally venture along a new route. Once in a while, alter the order of your day.
3. **Travel:** Unfamiliar places and situations may make you uncomfortable, but that is the point. Dealing with unfamiliar customs, trying to speak the local dialect, and learning about new cultural wonders all earn you major brownie points from your cortex.
4. **Meet smart folks:** Talk to smart people—really talk to them. Engage in conversation that challenges your political or spiritual views and forces you to see other people's perspectives. Ask questions; debate issues. Trading ideas forces your mind to question and investigate, and that is always good.
5. **Get shifty:** University of Toledo researchers found that if you move your eyes left and right for 20 seconds, as if you were watching a tennis match, you stimulate the frontal lobes of your brain and enhance your ability to remember selective recent personal events. Scientists guess this movement improves connections between the brain's right and left hemispheres.

▶ Naming and Renaming

Giving familiar objects new names helps open your awareness by playing with your perceptions and challenging you to see and hear things in new ways. Learning to name things accurately is one of the first tasks of our young lives—pointing, asking, enunciating, and repeating until a name is fixed in our brain. The creature with long whiskers who sleeps all day on the couch becomes "cat," and the great discovery is that there are many different cats out in the world.

Once you lock in your perception of something, you can experience fierce internal resistance when you try to rename it. Because you've created a hardwired connection between the thing and its name—and have done so intentionally and repeatedly—a challenge to that reality is met with immediate dismissal by your brain. The renaming exercise that follows is silly and fun, but it can help give you greater flexibility when you take on "renaming" the larger ideas and experiences of your life.

The point is to help you see that the names you have for things can be investigated and challenged—that it's possible to see everything from a different perspective than the one you've held forever, even if that new perspective is just a bit ridiculous. Another great way to make your brain more versatile is to study a new language—to literally learn new names for common things. Buy a set of flashcards containing words in a language you don't know, and concentrate on learning them all. Or rent a film in a language you don't know (with subtitles turned off) and try to enjoy the sense of disorientation you'll feel. Try, too, to grasp as much of the story as you can.

RENAMING GAME

1. Look around and give new names to the things you see.
   Give each thing a name that normally belongs to something else. For example, rename the window "hamburger" and the pencil "horse." The only rule is that the new name can't be associated with the object in any way. In other words, the window shouldn't be named "door," and the pencil shouldn't be named "pen."

2. For more fun, try this with a friend and make it a game. Take turns pointing out objects to name, and score a point each time you successfully rename an object. The person with the highest number of points wins the game.

MUSIC DRAWING

1. Choose recordings of three stylistically distinct instrumental songs. For example, you might have a lighthearted polka, a soft lullaby, and a booming orchestral piece.
2. Sit comfortably, eyes closed, and quietly listen to one of the songs. Notice any colors or feelings that come to mind.
3. Gather crayons in colors that seem to represent the music. Now, play the piece again, this time "drawing" it on a piece of paper. Let your hand move freely in response to the music.
4. Do the same thing for the other two songs.

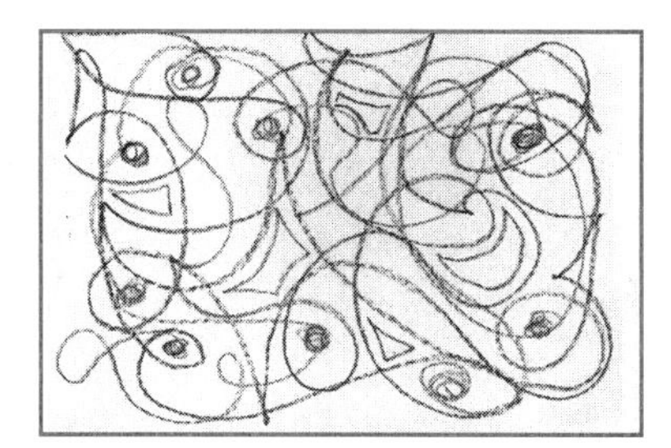

LOOKING FROM BOTH SIDES

Here's an exercise you can do anywhere to help expand your perceptions and open your mind to new possibilities. It's fun to surprise your brain and challenge yourself to see things from a new point of view.

1. Think of something nonhuman in your home with which you interact on a daily basis. It could be an object (such as a TV or a toaster) or maybe a beloved pet.

2. Now, write a complete description of this thing, telling all about how it looks and acts.

3. Then, write a description of yourself from the point of view of the object. How do you look from its perspective?

CREATIVE SHAPES

1. Take a look at these shapes. How many different objects do you see?
2. If you see three, try looking again. Think of things that the shapes remind you of—maybe the square is a TV, for example, and the circle is a penny.
3. Draw on the following shapes to turn them into something new.

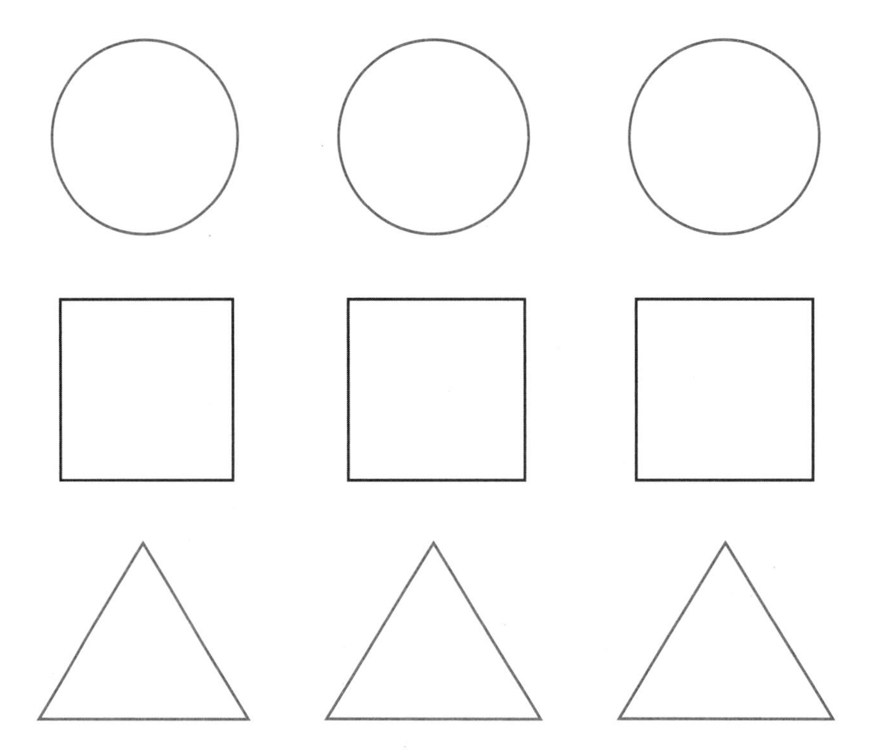

Challenging Assumptions

Simple games and exercises for your versatile brain demonstrate just how hard it can be to step outside of deeply ingrained patterns of thought. Given how challenging it can be just to call an object by another name, imagine the brain mastery you need to change your thinking about more complex concepts.

From now on, when you hear yourself make inflexible pronouncements about your self-identity, preferences, beliefs, and how things should be, bring a more flexible and versatilized brain to your thinking. Question assumptions that felt immutable in the past.

How do you describe life experiences in ways that lock you into a dysfunctional or unhelpful idea? Perhaps the worst experience of your life has always been described in terms that make you the victim. But if that experience actually made you stronger, try framing it in a new way the next time you recount it—as the difficult but refining experience that changed and empowered you.

Do you identify yourself in ways that can be challenged? *I'm not a morning person.* Is that true, or simply an image you've created? Have you misidentified your life challenges? *Earning more money requires working longer and harder hours.* It may surprise you to learn that in many people's experience, this statement is untrue. Do you hesitate to experience a better life simply because you mistake the order in which things need to happen? *I'll know peace and happiness after I accumulate wealth.* Do you emphatically state beliefs that are blatantly unhelpful? *I don't like to exercise.* Wouldn't you like to change that image of yourself for the sake of your physical and emotional well-being? *One person can't make a difference in the world.* Millions of individuals who make a positive difference every day would strongly disagree.

You benefit from rethinking how you identify things—especially when your old thought patterns don't serve your health, peace, or happiness.

Extending Your Competence

We all need to guard against a kind of intellectual, physical, emotional, and spiritual laziness that can slip into our lives if we aren't careful. This slide into lackadaisical patterns shouldn't be confused with peace and tranquility. When we're complacent, we experience limitation and restriction rather than freedom. Freedom and an engaged and flexible brain are what bring true and lasting peace, and the kind of tranquility each of us desires.

I encourage you to recognize when you're in a rut and to snap yourself out of it by taking on something that's foreign to you. I understand how good it feels to be competent at something—to know what you're doing and to do it well. But if you rarely extend beyond what you've already mastered, your life becomes much smaller than your real potential. What don't you do well? What do you avoid doing at all costs? What is so far beyond your natural comfort level that even thinking about it gives you cold sweats?

The things you name as you answer these questions would make a wonderful "must-do" list, wouldn't it? Imagine how empowered and capable you'll feel when you successfully take on these challenges and accomplish what you formerly thought you couldn't.

You don't have to become proficient at everything that intimidates you. But if you make even a little progress, or just shed your fears, you'll awaken a part of your brain that's been dormant. You'll become more comfortable in general with the idea of trying things that don't come easily to you, and that alone will help you face your challenges head on. Never again will you shrink away from mountains you haven't yet climbed.

Set Yourself Free

Your authentic self knows who you truly are. But if your essence is buried deep in your brain under tired ideas and unhelpful patterns that limit you, it's almost impossible for you to express that authentic self. When you accept responsibility for your brain and your life and work consciously with your brain's ability to change, you are the creator of your experience.

The bad news about your changeable brain is that bad habits and sloppy thinking create well-worn pathways that are difficult to redirect. It takes persistence and practice to change. The very good news is that in working to upgrade the quality of your life by rewiring the hardware of your brain, you can use its neuroplasticity to permanently upgrade your thoughts and your daily habits.

Don't cage in your awareness or limit your expectations about what you can accomplish. Set yourself free, knowing that if you try something new in one area of your life, you'll experience an openness in your brain. As a result, other areas of your life will become more creative and fun as well. Get over old ideas about your limits and try new things, and you'll mature and grow in skill and awareness.

We are what we think. We are what we repeatedly do. We are as conscious or unconscious as we choose to be. With more information and more practice, you can work with your brain's amazing neuroplasticity to improve your life. You are the master of your own life. Your task is to actualize your Power Brain—and your best life.

CHAPTER 9

Step Three: Brain Refreshing

Let me tell you a story that comes from ancient Korea. A Buddhist monk was traveling on foot to a distant land, and as night fell, he grew very weary. Exhausted, he stumbled into a pitch-black cave and decided to stay the night. In the darkness, he felt his way along the floor of the cave and found a small bowl filled with the most delicious and refreshing water he had ever drunk. His thirst thoroughly quenched, he lay down and slept deeply. He awoke in the morning feeling refreshed.

But in the early light that dimly illuminated the cave, to his horror he saw that the bowl he'd drunk from the night before was actually an upturned human skull, filled with brackish water. Suddenly, the thought of the delicious water he'd consumed only a few hours before made him sick to his stomach. Startled by this experience, the monk was enlightened about the nature of perception and the power of the human mind to transform reality. This monk, Wonhyo, later became a significant figure in the Korean Buddhist tradition.

Brain Refreshing is the process of discovering—like Wonhyo—how you can free your mind of limiting negative preconceptions and emotional residue from past traumas. The goal is to have a more positive state of mind and greater, more productive control over your emotions and thought patterns. This step is designed to develop three important skills. The first is to become fully aware of your emotions and moods. The second is to clear troublesome, harmful emotions from your mind. The third skill is to change long-term temperament patterns. Brain Refreshing is an exciting and liberating component of Brain Education, one that offers true freedom from the past and ensures that positive change is always possible.

Working Skillfully with Emotions

Before we proceed, I want to be very clear: life would be pale indeed without emotions. When you imagine a life without laughter, excitement, apprehension, or sorrow, it's flat and formless—it hardly seems to be life at all. In your own life, isn't it clear that you bring valuable emotion to the most important decisions you make? You seek strong relationships, success, and money in large part because you desire the emotional experience of being loved, respected, and secure. At their deepest core, humans want to be joyful, and rightly so, because joy is the most sublime of emotions. Yet emotions can also lead you to make decisions you regret; they can prevent you from seeing an issue clearly, and even paralyze you with fear when you clearly need to take action.

Even though you know that emotion arises within your brain, you may tend to look outside yourself for its source. "My husband makes me angry," you might find yourself saying—or alternatively, "I love it when he brings me flowers." But neither flowers nor husbands are inherently good or bad. You experience them in a positive or negative way far more because of you and the state of your brain than because of them. How you react emotionally depends entirely on the preconceptions and expectations existing within you. While you may be able to empathize with others, and they with you, ultimately your emotional experience is unique to you.

Here's another example. Imagine that your car is in the shop and you're forced to walk the two miles from your house to work. If you're running late, on edge about tasks that must be done, or wearing uncomfortable shoes, your anger and frustration may increase with every step. But if you're relaxed and comfortable, and have time to enjoy the fresh air and exercise, your walk may be quite invigorating. It may remind you how good it is to get out of your car. These two quite dissimilar experiences have nothing to do with the blocks between home and office somehow having radically changed from one journey to the next. The only changes are emotional and attitudinal—and they come entirely from within you.

The important lesson is that when you look outside yourself for the source of your emotions, you surrender your personal power by believing you're at the mercy of external circumstances. But when you look only to yourself as the source of your emotions, your focus shifts to something over which you do have control. You can't be in command of external events or other people, but you can play an enormous role in determining how they affect you emotionally.

Emotional Intelligence

I've heard many people say, "I choose not to exercise control over my feelings." Often, this attitude is born of a sense that negative emotions are just part of who we are—that persistently feeling angry or sad is the natural result of life's hard knocks. But how sensible is it to continue harboring such ideas when they wreak havoc on our bodies and our energies? The path of personal wisdom is to harness the brain's great powers of self-awareness—the watcher watching the watcher—to uncover the hidden patterns of emotion within us and to change how we view the world. We have the power to change our set points, as it were.

With Brain Refreshing techniques, you'll begin to hone your emotional intelligence, a term popularized by author and psychologist Daniel Goleman. Emotional intelligence—the ability to perceive, assess, and manage your own emotions, as well as to deal with those of others—is one of the most valuable skills of the mature individual.

When we're adolescents, adult passions appear in our minds unbidden: sexual longings, risk-taking urges, the desire to acquire expensive, beautiful things. But because our prefrontal cortex—the area of the brain that lets us make social judgments and develop foresight about the possible outcomes of our choices—doesn't mature until about age 25, emotion and passion can overwhelm us when we're young. Many young people lack the emotional intelligence to understand or control their powerful emotions. Instead, they are often on autopilot, led by their hormones and desires.

As we age, unfortunately too many of us swing to the opposite extreme. Because of some trauma we've experienced in life, we shut our emotions down out of fear. We live in terror of admitting to our emotions. But this isn't living. Despite the Western emphasis on intellect, ancient wisdom tells us that people are complete only when ruled by their emotions as well as their intellect—when their passions and their judgment are given equal weight. Yet many adults, especially as they grow older, become afraid of their feelings.

Emotional intelligence is the ability to assess one's emotions as they occur, to understand why they are occurring, and to manage their effects in real time. This deep level of self-awareness is accessible through Brain Refreshing. The human brain has an extraordinary ability to reflect on its own functioning, and people with strong emotional intelligence can identify pessimistic feelings as they occur and place them in proper perspective.

Imagine being able to perceive your feeling of irritation when speaking with a friend who taxes your patience, as if observing from the outside. You still experience the feeling, but you have the presence of mind to know where it's coming from and to remind yourself, "He doesn't really mean to be irritating; it's best to let that feeling go." This lets you set aside the unhelpful emotions and retain your positive outlook toward other people.

When you're able to face painful memories and let them wash out of your mind, you see the power that you once granted them. You discover that those memories have no power of their own, only the power you gave them. You're now in control of what triggers your emotions. You could say that you are achieving the highest potential of your emotional brain. Your mind becomes free to pursue its higher purposes—love, compassion, creativity, health, discovery, healing others. This kind of emotional awareness can renew lifelong relationships by allowing you to let go of meaningless grudges and focus on the positive, affirming traits of the people in your life.

Freedom from the Past

Your brain constantly receives information from the world around you. It's how your brain responds to information, rather than its intrinsic positive or negative value, that determines what the information "means." It may trigger fears and seem quite harmful, or it may appear to offer nurturing help and support. It all depends on your brain—which you, of course, can control. And as the ancient monk who drank from the skull discovered, when you allow a preconception to rule your behavior, you're allowing your past to control your present and even your future.

The past exists in the present only as information stored in your brain. The past can't be changed, because it doesn't exist except as neural memory, yet its influence on the present can be enormous. We often mistakenly think that the past has the same physical substance as the present. But whether it comes in the form of a book, a photograph, a film, a story you tell someone, or a scar on your body, any past you can think of exists in the present only as a form of information. Recognizing that the past really is only information is the first step toward freeing yourself from it.

We could divide the information of the past into "facts" and "interpretations." In many cases, what actually hurts most and makes us suffer longest isn't the incident or the fact, but how we interpret it. And interpretations don't end with one go; things get reinterpreted again and again, and new versions are constantly being written. We rewrite them several times a day! Know that the information that controls you isn't facts, but rather your interpretation of them. You can interpret something differently or erase it if necessary, because you are the author of the interpretation.

Knowing you can do that and discovering the power to do it must come through the process of refreshing your brain. I'm not saying that the past isn't important. But the past should be a steppingstone enabling us to get to where we are now, and a reference for the choices we make now and in the future. The past shouldn't be a source of unreasonable fear that limits our personal potential.

Imagine adding the monk's insights to your own life. Freed from the memories of intractable arguments over the years, wouldn't you delight in being able to love your father simply because he's your father? Or what would it be like to learn to swim at last simply because you want to enjoy that pleasure, free from the memory of the terrifying experience you had in a pool when you were small?

Imagine, too, putting your life story down in writing as you've always wanted to, free from the memory of a teacher who claimed you wrote poorly. Hundreds of liberations become possible when you discover simple methods for releasing your brain from the emotional connotation of negative memories.

Letting Them Go

I don't argue with those neuroscientists who suggest that it's quite difficult to gain control over certain "automatic" emotional responses. When you hear the sound of a window opening in the middle of the night, you're virtually certain to respond with fear. In that particular instance, it's an important and self-protective response. But if the memory of that fear never recedes and it prevents you from buying a house that's right for you, for example, a once-appropriate emotion becomes a serious obstacle to living your best life.

You wouldn't consider letting your trash pile up and go uncollected for weeks or even years. It would be unpleasant, unhealthy, and very much in the way of living the life you want. Yet many people fiercely hold on to emotional memories that serve them no better than rotting garbage. Do you find yourself unwilling to begin a new relationship because the memory of a failed relationship is too painful to let you move forward? Does the anger you harbor at being unfairly terminated from an important job keep you from making the most of your career? Are there other circumstances in which you find yourself limited by emotional memories from long ago?

Recent scientific research has demonstrated that chronic negative emotions significantly affect our memory and learning functions, and even reduce the overall mass of the brain. That's how harmful they can be. But the good news is that you aren't forced simply to endure them—or worse, to pretend they aren't there when you experience their presence in a variety of debilitating ways each day. Instead, you can develop the dependable habit of releasing emotions as soon as they're no longer useful to you.

Brain Cleansing

The Brain Cleansing Exercise uses imagination and energy to purify the negative and self-limiting memories of the past. The power to imagine is the most creative and perhaps the highest function of the brain. Imagination in itself is a wonderful brain exercise. To maximize the benefits of Brain Education, it's important to maximize your imaginative abilities. You also need to believe that a combination of imagination and energy will truly bring about certain changes in the brain. Change comes in no small part from believing that it is possible.

As you undergo the Brain Cleansing Exercise, you'll recall many memories—some of them painful and raw. This is a natural phenomenon of the "refreshing" process of Brain Education. Don't try to force these memories to disappear; watch them roll out in front of you as if in a movie, and they'll soon lose their power to negatively affect you. Only when you put some distance between yourself and the memories that have limited you will you be truly free from the emotional prison that often acts as our internal glass ceiling.

BRAIN CLEANSING EXERCISE

1. Sit comfortably on a chair or on the floor. Relax your body.
2. Raise your hands in front of your chest, and activate your sense of energy with Energy Sensing Exercise (page 122).
3. After a few minutes, bring your hands up to your head, and imagine that you slowly lift your brain and lower it down in front of your chest. Trusting what you see in your mind's eye, observe which parts of your brain are hurt, distorted, or blocked.

4. Now, imagine a trickle of pure spring water washing over your brain with cool freshness and purity.
5. With your hands, wash away the dirt left by emotions from long ago.
6. Then, hold your brain, and rinse away stagnant and spent energy with the pure water. Gently shake your brain in the stream, loosening and shaking out all the dirt.
7. Now, gently guide your glowing brain back into your head.
8. Breathe in and out deeply three times. Rub your hands together briskly until they're warm. Gently massage your face, head, and neck.

Brain Breathing

As I've explained, we each have a system of meridians, pathways along which energy travels through our bodies. Energy points are the gates or openings through which energy enters and exits. The top of the head is the location of the energy point called the Baekhwe. When you concentrate on the Baekhwe point along with the natural rhythm of your breathing, you can start to feel energy coming in through the top of your head. The process of using this energy to refresh the brain is called Brain Breathing. After doing this exercise, you'll notice that your brain feels lighter and more refreshed.

Once you get used to breathing in with your Baekhwe and breathing out through your mouth, you can practice the same exercise using other energy points, such as your temples (Taeyang) or your third eye (In-dang). Imagine energy coming in through these points while stagnant energy goes out through your mouth.

Brain Breathing is designed to maximize the naturally occurring exchange of energy by using the power of your imagination. The livelier your imagination, the more effective this exercise will be.

BRAIN BREATHING EXERCISE

1. Sit in a comfortable position and place your hands on your knees, with your eyes closed. Relax your body and mind by taking several deep breaths. Feel the stream of energy move from the top of your head down to your chest, and then to your lower Dahnjon.

2. Concentrate on the top of your head, the Baekhwe energy point. As you breathe in through your nose, imagine a stream of energy entering through the top of your head, circling around inside your head, and cleansing your brain of stagnant or negative energy.

3. Breathe out through your mouth with a soft "whooh" sound as you imagine stagnant, negative energy being expelled from your body

4. Slowly breathe in and out three times as you imagine fresh energy entering and stagnant energy leaving.

5. Open your eyes and rub your hands together until they are warm. Gently massage your head and face.

Brain Releasing

Among your brain's many astounding capabilities is the way it retains experience as both memory and emotion, storing an extraordinary amount of information about what occurred in the past and what it meant emotionally. Every memory, in fact, carries associated emotional energy, even in instances where the emotional component seems very small. And it's the nature of emotional memory to cast experience as either positive or negative—note how few past events you think of in an entirely neutral way. Neutral experiences tend to flow through the body and mind. It's the high and low points that stay with us.

Experiences are crucial to learning, development, and growth—we simply can't live our best lives without them. The key is to retain those remembered experiences without the negative emotional memories that impede present progress. You keep the memory of the event but clear away your negative and self-limiting emotional response to it.

▶ Releasing in the Present Moment

Like most people, in difficult situations, you probably tend to respond emotionally in one of two ways—with repression or expression.

When you attempt to repress an emotion, you work hard to find a way to stuff it, ignore it, or pretend it doesn't exist. That may seem like a rather responsible thing to do—lots of us are trained to keep quiet when things bother us, after all—but burying an emotion doesn't do away with it. It simply turns a current emotion into an emotional memory that can remain in your brain indefinitely, constantly finding ways to disrupt your life. Sometimes, buried emotions fester, then suddenly find expression in violent physical or verbal outbursts that traumatize both you and the people to whom they're directed.

On the surface, the outward expression of a negative emotion might seem to be a good way of contending with a crisis or challenge. At least shouting at someone or punching a wall "gets it out"—but this still allows the emotion to return unbidden at some other time. And, of course, you run the real risk of injuring someone when you release an unwanted emotion with verbal barbs or clenched fist. By acting so impulsively and recklessly, you emotionally damage yourself, too.

Is there a better way to respond to life's challenges and the negative emotions they engender? There truly is. When you simply release those emotions rather than repress or wildly express them, you immediately go a long way toward taking control of a complex situation. You also help remove the emotion itself from the role it may be playing in making the circumstance difficult.

But when you're suddenly angry, you're angry. When you're afraid, you tend to be very afraid. Doesn't it take extraordinary willpower to release powerful emotion such as anger, fear, and sadness right when you're experiencing them most powerfully? Actually, you don't need to be an Eastern mystic with a lifetime of meditative experience to learn how to release emotion. All you need is a tool you already possess, but which—if you're like most adults—you use far too seldom. That wonderful tool is your smile.

▸ The Power of a Smile

When you smile, your blood pressure drops, your chest relaxes, and you breathe more easily. Smiling causes your brain to release important neurochemicals—serotonin, which improves mood, and endorphins, which reduce the sensation of pain. Studies show that forcing yourself to smile triggers the same neurochemicals that a spontaneous smile does. When you smile, your brain immediately initiates a "joy response" that dramatically shifts your outlook. And as your mood improves, you open yourself to new possibilities; emotions such as anger, fear, and even sadness recede.

Smiling is a great exercise. Your brain has to initiate a complex series of physical and psychological actions to create a smile. In fact, studies have shown that three to four minutes of smiling are equivalent to a full physical workout for reducing stress. Smiling sends oxygen rushing to your brain and lifts your spirits. Perhaps even more importantly, it's the single most important key to being able to take control of your brain.

Am I suggesting, then, that you've got to find a way to be endlessly and constantly happy in order to make the most of your best brain? No, I'm not. What I've come to understand in my studies and my work is that

5 WAYS TO BUILD YOUR EMOTIONAL RESILIENCE

Practice the following to regain your emotional balance effectively after a setback rather than wallowing in anxiety, anger, or depression.

1. **Know yourself:** Explore who you are as an emotional being. What makes you angry, anxious, or depressed most? When do you feel happy, joyful, and content? With self-knowledge comes the ability to make choices and decisions that will help build resilience.
2. **Keep good company:** Feeling connected to your family members, friends, or colleagues is essential in building emotional resilience. Accepting help and support from those who care about you and will listen to you strengthens resilience.
3. **Pump up your positivity:** Practice optimism and actively seek the good side of a bad situation. Look at adversity as an opportunity to learn and build the habit of moving toward adversity instead of running away from it. Keep things in perspective. Learn from your mistakes and think long-term.
4. **Take care of yourself:** Pay attention to your own needs and feelings. Engage in activities that you enjoy and find relaxing. Exercise regularly. Eat well and sleep well. Looking after yourself helps to keep your mind and body primed to deal with situations that require resilience.
5. **Practice detached watching:** Observe your thoughts and feelings as a nonjudgmental witness. Avoid making any judgments about the rightness or wrongness of them—just watch them from a distance. This practice gives you insight into the inner workings of your own mind and how to improve them.

the ability to smile when we're happy is simply one of the great divine gifts each of us is given. It's smiling when we're not happy that we're called to learn as we seek creative fulfillment and peace.

It's easy to smile when we feel happy. Then what about smiling for no reason? Would that seem awkward or unnatural? Instead of smiling because we're happy, is it possible to become happy by smiling? Yes, absolutely. I'm not suggesting that smiling when a loved one has died, for example, can transform your sadness into a kind of giddy reverie. It cannot—and you wouldn't want it to. But in the midst of that pain, smiling as you remember the person you've lost can indeed transform a raw and aching emotion into one that's bearable and that more accurately reflects the intertwined joys and sorrows inherent in being alive.

Almost certainly, you've experienced how unexpected joy or laughter can lighten a deeply sad moment and offer you both peace and perspective. The challenge is to take that understanding and learn how to intentionally smile exactly when you most need to—not just when you're already happy.

Practice smiling every day, and watch your face physically change. It will. Watch as your health changes for the better. Notice, too, how your goals become easier to reach. Don't be stingy with your smiles—share them freely everywhere and with everyone—and don't hesitate to smile because you're alone. Your brain is hard-wired to initiate a smile at the blink of an eye. Don't struggle to prevent it; the joy and happiness expressed in your smile are your natural states of being.

▶ Brain Releasing Exercise

Despite its many extraordinary capabilities, your brain finds it very difficult to produce two opposite emotions at the same time. Your brain is designed for you to experience one emotion powerfully without interference or competition. This is the brain's protective mechanism to keep our judgment from being paralyzed by confusion. Imagine what it might have been like if the first humans were both terribly afraid of saber-toothed tigers and happy to see them. The resulting emotional confusion might well have spelled the end of our species before it had advanced very far.

This brain characteristic means that we can't hold on to negative emotions when we're feeling happy. We can't feel sad or angry while we genuinely smile or laugh. Conversely, we can't smile and feel happy while we're in the throes of negative emotions. When you consciously attempt to express happiness by smiling even when you're not already happy, your brain is momentarily caught up in the tension between emotions. But your brain seeks comfort and peace, so it naturally desires the positive emotion over the negative one.

Thus, a smile isn't just a simple movement of facial muscles. A smile has real power to positively affect your life. And research shows that merely raising the corners of your mouth in the physical expression of a smile provokes a positive neurochemical response in your brain—even in the midst of negative circumstances or emotions. Admittedly, it isn't always easy, but the reward is a happier life.

This exercise is designed to help you use your breath, your smile, and the strength of your will to limit negative emotions. While these three things are effective individually, in combination they are even more powerful tools for emotional release. With practice, you'll learn how to release negative emotions and stress from your everyday life with ease. And when you're confident of your ability to release them as you choose, you'll begin to conduct your emotions in much the same way that an orchestra conductor leads her musicians to make beautiful music. Your emotions can enrich your life rather than chain you to the negativity and failures of the past. You'll discover that harnessed and nurtured emotions give you the freedom to transcend suffering and experience greater joy.

BRAIN RELEASING 1: SMILE AND LAUGH

1. In any position, relax your shoulders, close your eyes, and let a smile float on your face. Feel your body and brain relax. Feel the relaxation in your chest spread upward to your head.

2. Now, frown as intensely as you can and feel the tension generated in your body and brain.

3. Smile, then frown suddenly. Repeat this several times and note your body's reactions. You may feel yourself relaxing and your mood improving.

4. Now, start with a smile and then nurture that smile into a big laugh, taking note of the changes in your body.

5. Laugh as loudly as you can. Let your whole body laugh, from your face to your toes. Feel the refreshing sensation filling your brain.

BRAIN RELEASING 2: SMILE AS YOU BREATHE OUT

1. Sit comfortably and shrug your shoulders up and down to relax.
2. Breathe in and out several times, massaging your face to release the tension in your facial muscles.
3. Now, breathe in, gently close your eyes, and breathe out while forming a slight smile.

4. Continue to breathe deeply and naturally, combining your exhale with a widening smile. Repeat this several times, focusing on the motion of your smile as a light breath escapes through your lips, like a gentle wind.
5. Slowly shift your consciousness to your brain. Feel your brain as you breathe out, smiling. You'll feel it become lighter and more refreshed.

BRAIN RELEASING 3: TRANSFORM MEMORY INTO LEARNING

1. Bring up an emotionally traumatic or difficult memory. Reenact the scene in your mind, observing every detail. Let the emotion of the experience flow through you once again.

2. When you feel yourself immersed in the emotion, breathe in deeply, and then smile as you breathe out. Have your palms facing each other at about the level of your solar plexus (upper abdominal area). Spread your hands apart as you breathe in, and bring them closer together as your breathe out. Try to synchronize your breath, smile, and hand motions.

3. Begin with a slight, barely observable smile. Then, make it bigger each time you breathe out. At first, your smile may feel artificial, heavy, and reluctant. Your face may twitch, your lips tremble, and your eyes water. The smile might fade and struggle in the face of past negativity. But nurture the smile until it finally prevails!

4. Eventually, you'll feel the tension leave your face, as if a taut rubber band has relaxed. Your whole face will smile and become a bright flower. You might feel an internal barrier shatter, letting in a stream of light. Feel your head clear as negative energy escapes through your temples and Baekhwe.

   At this moment, you are relieved of the negative emotions associated with the past experience. All that's left is the objective reality of the experience itself, without the painful emotions. You are finally liberated from the emotion and are ready to see the experience as part of a learning process, offering valuable lessons to further your life journey.

BRAIN RELEASING 4: RELEASE IN EVERYDAY LIFE

1. Now, spend some time clearing your brain of the negative emotional energy that you've unwittingly stored in your brain. Make a list of different negative emotions you want to release, such as anger or sadness.

2. Write down as many past experiences that correspond to each emotion as you can think of. You don't have to include all the details, but jot down a key word or two that will jog your memory about the experience.

3. After writing down your memories, go back to one of the emotions on your list, and for each memory, release the associated negative energy through the power of smiling and breathing.

4. With enough practice, you can shorten these steps into just one. You'll be able to think of a memory and chase away any negativity with a single smile.

5. Try to purify each negative emotion, one by one, until you've gone through your entire list. Afterward, you'll be able to release negativity at the moment it occurs. Make releasing negative emotional energy an everyday habit.

Acceptance and Forgiveness

Acceptance and forgiveness are among the most difficult yet important tasks in the process of refreshing the brain. Acceptance means recognizing things exactly as they exist now. If you're stuck in a particular situation, in order to move on, you first need to accept the situation. Once you accept it, the way to get out of it can become clear. But if you continue to deny that you're in trouble, insisting that everything's all right, then you're denying yourself the opportunity to change.

The opposite of acceptance is rejection, which is a kind of attachment. When you are attached to something, you hold onto it. Usually, you hold onto something in order to keep it close to you because you like it. But when you reject something, you are holding onto it, at arm's length, in order to keep it away from you because you don't like it. Acceptance means recognizing and acknowledging as one part of your life that which you're holding onto. Holding onto something requires attention and energy, which gives that something power. By letting it go through acceptance, you remove the power behind it. Then, it can truly disappear from your life.

Forgiveness also takes power away from situations and people that have been a source of pain. However, it is more than simple acceptance. Forgiveness requires remembering and recognizing something deeper and more important than any justified pain you may be experiencing—your authentic self. Regardless of the source or circumstances, this self can only thrive when it's free from negative emotions. Forgiveness means choosing your authentic self over justice or righteousness and changing the energy of pain to the energy of love. Forgiveness is the ultimate self-love.

If you want to free your authentic self and forgive by loving yourself, start with gratitude. Rather than focusing on the wrongs that have been done to you, think of the things in your life that you are thankful for. Then, recognize that all of the people and events that have touched your life until now have made your life what it is, and say thank you until you feel grateful for all of them. The energy of love springs from gratitude.

Love naturally extends beyond yourself to every person, allowing you to feel sympathy and good wishes toward them, regardless of how they have treated you. You may even feel regret for the resentment you had been holding onto, which had primarily impacted yourself. Through forgiveness, your body and brain are relieved of the chronic stress of negative emotions and are given the chance to heal. This change in emotion from resentment and anger to gratitude and love is an important step toward making changes in your life.

The Balance of Freedom and Control

Think of your emotions as a powerful horse. When they're wild and unharnessed, lacking any constraints, your emotions are formidable—sometimes frightening, unpredictable, and even dangerous. But when you gently tame them and harness their enormous energy, you're able to maintain a balance of freedom and control that can carry you a long way toward your life's goal. It's important never to deny or disown your emotions, but rather to master them in ways that let them serve you precisely as you choose while still moving freely through you as a rich and meaningful part of life.

If you're prone to emotional outbursts, you clearly have work to do in this regard. And if you believe that you're already fully in control of your emotions—because you virtually never have emotional outbursts—you may simply be very good at repressing and suppressing them. Holding your emotions in masterful control means being fully aware of them, staying present with them, and maintaining the self-discipline to redirect their energy in a constructive way. It's a challenge that requires dedication and practice, but the rewards are profound.

Begin by resolving to process and release your emotions as soon as you're aware of them and the effect they're having on you. When your emotions get the better of you, quickly acknowledge this, gently forgive yourself, and work to release them as soon as you can. Let go of the need to let emotions flood out of you; instead, practice simply experiencing and naming an emotion when you feel it. Then, ask yourself, "How can I use this emotion well?"

You can turn anger into motivation to accomplish something positive. Jealousy can be directed toward greater attentiveness to yourself or someone else, and sadness toward deeper awareness and compassion. At first, it may be difficult to redirect your emotions in a constructive way. You may find yourself returning again and again to a harmful and stressful emotion, even though you've worked hard to control it. Understand that it's only a habit of your brain that keeps bringing you back to your old way of reacting. Catch yourself when you go off track, and keep practicing your new skills until they are second nature. It will happen.

Be patient, forgive yourself often, and keep working to find the positive action that can replace the negative emotion. It's often helpful to create a symbol that represents your pledge to work skillfully with your emotions. Wear a ring that reminds you; place in a prominent location a photograph that reflects the emotional mastery you seek to achieve; hold a stone you've collected as a reminder of your goal. Remind yourself to redirect your efforts in a positive direction, and celebrate the progress you make with a joyful heart. It's a practice that may take years to fully master, but when you work in partnership with your brain, you also can experience immediate breakthroughs.

The Internal Conversation

The more adept you become at working with your Power Brain, the more aware you'll be of your internal conversation. Your dialogue with yourself becomes increasingly articulate and conscious, and with practice you become the master of this inner conversation. Wisdom doesn't mean retaining lots of information or performing well on tests. Wisdom is the ability to make use of information in novel and productive ways. It's about being able to create—and creation requires experimentation, risk-taking, and invention.

When you find yourself up against an old pattern of thought that limits you, don't surrender out of habit. Engage with those ideas from a higher and wiser part of your brain. Talk to yourself within your brain to bring your thoughts into sharper focus. Ask yourself these questions:

- What stops me from doing what I really want to do?
- What emotional patterns prevent me from pursuing my dreams?
- What makes up my present ideas about my personal identity?
- Who and what influenced the creation of this identity?
- What parts of my identity are an image I've created, and not who I really am?
- What limits do I place on myself because of preconceptions and false ideas?

As you investigate these questions, be aware that nothing is more important than self-knowledge. You're not being self-obsessed or narcissistic when you explore your own depths. You can't bring anything of value to others and to the world unless you first become the master of your own brain and your own life.

The process of letting go of illusions and old ideas is something you'll find challenging but also exceedingly interesting. You'll need to experiment, to grow comfortable with failure, and to build the courage to try again and again. But when your knowledge and experience coalesce, you'll become aware of big breakthroughs taking place deep within your consciousness, and you will have wonderful moments of pure insight. There's a reason why we often represent the birth of an idea with the symbol of a light bulb above someone's head. Remember that in Korean, Noe—the word for brain—can also mean lightning, electricity, brightness. That's what you'll feel as your new awareness evolves—light and bright and full of creative ideas.

CHAPTER 10

Step Four: Brain Integrating

Reaching beyond your present limitations to shape the life you want is a profoundly interesting and joyful way to live. It requires assimilating what you've learned and becoming comfortable with a better version of yourself. As you transform yourself from deep within your brain, you'll function at a higher level than before, and you'll be able to redefine yourself and recreate your life according to your largest dreams.

The joy of changing and improving comes in living as a fluid and flexible work-in-progress. When you cling to an old identity because it's comfortable and easy, you aren't supporting real growth and change. But when you let your new identity be reinforced by the energy of life, the new information you embrace, and the direct action you take, transformation works inside you as a healthy, ongoing process—one that continuously nurtures your body and mind.

In the previous step, you learned how to empty yourself in order to experience the restorative power of refreshing your brain. By cleaning your mental house and moving past the limitations of negative emotions and beliefs, you've made yourself ready to experience a creativity that will fill you with possibility. This is a place from which you can create anything out of nothing—by tapping into powerful energy that's big enough to organize the universe but also personal enough to be working within your brain at this very moment.

Integrating Your Brain

In this fourth step of Brain Education—Brain Integrating—you'll work to reunite the diverse processing centers of the brain. Reviving dormant connections between thought, emotion, and reasoning will help you discover the best version of yourself. There are two ways to approach brain integration: the hardware method and the software method.

The hardware method consists of stimulating the brain through three elements of energy. Utilizing the power of light (energy patterns or circuits), sound, and vibration, you'll awaken the elemental life energy in your brainstem and reintegrate the three layers of the brain. The energy training methods in this book will assist you on your journey by enabling you to access the infinite life force of your brainstem, the emotion of your limbic system, and the intellect of your neocortex.

Since Brain Integrating requires that you delve deeply into yourself, you must believe in yourself and have the ability to concentrate for long periods of time. You must also have a sincere desire to get in touch with your inner being—your authentic self. When your brain reaches a relaxed and alert alpha state, you'll be able to quiet your mind and enter more deeply into an understanding of who you truly are.

The software approach to Brain Integrating is about reviewing the kinds of information that define you—Who am I? What do I really want with my life?—and interpreting your identity from a new perspective. Your sense of who you are is based on your essential self, who you are at your most whole and authentic level. This aspect of yourself is always present and may be familiar to you or something of a stranger, depending on how self-aware you are and how much work you've done to be in touch with yourself.

When you choose your own identity, or who you are in this world, your brain will act to support that identity and help it to manifest itself. Through this process, you can reexamine old preconceptions and information to determine whether they're helpful or harmful to your new sense of self. Then, you have to decide what to keep and what to throw away. You'll be reinventing yourself based on your own decisions rather than what others expect you to be. This is the ultimate self-liberation—and it's within your power to attain.

This world presents us with seemingly endless challenges and information, but our brain is more than adequately equipped for its tasks if we integrate the various parts of the brain system. I like to think of brain integration as taking place along two dimensions: the "horizontal" axis of left and right hemispheres, and the "vertical" axis of the brainstem, limbic system, and neocortex.

Horizontal Integration of the Brain

You've heard about the functional differences between the brain hemispheres: the left brain as logical, analytical, rational, linear, and verbal, and the right brain as intuitive, holistic, symbolic, and impulsive. You may have been told that you're more oriented to one hemisphere than the other, or you might have adopted this view as one of the images that reinforces your identity. Perhaps you take pride in being predominantly left- or right-brained—or perhaps you use this idea about your innate gifts and limitations as an excuse to remain as you are.

With advances in brain science, we now understand that when one hemisphere is damaged, the other hemisphere sometimes can compensate for the loss of a particular function. We're also learning that there is no such thing as a left-brain or right-brain personality. We're not left-brained or right-brained; we're "whole brained." While this right- and left-brained idea is valuable as a shorthand way of expressing basic aspects of brain function, it will be wiser to embrace the traits of both sides in a new and creative way.

Each of us possesses a unique combination of multiple intelligences—linguistic, logical, mathematical, spatial, kinesthetic, musical, interpersonal, intrapersonal, naturalistic, artistic, and inventive. Some are dominant tendencies and abilities, while others are dormant and in need of awakening. If you're talented in some of these areas but not "naturally" adept in others, imagine what you can create in your life when you open yourself up to thinking that you can be better at *all* of them.

Better integration could lead to better problem-solving. Suppose the left side is analyzing the complex features of a particular problem. The right side may suddenly come up with a wildly creative solution. The left argues why it won't work, then the right suggests another solution. If the two sides are communicating effectively, the brain will eventually hit upon a solution that's both creative and realistic. When our brains are integrated on a horizontal plane, the left and right brains work together harmoniously to come up with the best idea.

Horizontal brain integration is also about improving communication and interaction among the functionally differentiated areas of the neocortex. The outermost layer of the brain, the neocortex, is divided into five different lobes: prefrontal, frontal, parietal, temporal, and occip-

THE BRAIN LOBES AND RELATED ENERGY POINTS

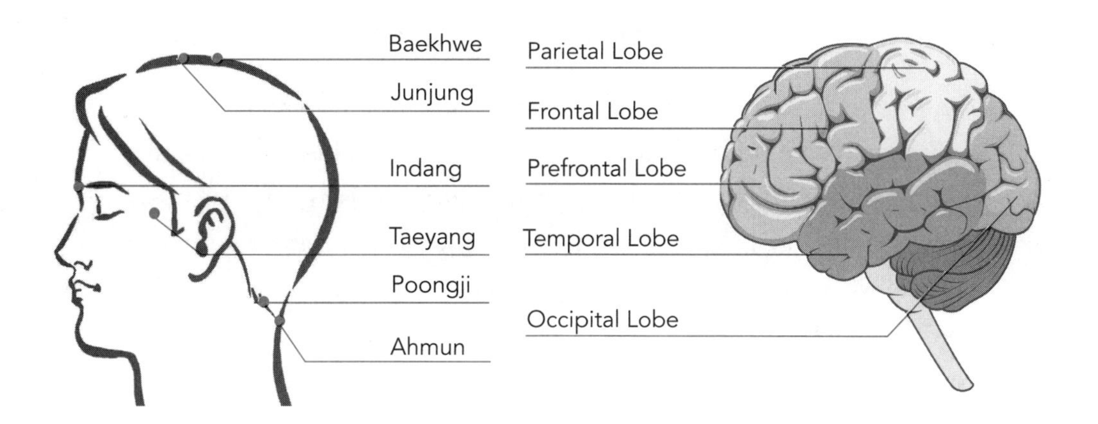

ital. The *prefrontal lobe* is at the center of the front of the brain, around the region of your forehead. It controls the highest human cognitive functions, including judgment, decision-making, abstract thinking, social interaction, and personality expression. The prefrontal lobe is a part of the *frontal lobe*, the rest of which acts as a control tower, watching over and controlling all conscious mental and physical activities. The *parietal lobe*, toward the top of the brain, controls the sense of touch, pressure, temperature, and other similar sensitivities. The *temporal lobe* refers to the left and rightmost regions of the brain, controlling memory and hearing. The *occipital lobe*, in the back of the brain, controls sight. Improved integration among these lobes will make the brain more effective and efficient.

Interestingly, we have energy points on our heads that are closely associated with the five regional lobes, as shown in the diagram above. Don't worry about memorizing all their names and locations; you don't need to try to find the precise energy points on your head. Just tapping here and there all over your head with your fingertips is enough to help activate and integrate the different lobes of your brain. This simple exercise gives your brain a powerful energy boost.

Vertical Integration of the Brain

I've worked for decades helping people not just to integrate the left and right hemispheres of the brain on the horizontal axis, but to consciously and intuitively integrate the brain on the vertical axis as well. This only *sounds* complicated. With focused attention, you'll be able to feel the truth of what it means to integrate your whole brain.

Consider whether the things that you like are also the things that you consider to be right. The answer to this question speaks to whether your neocortex (thinking brain) and your limbic system (emotional brain) are interconnected. This is what I call vertical integration. We can also use the analogy of the connection between the heart and mind; if this communication isn't free and natural, we'll face an inner resistance to everything we do, and our actions will lack power.

A person whose sense of "rightness" coincides with their "liking" is truly fortunate. The problem occurs when the two aren't the same. This can bring great turmoil, as we've all experienced. When heart and mind aren't one, we have no passion and can't reach our goals. How we overcome that dissonance is an important indicator of our level of brain mastery.

At the very bottom of the brain structure, vertical integration also includes the brainstem (life brain). If your reasoning and emotions work harmoniously, with no conflict between them, you can better access the power of the primal life energy within your brainstem.

When you improve the integration of all three layers of your brain, it will support you in feeling safe and strong, working skillfully with thought and emotion, and using your imagination and skills to act in powerful ways.

You can bring this conscious integration of your brain to the choices you make every day, and to the intuitive shifts of awareness you invite into your life. Imagine your brain as integrated horizontally, between left and right brain, and now also vertically, from brainstem to neocortex. Appreciate how this more complete sense of yourself will give you greater access to your potential.

Energy Circuit Exercise

Everything in the universe has its own characteristic pattern of energy flow, according to its shape, color, mass, and size. The world's wisdom traditions make use of patterns and shapes that repeatedly find their way into the art, textiles, and worship of every culture. Think of mandalas, labyrinth patterns, and the floors of ancient cathedrals.

The uniquely repeated patterns of these energy-flow circuits induce a calm and peaceful mental state in the observer. As you relax and trace the patterns, the stagnant and chaotic energy of your brain is released, and a more harmonious energy is restored. From dawn to dusk, we're engaged in demanding and complex cognitive tasks. We're bombarded with demands for our attention, in a world full of visual, aural, and tactile stimulation. Learning how to quiet our minds and focus our attention is more important in the twenty-first century than ever before in human history.

The following shapes look simple. The peace they provide is equally simple, and something I'd like you to experience before you move on. This exercise is especially helpful when you're faced with intense emotion.

It's harder than it looks to make each shape balanced and even; it takes concentration and practice. Work at it until you're calm, relaxed, and energized—almost in a trance state.

ENERGY CIRCUIT DRAWING

1. Sit comfortably, breathe deeply, and relax.
2. Copy the pattern of the circuit on a blank piece of paper in the direction the arrows indicate. Start by drawing the shapes large. After you get used to drawing the shapes, draw them in varying sizes. When you're satisfied that the patterns and shapes flow freely, try switching to your nondominant hand. Then draw with both hands at the same time. Repeat at least five times with each hand and with both hands.
3. Gaze at the pictures of the circuit pattern. Try to feel the energy emanating from them. As you sink into a deeper state of concentration, you may even observe an aura around the circuit.
4. Now trace the circuit with your eyes, as you'd draw it with your hand. Feel the complex thoughts and emotions crowding your brain fade into the background, to be replaced by a feeling of peace and calm.

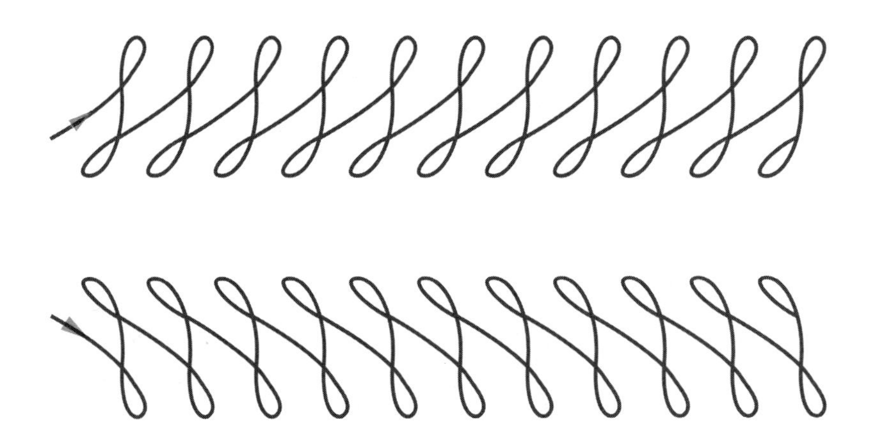

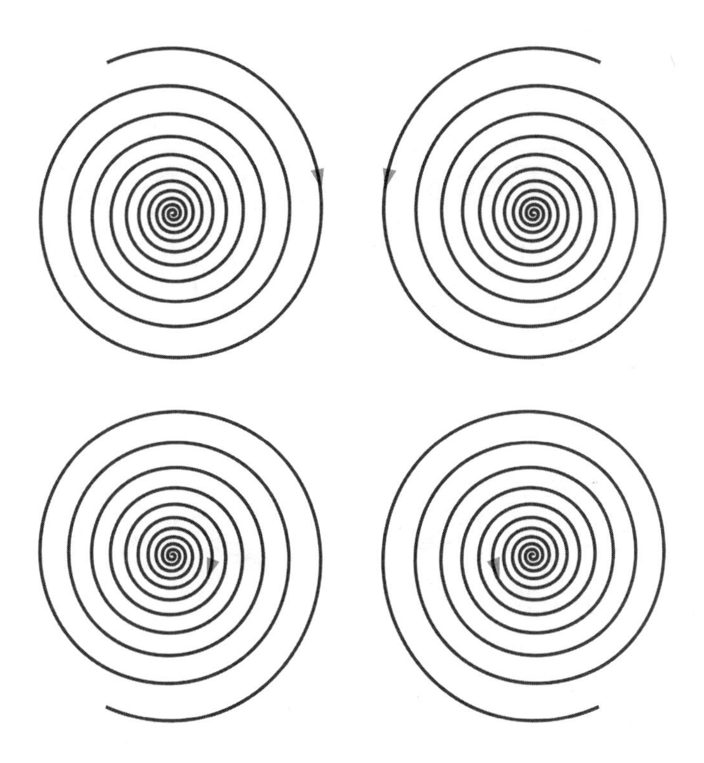

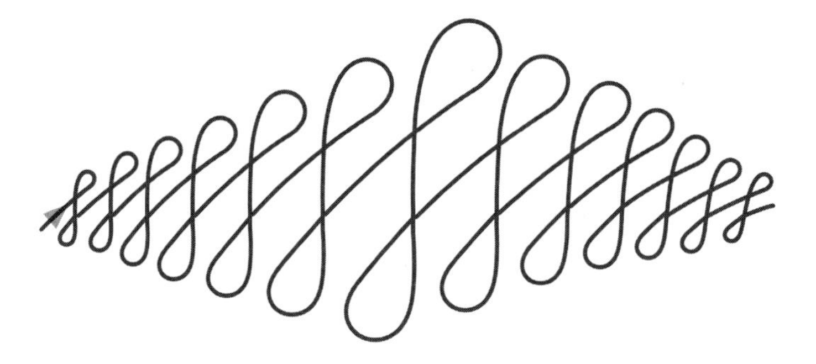

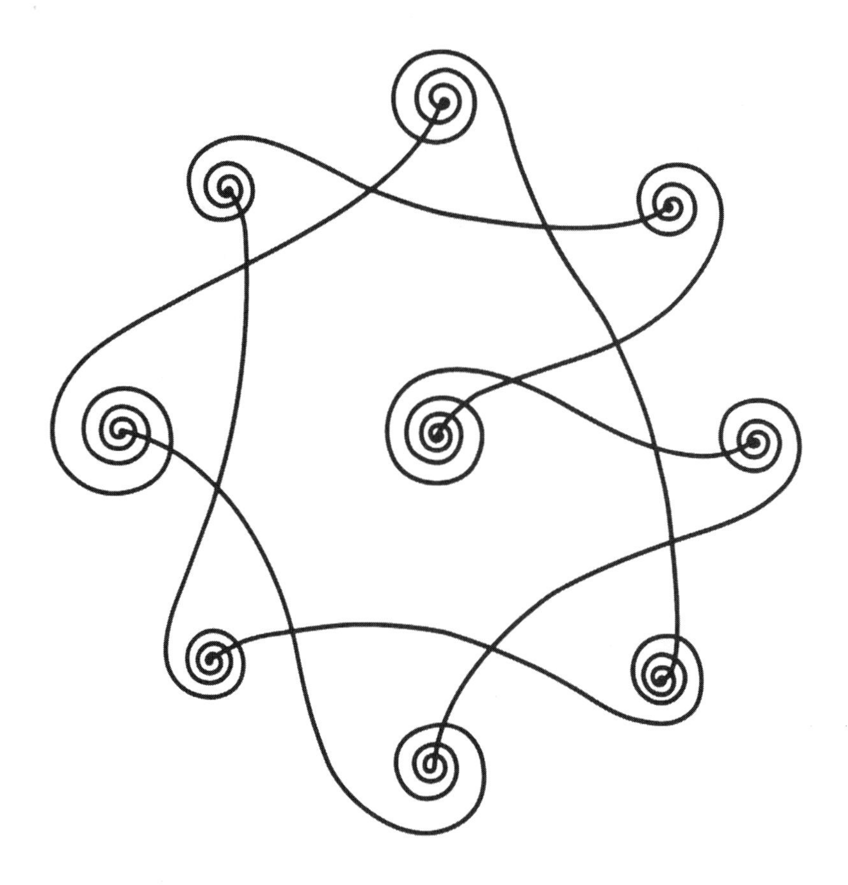

Helpful Hint: Turn Your Doodle into an Energy Circuit

Doodling helps you stay focused. A 2009 study found that people who doodled while listening to a phone call were able to recall 29 percent more information afterward than those who simply took notes. This suggests that a slightly distracting secondary task may actually improve concentration during the performance of dull tasks that would otherwise cause a mind to wander. When you are bored, doodle! Your doodles can act as powerful brain energy circuits.

Sound Vibration Exercises

Before creating the unencumbered information you'll be adding to your awareness, let's tune up the body and brain again. Our overactive neocortex is hungry to connect with the elemental life energy provided by the deeper brain structures. To get to breathing deeply into your lower body, try an elegantly simple exercise that helps induce the alpha mental state. Doing this exercise well increases the oxygen supply to your organs, including your oxygen-hungry brain, and settles you into a place from which you can do your best intuitive and cognitive work. It also helps you manage your emotions better.

Every sound has its own frequency and energy vibration. According to the ancient Asian healing traditions, there are specific sounds that have a positive impact on each of the body's organs. For example, when you make the sound "Ah," you'll soon feel the fire energy of your heart being released.

Expressing ourselves through our own voices happens naturally without even thinking about it. Ahhhh! We let out a sigh when our chest feels blocked. Woo hoo! We shout out with joy when we are excited. You can intentionally use your own self-created sounds to bring better integration to your brain. By creating and focusing on long, sustained vocal sounds, you can massage and recalibrate your body and mind from the inside out.

One special sound, "Om," incorporates all five elements of energy, stimulating all the internal organs, including the brain. It's a very effective sound for slowing down the flow of thoughts and emotions and creating a space in which to concentrate on your body, mind, and energy.

You can consciously incorporate the meditative practice of making sounds that release tension and invigorate both body and brain. Tune into your body by sitting with your eyes closed, breathing deeply, and making these sounds repeatedly and with different levels of volume and intensity. You'll develop a heightened sense of how they feel in your brain and your whole body.

FIVE-ORGAN SOUND VIBRATION

The key to maximizing the benefits of this exercise lies in your ability to focus. Maintain focus on the organ that you are working on, and feel how your sounds shift its energy. At the same time, imagine old, stagnant energy leaving that organ. You will feel more balanced and restored as your own sounds stimulate it. Say, "Thank you," to the organ before moving on to the next one.

1. Make yourself comfortable in a sitting position. Close your eyes.

2. Place your palms over your heart on the left side of your chest, and make an "Ah" sound for at least five seconds. Repeat five times or more.

3. Place your palms on both sides of your chest, over your lungs, and make a "Eu" sound for at least five seconds. Repeat five times or more.

4. Place your palms on your stomach, which is on the left side of your abdomen, just underneath your ribcage. Make an "Uh" sound for at least five seconds. Repeat five times or more.

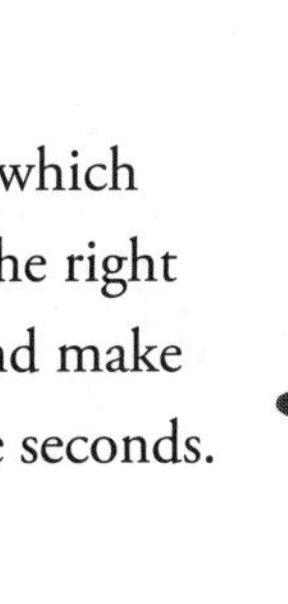

5. Place your palms on your liver, which is underneath your ribcage on the right side of your upper abdomen, and make an "Woo" sound for at least five seconds. Repeat five times or more.

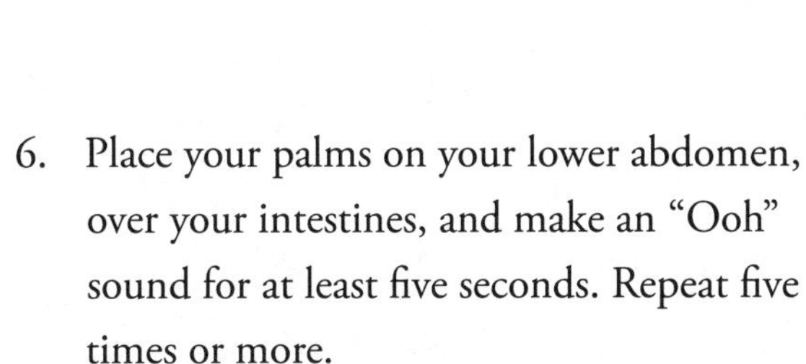

6. Place your palms on your lower abdomen, over your intestines, and make an "Ooh" sound for at least five seconds. Repeat five times or more.

7. Place your palms on your lower back on either side of your spine, over your kidneys, and make a "Eeh" sound for at least five seconds. Repeat five times or more.

8. Repeat the whole cycle three times or more to get the most out of this exercise.

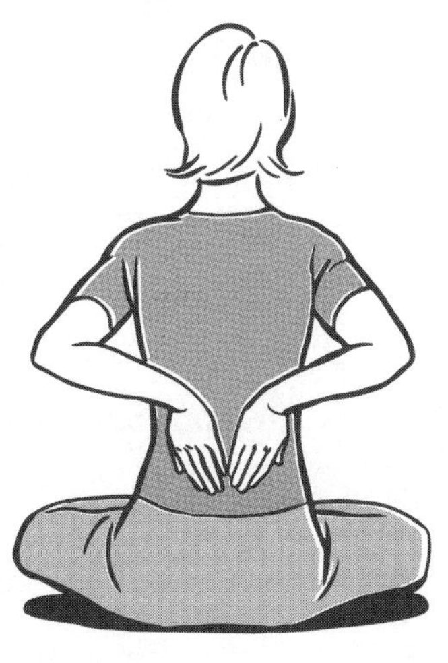

OM VIBRATION

1. Make yourself comfortable in any position—lying down, sitting, or even standing. Close your eyes and whisper the sound "Om...Om." Observe what effect this has on your brain.

2. Don't cut off the sound, but let it linger. Concentrate on the subtle vibrations in the sound as it rings in your chest and echoes in your lower abdomen. Let the vibration seep into your brain; feel its effects on the brain cells.

3. Place both hands on your chest and make the sound with all your heart. Let it linger as long as possible. With practice, you'll be able to increase the duration.

4. Now, voice the sound rhythmically. Use any rhythm and tune you want. Let your voice become an instrument, singing the song of "Om." Imagine yourself inside a huge bell that's ringing the "Om" sound. Let the vibration envelop your whole body.

5. When you're finished, breathe in and out three times. Rub your hands together briskly, and massage your face and neck.

Brain Wave Vibration

Your brainstem is like a hidden conductor of the great symphony that makes up your body's intricate systems. Without any conscious direction from you, it sends out messages telling your heart how fast to beat, commanding your white blood cells to spring into action, directing your digestive system to go to work, and coordinating myriad other bodily functions that support your health and well-being. Essentially, the role of the brainstem is to maintain your state of equilibrium.

However, modern life puts each of us at war with our own brainstem as we suppress our pre-rational, subconscious side in favor of rationalistic obsession. The thinking mind has become so central to our lives that it often carries us away from ourselves into patterns of negativity. Constantly judging everything that comes our way, we send our bodies into a state of continual alarm and lack of equilibrium.

In my experience, I've concluded that people's health and happiness are greatly compromised if they have a busy head full of facts and figures but no tools to help integrate the thinking brain with the emotional and subconscious brain. Just as the neocortex, limbic system, and brainstem have separate roles, each responds to a unique energy frequency. Proper selection of and control over energy frequencies makes it possible to stimulate or stabilize different parts of the brain.

Generally, the neocortex responds readily to intricate musical pieces with diverse sounds, such as symphonies, while the brainstem responds better to more primitive, simple, driving beats of ancient indigenous music. Light has a calming effect on the neocortex, and sound has an immediate influence on the emotional control of the limbic system. Vibration in the form of a simple, powerful beat has a noticeable effect on the brainstem, because the brainstem is the seat of the rhythm of life. When our consciousness is able to penetrate the layers of the neocortex and limbic system and enter into the brainstem, we are able to meet with the energy of life.

Meditation is essentially the practice of slowing, or even stopping, the thinking mind. Meditation gives our brain a much-needed rest from the constant mental chatter that keeps us stressed. Brain Wave Vibration is the form of moving meditation that I most frequently introduce to people to calm the thinking brain and awaken the brainstem. It uses repetitive rhythmic vibration to tone down the activities of the neocortex, activate the limbic system, and allow you to meet the life energy residing in your brainstem. Brain Wave Vibration also releases negative emotional content and replaces it with positive information. The rhythmic vibrations and spontaneous movements can also help activate creativity and imagination as you are transported to a place beyond the rational mind.

▶ Restoring Your Autonomic Balance

When we're under a lot of stress, we often feel tension in our shoulders and the backs of our necks. When you've experienced this, have you ever massaged the back of your neck with your hand, or moved your head from side to side to release the tension in your neck? These are things that everyone does naturally, without being taught.

The neck and the back of the head are the first areas to tense up as blood surges to the head when we're under stress. In particular, the concave point below the back of the head, where the skull and cervical vertebrae meet, reacts very sensitively to stress. This is the location of the medulla oblongata, which regulates autonomic activity most directly. Not only does this part of the brain play a central role in maintaining life—regulating respiration, circulation, and digestion—but its connection with the spinal cord makes it an important pathway of movement and sensation.

Because the medulla oblongata plays a central role in the autonomic nervous system, when it becomes tense, autonomic balance is obviously broken. In other words, the hyperactivity of the sympathetic nervous sys-

BRAIN WAVE VIBRATION AND THE MEDULLA OBLONGATA

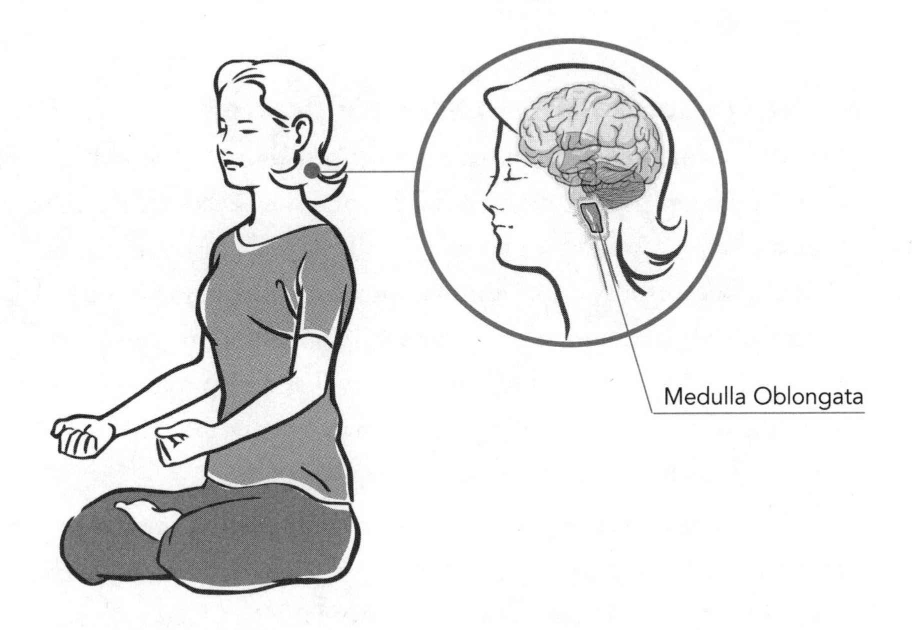

tem, distributed along the spinal cord, continues. And tension in the medulla oblongata and sympathetic nervous system inhibits respiratory and circulatory function, which results in blood and hot energy continuing to rush toward the head. Unrelieved, this tension leads to headache, insomnia, high blood pressure, and other problems. Brain Wave Vibration relaxes the medulla oblongata and the overactivated sympathetic nervous system with simple, repetitive movements. It helps you release the tension in your head and the back of your neck and bring your body and mind back into balance. By tapping into your body's inherent rhythm, you're able to reach a state of deep relaxation similar to that achieved through traditional sitting meditation.

This exercise also helps you restore the optimal Water Up, Fire Down energy balance in your body. Try this several times, and you'll really experience the amazing power of these simple movements. They unplug feelings of incredible stillness, peace, and the joy of life, which then well up from within you.

▶ Preparation for Brain Wave Vibration

When trying any unfamiliar exercise for the first time, it's natural to feel slight discomfort as your body adapts. You might feel a little dizzy as you shake your head when you first do Brain Wave Vibration. Stop moving, and control your breathing as you rest with your chin tucked in slightly, and the dizziness will subside. Be careful not to shake your head too quickly or for too long at first. It will also help to open your mouth slightly and keep exhaling the stagnant energy and air from your head and chest.

It's easy to feel dizzy if excessive work or stress has created severe tension in the cervical vertebrae or the back of your head, or if your chest feels constricted. If you have headaches, anemia, high blood pressure, or low blood pressure, be extra cautious and adjust the speed and duration of the movements accordingly. Even slow, gentle back-and-forth movement is effective for releasing tension in the brain and cervical vertebrae; it doesn't have to be fast. Once you've gotten somewhat comfortable with the motion, try to increase the speed a little bit—but don't overdo it.

If your physical condition is very weak or you feel too tense, relax your body by slowly turning your head left and right and rotating the shoulders forward and back before starting Brain Wave Vibration. You can also do a few stretching exercises before you begin. If you stand during practice, make sure your feet are planted solidly on the ground.

Brain Wave Vibration practice doesn't require music. It's all about your own internal rhythms, not about moving to a beat. But music can be helpful when you begin. Obviously, slow and sentimental music isn't suitable. The most effective music for Brain Wave Vibration has a strong, basic beat—as found in many forms of traditional drumming. I find Korean *samulnori* to be especially effective, because it awakens the brain with a lively combination of sounds from gongs and drums, generating a powerful vibration felt throughout the body. Percussive folk instruments from Africa and South America also offer a simple, primitive repetition of sound that replicates the basic rhythms of life.

Music is helpful for inducing the proper state of mind for Brain Wave Vibration in the beginning, but as time goes by, the rhythm of the body should overpower the rhythm of the music. Be sure to focus inward at all times and allow your own rhythm to come forward.

RESEARCH ON BRAIN WAVE VIBRATION

Initial research on Brain Wave Vibration has shown that it helps you be more positive, reduce stress, and thicken your brain's gray matter.

1. **It promotes positivity:** According to a study conducted by scientists from various national research centers in South Korea, people who engaged in a regular Brain Wave Vibration practice were less stressed and displayed more positive emotions. Stress factors, such as depression, anger, and the manifestation of psychological symptoms in the body, were also significantly less in the meditation group than in the control group.This study was published in the June 2010 issue of *Neuroscience Letters*.

2. **It reduces stress:** Research in 2012 by the University of London and the Korea Institute of Brain Science confirmed that Brain Wave Vibration improves stress levels, as well as overall mood and vitality. In this five-week comparative randomized controlled trial with Iyengar yoga and Mindfulness practice, Brain Wave Vibration was unique in improving depression and sleep latency. The study was published in Volume 2012 of *Evidence-Based Complementary and Alternative Medicine*.

3. **It changes brain matter:** A study comparing a control group with people who'd done Brain Wave Vibration for at least three years showed increased cortical thickness in the frontal and temporal lobes—centers of thinking, judgment, and emotional regulation. This indicates that Brain Wave Vibration may be effective for preventing dementia and other degenerative brain diseases, and may have an anti-aging effect. The study was published in the May 2012 issue of *Social Cognitive and Affective Neuroscience*.

BRAIN WAVE VIBRATION—BASIC FORM

1. Straighten your lower back, comfortably relax your chest and shoulders, and rest your hands on your knees, palms up. Gently close your eyes and pull your chin in slightly so that your spine and head are aligned.

2. Mentally feel the inside of your body, slowly scanning from the top of your head to your neck and down along your spine. Then, let your concentration rest inside your lower abdomen.

3. Make loose fists and gently tap your lower abdomen with your fists, palms up, alternating between left and right hands. You want to tap two inches below your navel, on your lower Dahnjon. This is your body's energy center, and tapping strengthens its energy and makes it warmer.

4. As you continue to tap your lower abdomen, move your head, spine, and upper body to a natural rhythm. You'll get the feeling that you're pounding a drum to some beat, and you'll sense an inner rhythm and excitement rising up.

5. When your movements become rhythmic, begin shaking your head gently from side to side. Without moving too forcefully or rapidly, try to feel your central axis. That's where your spinal cord passes and the center of your autonomic nervous system is located. Starting there, let go of the tension from your neck to your shoulders through the movement of gently shaking your head. Shake slowly at first, then a little faster once you're comfortable with the exercise.

6. Don't think about anything at all. The point is simply to shake your head, imagining that you're shaking out all thoughts. If you feel any weariness or hot energy in your head, keep breathing it out through your mouth.

7. Continue exhaling through your mouth. Feel your breathing getting lighter and more natural as the blockages in your chest open up and tension is released through your exhalations.

8. Once your lower abdomen feels somewhat warmer, use your palms to pat any places on your body that seem to have blockages, opening the energy points. If you have a stifling feeling in your chest, pat your chest. If your legs don't feel good, pat your legs. When the senses of your body have been revived, your hands will automatically go to the places that hurt.

9. Once your body feels fully relaxed, gradually slow your movements and sit quietly. Calm your breathing, and let your consciousness dwell in your lower abdomen.

10. Try this exercise for five minutes in the beginning, gradually increasing to 30 minutes.

▶ Immersion in the Rhythm of Life

Once you're familiar with the basic form of Brain Wave Vibration, try Full Body Brain Wave Vibration, in which you entrust your whole body to the rhythm of life. The goal is to create full relaxation and a calm, meditative mental state. As you practice the basic form, you'll be able to go deeper into the vibrations and experience greater benefits. You'll eventually be able to grow the vibrations to include your whole body, changing your posture as seems intuitively appropriate. There's no specific time requirement for Full Body Brain Wave Vibration, but you might start with 10 minutes and work up to 20 to 30 minutes.

During Full Body Brain Wave Vibration, you need to experience the vibration with your body without analyzing it with your intellect. Like a large boat slowly sinking into the ocean, let your awareness sink into your own body. You'll find that your awareness isn't separate from, but rather is in tune with, the vibration coursing through your body.

The vibration will shake up your energy, which will naturally drift down and gather in the lower abdomen. In this energy state, and with your awareness in your body, you will feel more comfortable in your body. People often mistakenly believe that resting is more comfortable than moving. But the opposite is actually true. The human body is meant to be in motion. Activity is our natural state of being. Our lives and energy become stagnant when we forcibly repress the body's naturally-occurring motion. In this exercise, allow your body to express itself fully, and observe what movements it produces. You'll soon notice that your motion will follow the flow of energy and seek to strengthen the weakened parts of your body. It will reinforce the sturdy parts and heal the painful parts. Natural body motions will work to restore balance in your body.

Once the vibration becomes natural and familiar, you will become increasingly aware of the movement of energy within your body. Allow yourself to follow that flow. Just like hitting the accelerator in order to speed up a vehicle, this increased energy will speed up and strengthen the waves of the vibration in your body. While the movements tend to get bigger at this point, they will also become more graceful and free-flowing. Your body's natural healing instincts will take over, and you will find that you automatically assume unique postures that promote healing for your particular bodily condition.

During the Brain Wave Vibration exercise, you'll find that the focal point of your body shifts continuously. From the elbow to the knee, from the heels to the leg—this is part of the body's process of healing itself and restoring its balance.

Don't try to control your breath. Let it flow. You'll notice that your breath has a rhythm of its own. Focus on exhaling completely, because this will help you release tension from the body. Also, open your mouth a little bit to allow your breath to flow freely. Imagine that you are expelling all the negative energy from your body through your mouth and nose.

As you become more comfortable with this exercise, work on letting go of your inhibitions. Don't be concerned with how you look or whether you're doing things correctly. Release any self-consciousness that interferes with giving free rein to your movement. Let this become like an improvisational dance in which you express your inner being. Don't be bothered when stray thoughts and emotions enter your mind—just let them pass by.

Although the goal of Brain Wave Vibration is to quiet the mind so that the latent powers of the brain can come to the forefront, this is not so easy for most people. Many are accustomed to constant, habitual chatter in their minds. Instead of vainly trying to shut off your mind, you can concentrate on a single positive thought during Brain Wave Vibration. Choose something highly empowering that relates to your personal vision. For example, it could be something as simple as, "I am free." Chant this to yourself, either silently or aloud, as a personal mantra while you practice.

FULL BODY BRAIN WAVE VIBRATION

1. Stand on a stable surface with your feet shoulder-width apart. Bend your knees to lower your hips slightly. Allow your arms to hang forward slightly, and relax your shoulders completely.

2. Close your eyes, and begin to bounce your hips up and down, following a rhythm that feels natural for your body. Let this movement expand until all parts of your body are shaking up and down in unison.

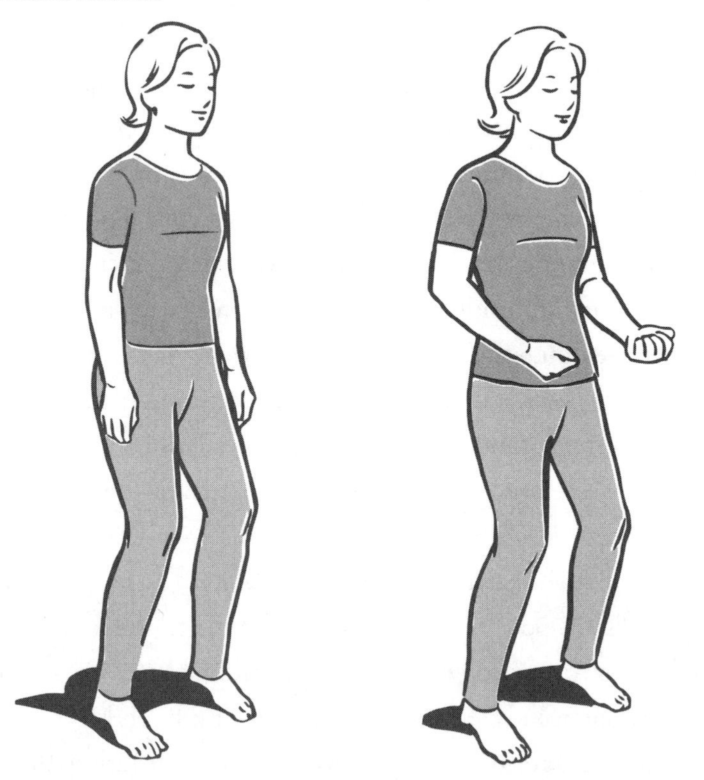

3. Tap your lower abdomen with lose fists while continuing to bounce your hips up and down. Focus on exhaling and releasing tension from your body. Continue tapping and bouncing for five minutes or longer, until your body feels fully relaxed.

4. Stop tapping your lower abdomen, and gradually let the body's natural vibration take over your movement. Quiet your mind, and feel your body as it creates its own rhythm. You may want to tap other parts of your body or feel compelled to make dance-like movements. Up and down, from side to side, twisting and rolling—all of these motions may come into play. Your breath will naturally become synchronized with your movements.

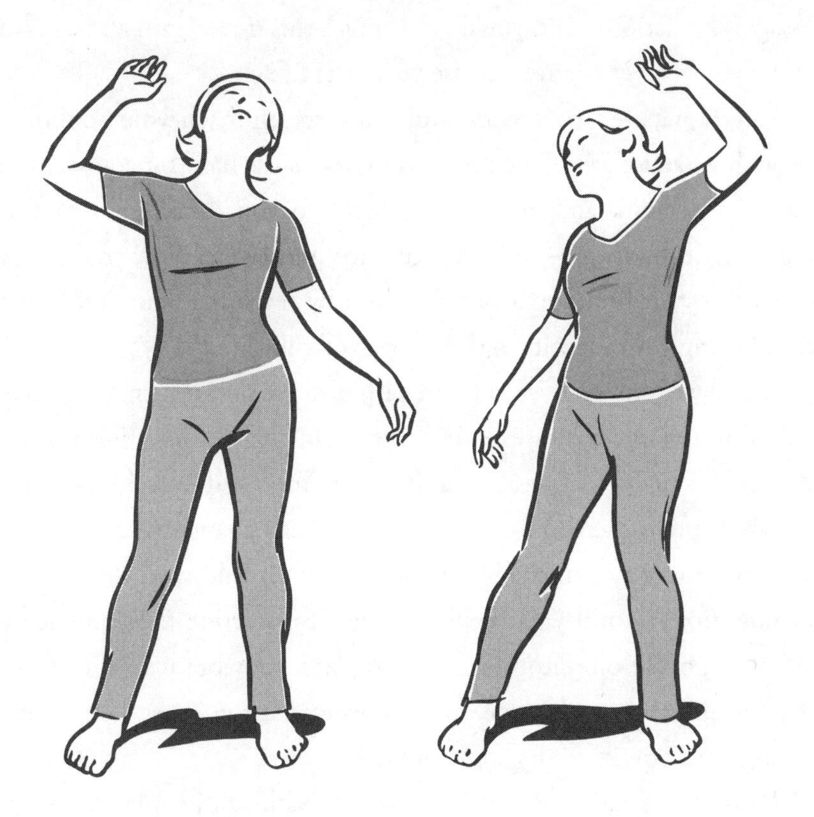

5. Once your body feels fully relaxed and loose, gradually slow your vibration and sit quietly. Calm your breathing, and gently focus your mind on your lower abdomen.

Upgrading Your Core Beliefs

Integrating, moving on, and moving up involves using your vital life energy—energy you can more readily access now that you've learned to quiet your mind. Brain integration also requires that you work with the new messages—information—that you're consciously adding to your awareness. And you must reinforce your new identity through action. This simple but enriching process is a continuous round of working with energy, message, and action—and you'll go through this cycle again and again as you use your Power Brain to create your best life.

You've prepared your body and brain to approach your soulful desires with greater clarity. The previous exercises use light (energy patterns or circuits), sound, and vibration to tap into your brain's potential by integrating its hardware—its different parts and layers. Now you're ready to integrate your brain on a software level by revisiting your core beliefs, reestablishing your identity and the value of your life.

In order to integrate your brain with positive new information about yourself and your life, it's essential to take in that information not just on an intellectual level but also emotionally. You need to feel it permeate your whole brain. Remember that your mind can change quite easily in a surface kind of way, but the brain will slip into its old ways despite your best intentions—until you deeply change. To override the tendency to slide through life on autopilot, go deep into your brain to find where self-limiting beliefs still reside, and to overcome the inner resistance restricting your power, clarity, and conviction.

From my experience working with thousands of people around the world, I can tell you that there are a few positive core beliefs that will provide you with incredible momentum, just as there are negative core beliefs that will hold you back no matter how hard you try.

When you know for certain that you are courageous, you're free to act courageously. When you forgive yourself for past mistakes, you're free to do something better in the present. When you love yourself, you're free to love others. When you believe you have value and are precious, you are more likely to treat others as precious. When you feel pure in the present moment, even when your past is not, you are able to create a more complete life. When you feel beautiful, you can then see the beauty in others and in the world around you.

But if at some deep level you don't feel courageous, or forgive yourself, love yourself, find yourself precious, believe in your essential purity, or feel that you're beautiful, you are bound to run into obstacles. You can set any number of goals, but you'll inevitably experience self-sabotage, both consciously and unconsciously, unless you change your core beliefs about yourself. The following exercise is a good place to start.

▶ Self-Affirmation Exercise

As you make the following statements, be aware of the feelings and thoughts that arise in you. You may find yourself trying to "sell" an idea you don't really believe in. You might experience the hope that a statement is true, but feel that it really isn't. You may feel strong emotions rise up later in the day, and your dream life may be stirred up after this exercise. Work with whatever emerges, and give yourself time. These foundational beliefs, negative or positive, took time to form within you. It will take time to reshape them, too.

- I am a courageous person.
- I forgive myself.
- I love myself.
- I am a precious being.
- I am pure.
- I am beautiful.

Keep repeating the positive phrases until they are deeply ingrained in your brain. Use any of the previous exercises that worked particularly well to ground yourself and provide a peaceful place from which to revisit these statements. Do this as many times as it takes to fully integrate the ideas. Some people find it useful to speak while looking into a mirror. If you have a close friend or partner whom you deeply trust, speak the words to them and then have them give you feedback about how convinced and sure you seem as you make each statement. You'll both know when you've shifted into really believing what you're saying.

Choose to believe these statements. Wire them deeply into your brain. With this important foundation in place, you'll be free to explore new choices about your life from a clean and clear place—free of negative preconceptions, self-limiting thoughts and beliefs, fixed and rigid ideas, and old information that doesn't serve your truest goals.

Establishing Your Identity

Of the countless forms of information we come across, what has the most decisive impact on brain function is information about our personal identity and life purpose. When there's a change in this high-level information—Who am I? What is the purpose of my life?—all other information starts to be reorganized around the new messages the brain has received. The information system of the entire brain changes, ultimately producing changes in thought, word, and deed.

Ask yourself what it is that's limiting your capabilities. At first, your answers will probably relate to so-called objective circumstances, such as your physical condition, academic record, finances, and time. Keep asking, though, and you'll see that what truly limits you is the "information on information" stored in your brain, the self-definition and self-image by which you assess, choose, and organize all other information. Take time to look into "the self I think of as me"—in other words, information about your self-identity. What's important here is that your information about yourself isn't fixed and unchanging. As the master of this information, you can use, assess, and revise it. You can also create or discard information.

▶ Who Am I?

I'm someone with a certain position at a certain company. I am somebody's husband and somebody's father. I am someone's wife. I'm a student at a certain school. I'm someone with a certain dream. I am someone's son or daughter, and somebody's friend.

How do such self-definitions form? If we look at them closely, we can see that they are related to the roles we're given by our environment—at home, at work, at school. Let's say that one person mostly thinks of himself as so-and-so's dad and that another person mostly thinks of herself as an executive of a certain company. If a conflict arises between work and family, what decision would each of these two make? The first person would make a decision that put his family first, while the second person is likely to put work first.

If we examine what it is that determines our thoughts, words, and deeds, we can see that it's ultimately information about our self-identity. To know who you are, not who you "should" be, you need to ask fundamental questions about yourself and your life. The effectiveness of this process depends on the depth and courage of the questions you ask yourself.

As you silence your critical, self-doubting mind, you'll begin to hear your brain speaking in an unfiltered way. This organ partakes of the larger truths about yourself; it's a link to a greater you and to your inner wisdom. Once you stop trying to influence the flow of that wisdom by what you find socially, politically, or spiritually acceptable, you'll see fresh truths. Not all of these will be comfortable. But approaching them with courage and honesty is the key to Brain Integrating.

To reveal who you truly are, I suggest that you reflect on your personal values and choose your core values. Core values are your convictions and philosophy, and they guide your actions and choices. They are a part of who you are, and they highlight what you stand for. They provide you with a personal code of conduct. Those who have their own core values live lives of consistency and integrity. People without core values have no standards guiding their actions, so their decisions are dictated by the situation, their mood, or the opinions of those around them. Their lives are confused and lacking in integrity.

Having core values is absolutely critical to living a life of meaning and purpose. When we have our personal values and consistently honor them, we feel satisfied and content. And we use our brains in a most productive way, by allocating their energy and abilities to what really matters to us. When we don't have core values or don't honor them, on the other hand, we feel incongruent and unhappy. And it's easy to waste our important resources, including energy, time, money, and the brain.

▶ What Do I Really Want?

When we feel unsatisfied with our lives, we usually think it's because we've failed to achieve what we want. But just as difficult as achieving what we want is *knowing* what we truly want.

"What do I really want?" is one of the most important questions you can ask yourself. It sounds simple enough, but few people ever answer the question honestly. Our brains become entangled in how we *think* we should be and what we want others to think about us. It's hard to look beyond the surface to see our own underlying motivations for life.

I urge you to ask yourself this question with great sincerity. And then ask yourself again. Try to really get to the core of what you want. This will free you from being caught up in the details of what you *think* you want so you can achieve what you really do want.

For example, maybe you'd answer the question by saying, "I want a successful career." But why do you want a successful career? There may be multiple reasons. Maybe you want to feel that you've lived a productive life, maybe you want to feel respected, or maybe you want to be financially secure. Now, ask yourself why you want these things. You may discover that you want to find meaning for life through productivity, or that you feel loved when people show you respect and when you're adequately compensated for your work. Ultimately, you may find that all the things and accomplishments you desire can be narrowed down to a few specifics, such as love or freedom.

Knowing what you really want gives you more options in your quest to find fulfillment, because now you can free yourself from the notion that particular details must be in place in order to achieve happiness. As you create your life, remember to look at the forest rather than the trees. If you get stuck looking at details—expecting them to be just so before you can move toward your dreams—you'll probably never truly advance.

▶ What's My Life Purpose?

After asking yourself fundamental questions about yourself and your life, it helps to organize your life purpose in the form of a personal vision. Just as a corporation has a vision guiding its activities, so you, too, should try to have a vision—one that will guide your life. Knowing your vision is knowing who you are, where you're going, and what will guide your journey.

You'll have goals, great and small, in your personal and professional life. Having such goals, though, doesn't mean you have a vision for life. A vision and a goal are different. A vision is something permanent that ceaselessly provides guidelines in the course of achieving goals. One way to distinguish between a goal and a vision is to ask the following question: "And then what?" Once achieved, a goal is finished. A vision, however, presents a clear direction for future action and helps establish new goals. Many people only have goals, without a vision. If that's your case, then it's easy to feel empty even when you achieve your goals.

Discovering your personal vision is perhaps the most vital activity in which you can engage. It is one of the most important keys to finding your path in life. Having a clearly articulated personal vision provides a template of purpose that you can use to initiate, evaluate, and refine all your activities.

As you ask yourself important questions and reflect on your answers, you'll discover new values, beliefs, goals, and abilities that had been hidden in the many layers of your mind. You'll see some of your cherished values and beliefs in a new light, rearranged and reconsidered. Through this process, you'll have the construction materials you need to build a clearer, stronger, more authentic identity reflecting your vast potential.

▶ Life Questions Exercise

Answering the following questions will greatly help you reestablish your identity. Try to answer each question honestly and bravely. Just write down whatever comes to mind, without trying to edit yourself. The key is to trust yourself and not shy away from what your deep self-exploration tells you.

▶▶ WHAT IS MOST IMPORTANT TO ME?

Ask yourself, "What is most important to me in life?" Brainstorm a list. What do you hold most dear? Integrity, love, abundance? Write down 10 things that come to mind, whatever they may be. For each item, ask yourself, "Would living this value make me feel really happy and fulfilled?" Then, choose the five things you think are the most important to you.

►► WHAT IS MY PASSION?

Ask yourself these questions: "What is my passion?" "What excites and energizes me?" "When does time seem to fly by?" Write down your answers. Our passions are desires or purposes that bring us joy. Passionate people are full of energy, have a zest for life, and motivate the people around them. Passion gives us the internal fire to succeed. It acts as a motivating force to help us do truly great things.

►► WHAT DIFFERENCES CAN I MAKE?

Think about what activities you most enjoy—in your personal life and in your professional life. What are your talents and skills? What do people say you're good at? Given your interests, talents, skills, and gifts, how can you contribute to others? How can you make this world a better place? What difference can you make? Just think of the possibilities.

►► WHAT WILL BE MY LEGACY?

What kind of legacy do you want to leave? How do you want to be remembered? What qualities and characteristics will people remember you for? What outstanding accomplishments will you have achieved? What difference can you make in the lives of others?

►► WHAT IS MY LIFE PURPOSE?

Take a look at your answers to all the previous questions and ask, "What does this reveal about me?" Ask yourself, "What is my purpose for being here on earth?" Take some quiet time to reflect and listen.

New Information to Support New Choices

Express your answers to these questions in whatever way suits you best, and enjoy the breakthroughs you experience. Your vision of who you want to be should fill you with joy. If it doesn't, you might be formulating answers you think will please others. Keep working to identify goals that aren't what you think they should be, or what others expect, but that are your own truth, whatever that may be. Be honest and courageous as you identify your vision. Stretch to make sure that what you describe will spur you to act at the highest levels of your abilities, at the edge of your knowledge, and with the depths of your wisdom.

You know who you are, and when the barriers and wounds of your personality and history are set aside, you'll emerge ready to take in new information about yourself. I've found that when the vision is clear and the feeling joyful, people discover that who they are goes far beyond their individual needs and the needs of their families. When people look at themselves with a clear lens, their own desire for health, happiness, and peace wonderfully expands into a larger desire to benefit the world with their particular gifts. As I mentioned earlier, in ancient Korea, this instinct was called Hongik, meaning "to widely benefit others."

I believe that Hongik is the underlying force in our lives. We're all different, with unique contributions to make to the world, and yet we share this powerful instinct to seek the original goodness within us. We want to support the health, happiness, and peace of others and even of the world as a whole. Although I've ceased to be surprised by how universal this desire is, I'm always moved by the miraculous improvements that come to people who embrace this enlightenment. Their lives are transformed gently and with a tremendous sense of wholeness and joy.

You've consciously worked to strengthen and expand the horizontal and vertical integration of your brain structures, you've reshaped and renewed the information you possess about yourself and your life, and you've deeply integrated your new and updated beliefs. With this foundation in place, you can continue to train your brain and realize your latent, unconscious, and powerful potential. You're ready to proceed with brain mastery—a process that will last for the rest of your life.

CHAPTER 11

Step Five: Brain Mastering

Now that you've discovered the life you truly want to live, you're ready to create a lifestyle based on the goals you develop through understanding that purpose. This is essentially a spiritual quest, because it requires continuous attention to the highest aspects of your character.

Brain Mastering cultivates the habit of continuous enlightened living, as opposed to brief, transient moments of awakening. During this phase, you'll continue to apply the four previous steps of Brain Education as you keep developing your body, mind, and spirit. When you practice these collective disciplines as a lifestyle, you'll have greater control over your brain and a greater ability to achieve cherished goals.

Once you've begun to take control over the internal workings of your brain, it's time to turn the power of your brain outward again. In short, it's time to act. Through action, you'll put everything you've learned to the test, and you'll hone and strengthen its effectiveness. Now is the time to build the life of your dreams through Brain Mastering.

The Master of Your Brain

To master your brain, first and foremost you must know that you are the master of your brain. You are far more than the collection of your emotions, thoughts, preconceptions, and all the information and memories stored in your brain. You are not your thoughts. You are not your emotions. You are not your body. You are not your mind. You are all these things, and something that goes far beyond them as well.

When you become one with this awareness, you come to understand in every part of your being that your brain is the extraordinary tool that helps you create the life you want. It's up to you, as your brain's user, to direct it. Your thoughts, emotions, information, memories, and body are simply the tools with which your brain leads you toward your dreams.

Your brain won't do what you tell it to just because you claim that you are the master. You have to earn its trust and respect. The way to do that is to constantly remain true to the principles of honesty, integrity, and responsibility. Then, your brain will finally start listening to you and serving you fully.

Having definite goals is equally important. Even if you're able to use all of your brain's great potential at will, that power will be meaningless unless you're clear about where you'll apply it. It would be like purchasing a computer with the highest possible specifications and then using it only as a decoration.

The best way to use the brain's latent potential is to give it a workload that forces it to wake up and work hard. To awaken your brain, increase the level of your needs. When you've established a great, clear purpose, your brain will start exhibiting its best ability to achieve the goal you've set. You need a goal that will fully motivate your brain to act to its full capacity. We can call such information a "vision." When your brain is focused on a vision, it can function at its optimal level.

Having a vision or established goals is just a starting point, though. Making a New Year's resolution to read more often or exercise daily or resolve a family dispute doesn't ensure that you'll do so. For your dynamic and deeply personal new vision to become truly you, you have to reinforce it within your brain. Otherwise, it's all too easy to revert to your old values, insecurities, and self-identity. It takes courage to break away from everything that's familiar, safe, and secure. To make enlightenment an everyday habit, you must practice until your brain becomes hardwired to the vision you've chosen.

To become the master of your brain, harness the power of intentional action. If you have trouble carrying out your plans, check how you're using your will. When you choose to do something, are you perhaps creating unconscious resistance? Do you have inner voices prophesying failure even as you set out to do something? If that is the case, then you are using energy to work on your plans and also to maintain your resistance. At the same time, you are using energy to overcome your resistance. You create your own unconscious resistance, then try to overcome it even as you maintain it. This makes the work so taxing that you may give up.

Although there might be other external obstacles, if you feel that it's usually difficult to carry out your goal, then you first have to resolve any internal obstacles and resistance. Obstacles within you can keep you from using all your energy, and they can keep you from achieving unity in your relationships with other people.

You have to be single-minded in order to achieve your established goal, focusing all your energy on it. This power to focus completely on your goal—your first intention—comes from a place deeper than any thought or emotion, a place deep within your belly: your Dahnjon. The character of this power is to "just do it" when you've decided something, and its most precious property is that once your mind is made up, it won't change.

When you really know what you want and have a clear, concrete vision to express it, when your brain has come to trust in you 100 percent through your honesty, integrity, and responsibility, and when you have the power to see something through to the end, then you can say that you are the master of your brain. All you have to do is trust your brain and let it work hard for you. Before long, you'll understand what a perfect tool of creation you have.

A Brain You Can Trust

Your thinking mind is only one aspect of your brain's myriad capabilities, but it's a very powerful aspect—something that sometimes serves you well but also can work to your detriment. When you think, "This is my utter limit," your brain won't try to propel you any farther, because your brain follows your mind, not the other way around. That's why it's critical to develop absolute trust that your brain will follow your true wishes, knowing it has the power to help you move past any limitation or difficulty. Trying to achieve anything significant without complete trust in your brain is a bit like driving a car with the parking brake on and then complaining about not being able to go as fast as you'd like.

This is a truth that you may never have considered: your brain can learn things you don't now know and do things you've never done, even things you can't yet imagine. I'm sure you recognize this at one level, but I suspect it's important for you to meditate on what it truly means. In the same way that the words of any language can be arranged to tell an infinite number of stories, your brain has limitless ability to grasp new information and to act on it in novel ways.

The brain has astonishing power to find solutions that aren't immediately obvious. You're never limited by what you don't yet know, never constrained by what you haven't yet experienced, never shackled by actions you haven't yet taken. Too many people live within the limits of the lives they've already known. They're afraid to attempt things outside the scope of their own knowledge and experience, and they don't trust their brains to take on the unknown and be enriched by it. This dramatically limits their potential, shrinks their lives, and leaves their dreams unfulfilled.

It's far easier now than at any other time in human history to learn, to experience the unknown, to widen your perspective. An extraordinary amount of information is available anytime you want it, at little or no cost. Long ago, people's worth was determined in many respects by how much information their brains possessed. But now, all that truly matters is how each of us chooses to use the information to which we all have equal access. Please consider what a great gift this is.

In order to gain true trust in your brain, go outside yourself. Flood yourself with new information and trust your brain to employ it wisely. Don't look for answers and solutions in the same old places. Be unafraid to ask your brain tough questions about the nature of your life and its ultimate meaning. Set a lofty goal that challenges your brain. Let your brain be as creative as it can be in ensuring that you achieve your vision.

The Power of Vision

If you have a vision that urges you to devote 100 percent of your brain to reaching your goal, you are truly fortunate. When you're tuned into the vision, you think about it anytime and anywhere, even in your dreams. You receive messages and inspiration from an array of sources in support of your goal.

It's even possible to access the life force in your brainstem—the very essence of life that drives you and makes you one with every living thing. Harnessing the power of this life force is key to manifesting your vision. When you bring deep intention to something you desire, it isn't simply that intention that helps bring it to you. It's the extraordinary power of the brain that's responsible.

I'm sure you've had fortuitous experiences in which a key piece of information or a missing component seemed to drop into your lap. This hasn't been a coincidence, strictly speaking. Instead, it's the result of your brain's ability to "move heaven and earth" as it channels cosmic energy to help you reach a particular goal. When something seemingly impossible is made possible, it's the creative power of your brain that brings about the good fortune. There really isn't any secret other than the truth that as the master of your brain, you can achieve whatever you choose.

The Vision Meditation on the following pages accesses your brain's creative power by planting a specific vision deep in your consciousness, then igniting your whole brain to work toward its fulfillment.

During the Vision Mediation, you use what I call your MindScreen. A MindScreen is a vast visual plane that you project onto your mind's eye. All great imaginative minds throughout history have been adept at using their MindScreen. In a sense, you are using your MindScreen all the time, whether you are aware of it or not. However, when you consciously use it, it can truly make a difference in your life. You can put anything, anyone, or any situation on your MindScreen and nurture your intentions by sending it energy. Your MindScreen, a 360-degree hologram, is a place to make your visualization more tangible with the great assistance of your attention and energy. Your MindScreen hosts and channels energy to whatever and wherever your mind directs it.

When you do Vision Meditation with your MindScreen, you are broadcasting your creative intention to the responsive universe. Your ideas, thoughts, and intentions are the seeds of creation, and your attention is the powerful tool that drives energy toward the object or outcome you want to create. Your positive emotions and passionate actions add power to this creative process.

Think about what you really want. What can propel you to overcome your personal limitations and engage with what most fulfills you? As you consider, remember that you can create many visions—for a lifetime, a relationship, an important project, or simply a way to luxuriate in peace and contentment.

Remember, too, that a vision needs to be bright enough to fill you with true joy just thinking of it. A vision must offer unrelenting motivation worthy of your time and effort, and it must require you to use your energy and abilities to their limits. A vision has to be attractive enough to hold your utmost attention, and it must be beneficial to others in order to gain their essential support. And a vision must be realistic enough to be evaluated by concrete methods. Always ask yourself whether a vision you're formulating comes from your authentic self.

If a new vision demands changing the life that you've led up to now, be prepared for doubt and hesitation—they are inevitable when you face great transformation. But worry and stress won't make your decision any easier. Ultimately, resolving to move forward comes down to a moment of choice.

So let me ask again. What is it you really want? What fills you with joy and delight? Dig deep and ask your heart; there's no one else who can tell you whether the vision you've chosen is right for you. If your heart tells you what you really want, or confirms what you've suspected, then ask your brain how to go about getting it. Your brain is the tool that's been given to you to complete your journey of self-actualization, and Vision Meditation is a way to converse with your brain to access the ideas and strength you'll need to make your vision come true. Your authentic self uses your brain to deliver its messages to you. When doubts arise, dig deep again and listen to be sure the messages come from a place that's authentically you.

VISION MEDITATION

Set aside a specific time for meditation. When you finish doing this exercise, record your ideas and thoughts in a diary.

1. Sit comfortably, and breathe in and out three times.
2. Lift your hands to chest level, and begin Energy Sensing Exercise (see page 122). Once you feel the surrounding energy field and quiet your thoughts and emotions, lower your hands to your knees.
3. Imagine a stream of energy entering the crown of your head (Baekhwe energy point) and shooting out through the third eye (Indang energy point) between your eyebrows. Imagine that it's projecting a bright screen in front of you, the MindScreen. Visualize what you want to create on your MindScreen as if a movie is playing on the screen. Visualize the outcome with all of your senses.

4. Imagine yourself being filled with joy as you achieve your vision. Keep concentrating, and you may be presented with ideas to use in reaching your vision.
5. Breathe in and out three times and open your eyes.

Self-Declaration

I encourage you to try self-declaration as a powerful brain mastery tool. A declaration is not an explanation or description. It is not tied to comparison or circumstance. It is pure choice. Your declaration reflects your being, here and now. No reasons or justifications are necessary.

Self-declaration is one of the most powerful ways to express your passionate goal or purpose. Your declaration creates a new possibility. Listening to your inner voice as thoughts and emotions recede into the background, you journey to the place of infinite possibility, the place of a new beginning. From there, you declare yourself to the universe.

Create your self-declaration to help keep your brain infused with the will to complete your vision. All you need to do is create a simple declarative sentence that will keep your mind in a positive state. In other words, it is a statement that helps you be the kind of person who naturally embodies the goal you are seeking. This statement is not the same as the goal itself: it is a statement of character, a simple "I am" statement.

This statement may be in direct opposition to the negative self-talk that is too often produced by your brain. For example, if your brain has habitually undermined your dieting attempts with thoughts like "I am useless," then replace that with a strong statement in the reverse, such as,"I am worthy." If you have a non–I am statement such as "I can do it" or "I love myself," that is absolutely okay, just go with it.

Surprisingly, you will discover your self-declaration if you listen to your inner voice. If it comes to you, just accept and grasp it. Again, no reasons or justifications are necessary. Once you have discovered your declaration, write it down. Say it over and over. Talk to a supportive friend or mentor about the life you envision. Declare yourself consistently, diligently, and sincerely. Your declaration is truth.

The Cycle of Self-Creation

Self-creation is the development and nurturing of a Power Brain by supplying it with information from your authentic self—information that reveals what you want to be and create from your innermost being. The new identity you've chosen and your new vision should be practiced in everyday life. You define who you are through your actions—actions set in motion by information in your brain. In turn, the information in your brain is reaffirmed by your actions, and a cycle of mutual reinforcement is established.

When information first enters your brain, it's not yet verified. Your brain doesn't have full trust or confidence in it and therefore doesn't translate it into action. But when your brain comes to trust information, it stimulates action. When that action, in turn, proves that information's worth, it becomes what I call decisive information—information that has the power to directly stimulate your brainstem and summon the enormous life-force energy therein. It's crucial for your new identity to be formed out of decisive information that's repeatedly reinforced through your actions and behaviors.

Information acquired by experience is far more trustworthy than information obtained by rote learning. When your words and actions become one and the same, then the nature of the experience is likely to become permanently etched into your brain. When the information is proven beyond a doubt, it's linked in your brainstem to the cosmic network of information that drives the universe, and you "move heaven and earth" to achieve your vision.

SELF-CREATION EXERCISE

Set aside a specific time in the morning or evening to do this exercise.

1. Sit comfortably, and breathe in and out three times. Lift your hands, and engage in Energy Sensing Exercise (page 122).

2. Once you feel the energy flow, begin Brain Energy Sensing Exercise (page 152) by moving your hands toward your head and then away from it. Feel your brain breathe along with the rhythm of your lungs. Rest your hands on your knees when you feel relaxed.

3. Talk to your brain about the vision you hold for yourself as if you were speaking to your best friend. You can speak aloud or silently.

4. Imagine that the vision is being accepted and acknowledged by your brain. Visualize brightly shining energy entering your brain, passing through the neocortex and the limbic system to reach the brainstem. Sense your whole brain illuminating magnificently as if it were promising you the very best support.

5. Ask your brain what you should do to achieve your vision, and listen to what it has to say. Notice the first feelings, sensations, or thoughts that come to you. They may offer new insights or ideas you need.

6. Repeat the following sentences out loud or in your mind: "My brain is productive. My brain is creative. My brain is peaceful."

7. Breathe in and out slowly three times, and then stop the exercise.

Upgrading Your Brain Operating System

I consider it useful to think of the brain as having an operating system. Every brain, like every computer, has an operating system through which it processes the information it receives. Your brain's operating system is the system of beliefs and behavior patterns through which you interact with the world. Sometimes, our brain operating system is programmed in a way that doesn't suit our life intentions. Look at the progress of your life so far, and it won't be hard to see if your own brain's operating system is working compatibly with your dreams.

Here are five basic principles that can help keep your Brain Operating System (BOS) in top running condition:

1. Good News Makes a Good Brain

Information is brain food. If we were as concerned about information for our brains' sake as we are about food for our bodies' sake, then the content and quality of the information we provide would be quite different.

What kind of information do you offer your brain? What kind of information was your brain exposed to today? Right now, negative news is the world's addiction. The media will continue to give us whatever transfixes us as we sit there, mesmerized by the light of the cathode ray tube.

Many people underestimate the influence such information has on their brains. "I'm all right," they think. In fact, even passing images leave impressions on our brains. When psychology and brain characteristics started being used in product marketing, cola companies inserted images of their products into movies at a speed too fast for us to detect, engraving the pictures on our subconscious. Although such advertising techniques were ultimately banned as mind tricks being used without viewer consent, they show how information affects our consciousness even when we're not interested in it.

It's not only information coming from the outside that's important, but also information produced inside you. This includes all sorts of things—thoughts, associations, memories, imaginings, beliefs. If you take just a little time every day to look within, you'll see this information created within you, and you'll develop the ability to control it.

For your brain's sake, try screening and managing the information to which it's exposed, from within and without, the same way you try to provide your body with healthy foods for your health's sake. You'll soon realize that the information you've been unconsciously accepting and generating has had an incredible impact on your thoughts and emotions, and on the condition of both your body and your brain.

There's no way your BOS can function well if you feed it a steady diet of doom and gloom. No matter how tough things get, you must find a way to keep giving your brain hopeful information about yourself, your life, and the future. No good news? Then make some good news! If you open your eyes wide enough, you'll see that you are surrounded by blessings.

2. Wake Up and Pay Attention

"Attention" is our brain's most expensive resource. It was the latest of the brain's features to form, evolution-wise, and more energy is allocated to the prefrontal lobes—the areas in charge of attention and complex thinking—than to any other part of the brain. As one strategy for using this resource efficiently, the brain limits how long external stimuli remain in the prefrontal lobes. Nothing remains there for long unless we intentionally focus. By focusing, we can selectively control how long information remains in our short-term memory.

Energy flows to the object on which attention is directed. You need to understand that when you mentally chase after thoughts or images that have little meaning—or to put it another way, when you're lost in fantasy or distracting thoughts—you're wasting your brain's most valuable asset.

"Wake up and pay attention" means being startled into awareness as you think, "What am I doing right now?" It means bringing your focus to truly meaningful and important goals.

Time is usually measured in length, but what makes time truly significant is quality, not length. Attention and focus are what increase the quality of time. Time management is considered crucial for business management and self-development, but unless the quality of time is managed by supervising attention and focus, time management can easily become outward busyness with little substance. "Wake up and pay attention" creates an incredible difference in the quality of the time you use.

3. If You Choose It, It Will Happen

This really isn't as magical as it sounds; it's common sense. Life, in short, is a series of choices. Nothing happens unless you make a choice. Imagine there's a little bell in front of you. Even though you know it's a bell, it's nothing more than a lump of metal unless you strike it. The most important thing is action—making the choice to strike it.

If what you want isn't happening, you should ask yourself, "Did I really choose it?" Truly choosing something means resolving to do it no matter what, not that you'll "give it a try" or "work at it." The difference between "I'll do it" and "I'll give it a try" is subtle, yet so fundamental that it determines success or failure. If your attitude at first is "I'll give it a try," though outwardly you seem to be working hard, a part of your mind is trying to come up with excuses just in case things don't work out. You can't use 100 percent of your energy, because your mind isn't united within you.

Conversely, once you've made up your mind that "I'll do it," your fear disappears and your mind grows lighter. You're able to use all your energy because you have no conflict over what you're going to do. And when you truly resolve to do something, your brain knows it and is already starting to act. When you tell your brain, "I will do this!" it starts to create situations that let you carry out that choice. The more intentionally you choose, and the longer you remain true to your choice, the more powerfully your brain reacts. Everything around you starts to change, new opportunities arise, and new encounters support you in your choice. You're simply manifesting in reality what's already been achieved in your brain.

If you've really chosen to do something, then your task is practically accomplished already. If you set an objective and take even a single step in that direction, then as long as you don't give up, you'll ultimately reach your goal. It's not a matter of choice or probability. It's as natural as a tossed ball falling to the ground as a consequence of the law of gravity.

4. Master Time and Space

While on this earthly plane, we live in time and space. Being aware of this means living as the master of those things. People generally tend to live lost in their own emotions and desires, or they become preoccupied by trivial events without being aware of space and time. That gradually leads to viewing themselves as small, weak beings and to living dominated by time and space. Are you living as the master of your time and space, or do they rule you?

If you look at how you use your time, you'll see how wisely and maturely you're living your life. You'll also see how well you're using your brain. Using your time well is about how you're using your brain in the time you've been given. Why are we always short of time? We're always busy, but the work never gets done on time. We live our days diligently, but the results don't meet our expectations. Most people in modern society probably have feelings like these.

Living without being driven by time pressure is a matter of priorities and timing more than anything else. Unless you establish in advance what you should do according to the values you've set, you'll find that you always spend your days dealing with the most urgent tasks. The first solution for properly using your time is setting priorities that are consistent with your purpose and values, with the principles and philosophy to which you wish to be true. You'll unconsciously waste your time on unimportant things unless you consciously invest it in what's important.

Next, get your timing right. We commonly invest an incredible amount of time and effort on things that we could have accomplished easily had we gotten our timing right. Unless we remain true to the principles of priority and timing, conscientiousness can sometimes be a well-packaged waste of time and energy.

Finally, begin with yourself. If you say you'll act when a particular thing happens or when someone else does something, ultimately you're making yourself dependent on outside conditions. Whatever the task is, if it's been entrusted to you, plan so that it's organized around you. Then, it will be much easier to elicit cooperation from others who need help.

You must be productive and creative in order to use your time more efficiently. The condition of your body and mind is of basic importance for this. Those who rush forward when their energy is depleted and their minds are filled with tangled thoughts and emotions aren't likely to create anything efficiently. Your body needs to have energy and vitality, and it's important to maximize your concentration on the work at hand by emptying your mind of confusion.

When your creativity revives, your efficiency will improve so much that you'll be able to do in a few dozen minutes what would normally take several hours. Because you'll be dealing with things speedily and with lucid judgment, creative ideas and solutions will pour out of you. In such moments, your brain will fill with the joy of creation. Through this sense of achievement, you confirm your own life and existential value.

People who've mastered time also remember to devote some of it to self-management and self-cultivation. They know that getting themselves in good physical and mental condition is actually a shortcut to using their time efficiently and productively. In such people, we don't feel a frantic busyness driving them to forget themselves completely. Instead, we sense an unshakable centeredness that gives them the composure to handle work efficiently, with a smile and with a passion for life.

To master space and time, you have to come to a realization about your existential meaning. Reflect on the question, "What is the reason I'm living now in this space and time?" Having a definite purpose and meaning in life will grant significance to the space and time around you, and you'll be able to make the most of your space and time. And when you're conscious of space and time, you'll come to have a deeper interest in the culture and spirit of the times in which you live. You'll come to think more seriously about the communities affecting and being affected by you. In its most fundamental sense, becoming a master of your space and time means awakening to the fact that you exist beyond their limits. Although our bodies are inevitably ruled by space and time, our essential substance—energy—transcends space and time, and thus is infinite and eternal.

5. Design Your Environment

Many environments make up the surroundings of your life: your living spaces (including your home and workplace); the people around you (including friends, family, and colleagues); the work you do and the hobbies you pursue; and even your own body and mind.

We always hope to live in good environments, but there's no guarantee that we will. It's a universal truth of life and the universe that environment is variable. You never know when a bad situation will come to someone in a good environment. Sometimes, people who've always lived in good environments give up more easily than others when confronted by difficult situations. In contrast, there are people who are able to change their environments even though they started out in a bad situation. Many of the people who've been successful in the world weren't handed good environments by their parents but overcame difficult conditions.

Live for a while and you find that life isn't all clear days and sunshine. It might rain, it might snow, and the wind might blow. Unhappiness and happiness can come into anyone's life. You might get sick, or the people you care about might get sick. While there are times when you feel great joy, there are also times when you feel lonely, sad, and angry. It's normal to feel such emotions as our environments change, because we prefer stable environments. You should realize, though, that emotions themselves are a kind of environment. As the master of your environment, you must be able to watch your emotions objectively as you experience change.

The ultimate master of our environments is our consciousness. If your consciousness awakens, you're able to use and redesign your environment instead of being ruled by it. This means you can change unhappiness into happiness, and adversity into hope. The power of your consciousness is manifested when you gladly accept your environment as the subject of study for your personal growth.

If you make up your mind to love your life instead of lamenting over your environment, in that moment—amazingly—your negative consciousness will be changed to a positive one. And when, through sustained practice, you begin to change your internal environment into something healthy and vigorous, your consciousness will gain even more resiliency. Remember, too, that you also participate in other people's environments. You can choose to be a good or a bad environment for someone else. It is your consciousness—the power of your brain—that makes this choice. When you share bright energy and unrelenting positivity with those around you in hopes that all of them—family, friends, colleagues, everyone around you—will become happier, you become a beneficial and reliable environment for them.

View Obstacles as Blessings

Throughout your life, you'll create new visions and refine and redirect existing ones. And in every case, as a master of your brain, you'll use these visions to propel yourself to action. Brain mastery means executing what you intend to achieve, consciously manifesting your intentions.

But there are certain to be pitfalls along the way. No matter how enthusiastic and confident you are about actualizing your dreams, difficulties will arise. For many people, these obstacles quickly put an end to dreams—or worse, keep them alive as dreams they somehow don't "deserve" to have fulfilled. For others, it's a case of "if it's meant to happen, it will"—that is until an obstacle comes along and "proves" it wasn't meant to be after all. Many people have a fairy-tale idea about how their lives should go.

But that's not really the way of life, is it? You'll encounter obstacles, and I want you to understand something very important: each obstacle you encounter, no matter how overwhelming, is a blessing. Instead of focusing on how hard the concrete is, we're better served when we marvel at the way flowers find a way up through the cracks. It's a mindset I particularly recommend if your goal is to truly blossom in your life.

In my life, every time I had to confront an obstacle, every time "bad luck" befell me, every time I truly suffered, I came away from the experience with a valuable perspective. I was aware of new and perhaps better avenues I could take toward my goal, and I was mindful of all that I'd accomplished already. In retrospect, I can't think of a single bad thing in my life that hasn't proven to be important to me in the end—and my whole life appears to be a blessing, comprised of the good and bad in ways that have allowed me to reach my goals.

Think for a moment of a difficult period in your life that you are well past now, or a huge obstacle that you've successfully overcome. Quietly consider the ways in which that event or experience ultimately was a blessing. Almost certainly, it will take you only moments to express what the particular blessing was and to see the ways in which the experience helped you.

Get Physical

You can derive great benefits from taking on physical challenges at the same time you work to push beyond your perceived brain limitations. Physical-fitness training is an excellent way to practice stepping beyond obstacles. "Limitations" imposed by your body are easy to identify. You might find that at the moment, for example, you can walk briskly for only 20 minutes before you're exhausted, or you can do six push-ups but absolutely no more. Similarly, it's unmistakably clear when you've overcome those self-imposed physical limits.

Choose aerobic walking, push-ups, or any other exercise you know you can't do beyond a certain limit. Then proceed to master it. In the beginning, accept without self-criticism what you can accomplish. If it's only a single push-up, that's fine. Congratulate yourself on that single push-up, and promise yourself that you'll add at least one more push-up every day. Then, set a goal of doing 100 push-ups without stopping.

If you can briskly walk for just 12 minutes before you have to stop, accept that accomplishment with grace. But walk for 13 minutes the next day, and then for 14 minutes the following day. With self-respect, diligence, and unwavering commitment, you'll quickly be doing a hundred push-ups without stopping or walking for 90 minutes or any of hundreds of other challenges, and you'll set a wonderful precedent for success in every area of your life. And the fact that you'll be in much better physical condition is simply one of the many great benefits brought about by mastering your brain.

Develop a Lofty Character

As you move toward your goal, remember that no one along the way will simply hand success to you. That's the stuff of unproductive fantasy. Success will only come via your own hard work and the refinement of your character—something that's really as important as the achievement of your goal itself.

You've heard this before, but that's because it's true: the only thing that turns a lump of coal into a diamond is intense and constant pressure. You'll be similarly transformed by the pressures you face on the road to your goal. Instead of becoming discouraged or destroyed by them, let them shape you into a stronger, more complete, more refined person. Like a diamond, you'll gain remarkable durability yet also remain clear and precious.

It seems to me that true greatness in life is actually a matter of character. Financial success, political prominence, and celebrity all have their place. But why do people like Marie Curie or Mahatma Gandhi or Dr. Martin Luther King, Jr. seem to tower above the rest of us? Do they possess intelligence or skills or stamina the rest of us simply don't have? I don't think so. I believe the attribute that truly set them apart was character.

They were ordinary mortals made up of flesh and bone, and they certainly didn't possess superpowers. Their brains were commonplace human brains. But they used their brains with astounding skill and focused their brains with conviction as pure and durable as a diamond, and it was the full measure of their character that made them so great. To use your brain to its fullest potential, you must develop a similar level of conviction about what you want to contribute to the world. Then, like a diamond that sparkles from every angle, you'll radiate pure light to everyone you meet.

▸ Brain Supermodels

It can be very valuable to model aspects of yourself and who you hope to become on someone you greatly admire. If you'd like to develop greater personal courage, perhaps it makes sense to study the lives of such people as Viktor Frankl or Nelson Mandela. If you need to learn selflessness, perhaps the life stories of Mother Teresa or Gandhi will inspire you. If you struggle to stay focused on your dreams, you can learn a great deal from the lives of people as diverse as actors, athletes, and political and spiritual leaders who've succeeded despite great odds. You might want to read a biography or watch a documentary about your role model.

Your grandmother, your father, or virtually anyone you know well can become a character model who makes a real difference in your life. Your brain is particularly well-adapted to model itself on others—that's how you learned to walk and to talk, after all. Let the lives of your heroes and heroines be an example by which you live your own life, and in the process, your own unique greatness will be ignited inside your brain.

Plan – Do – Check – Act

Sometimes, a person is called an overnight success, but that's never accurate. It may appear from the outside that something big has been achieved instantaneously, but that's because the hard work that went on behind the scenes wasn't apparent.

To achieve anything, you need a clear plan for how to get there, and you need the patience to carry it out. As the old proverb states, "A journey of a thousand miles begins with a single step." To achieve anything, you must be willing to take the necessary steps one at a time. The trick is to enjoy the present moment while keeping an eye to the future. Let your vision—your ultimate goals—be a constant inspiration and hope for you, but focus on your present challenges. Work on the steps that lead to your dream. View these as mini-visions, and take joy in your small successes. Before you know it, all your little steps will add up to one beautiful journey.

In a dynamic meeting of East and West, an American engineer, statistician, and author named W. Edwards Deming was able to revolutionize Japanese product design, construction, testing, and quality control procedures in the years following World War II. At the heart of Dr. Deming's success was the four-step problem-solving process he called the Shewhart cycle after its original developer, Walter Shewhart, but which become widely known as Plan-Do-Check-Act.

In an industrial context, the "Plan" phase involved establishing the objectives and processes necessary to deliver specific results. "Do" meant implementing those processes. "Check" included monitoring and evaluating the processes and results against the original objectives, then reporting on the outcome. And finally, all the steps were reviewed in the "Act" phase and modified as needed before the planning cycle began all over again. It was Plan-Do-Check-Act, or PDCA, that ultimately made the Japanese auto industry so successful and its products so sought-after around the world. Dr. Deming's simple yet remarkably inventive quality control methods by now have been successfully applied to virtually every human endeavor.

In the end, the process of brain mastery is very much akin to the PDCA model. It's vital to plan your vision and how you expect to attain it, and to prepare for the challenges you expect to face. Next, it's critical to proceed with power, resolve, and complete commitment. When you check the degree of your success, you engage your brain at its most dynamic level, allowing it to use the new information you've gleaned to improve both your vision and the ways you're seeking it. With each successive cycle, your mastered brain ensures that you won't repeat mistakes and that your truest creative self is free to bring you closer to your goal.

Working consciously with this four-part cycle has benefited me in every stage of my personal and public life. At its heart is a commitment to continuous self-improvement. It's that dedication to living in the most dynamic and fulfilling way possible that I believe is the greatest reward for pursuing your Power Brain.

▶ PDCA for Your Vision

Apply the PDCA planning process to your personal goals by breaking them into realistic, manageable steps. This will also give you a way to measure your progress. It's best to begin with the end result in mind. From there, work backward through time to create an achievable, step-by-step plan. What would you like to achieve in the next year? What can you do in one month to move your life closer to your dreams?

Once you've narrowed your vision to a specific, obtainable one-year goal, you can break it down into monthly, weekly, and daily PDCA steps. This is your P, your plan. Then, of course, you must actually do (D). After that, check (C) to see if your plan is really moving you toward your goal. Act (A) to revise the plan as needed, continually cycling through the PDCA process.

Feeling the Earth

Imagine that you traveled to a distant planet, then tried to explain where you'd come from. Would you say you were from California or Brooklyn Heights or the Upper Midwest? Would you describe yourself as an Asian, a Baptist, a Buddhist? Almost certainly, first you'd simply explain that you came from a planet called Earth. Because of our planet's enormous diversity, the sole identity we share with everyone on the planet is that we're all citizens of the earth. Men and women, rich and poor, Christians, Jews, Muslims, Hindus, and Buddhists—all of us are first and foremost simply humans who call this planet home. Nothing is more fundamental or important than that, because all the values and visions to which we devote our lives depend on this watery globe that orbits the sun. The earth is the source of all life.

I like to suggest to people that each of us and the earth itself share a great deal in common. It's true. Have you ever considered how insignificant your own life is compared with the enormity of the earth and the numbers of people for whom this planet is home? If so, you can commune with the earth in the knowledge that it, too, is tiny and insignificant. Our planet is simply part of a small system of planets circling a medium-sized sun in a rather unremarkable galaxy that's one of millions of galaxies in the ever-expanding universe. Yet despite the brain-boggling enormity of the universe and the potential for it to be teeming with many forms of life, it's certain that there's only a single planet precisely like this one. In that respect, you and the earth share something else as well: both are unique, and therefore singularly precious and worthy of extraordinary support and nurturance.

When you consciously commune with the earth, you can't help but be transformed into a guardian of her incredible beauty, her health, and all the life forms she sustains. In this profound experience of expanding awareness, you sense in yourself an overwhelming love and responsibility for the earth. You come to understand that all of us must work tirelessly to overcome nationalism, gender chauvinism, religious prejudice, and belief in ethnic or regional superiority. You recognize both consciously and deep in your brainstem that everything is one—not in an abstract sense but very literally, because the earth is made of everything that lives. We live because we're part of the earth.

The following exercise allows you to commune with and become one with the spirit of the earth. As you experience this exercise, note that the earth—like you—is a living being made of matter and energy, whose spirit thrives in the interlinked brains of all who call her home.

EARTH COMMUNION

1. Sit comfortably in a chair or on the floor. Breathe in and out three times to relax your body and mind.
2. Lift your hands to chest level, and begin Energy Sensing Exercise (page 122).
3. Imagine that the blue-green earth is between your hands. Imagine it contracting and expanding as you move your hands in and out.
4. Bring the earth toward your forehead. Imagine that it's the size of a ping-pong ball as it enters into your head through the third eye point between your eyebrows. Watch it rotate and revolve inside your head, emitting radiant blue-green light. Lower your hands to your knees.
5. Now, bring the earth toward the center of your chest. Let it settle within your chest, and feel the warmth and golden light of the earth's loving energy in your chest.
6. Let the energy of the earth move up to your brain and down to your lower abdomen, forming a column of bright, pure light that connects the length of your body. You will lose the sense of your body and become the light itself.
7. Imagine the light getting bigger and stronger, illuminating everything around you. Now, imagine the light enveloping the whole earth in a capsule, emitting enormous healing energy.
8. Breathe deeply in and out three times to end the training.

Enlightened Living

Although I studied anatomy and biology as a clinical pathology major in college, it was only through personal experiences that I truly came to understand my brain. The greatest lesson came during a difficult and even desperate search for the meaning of my life when I undertook a three-week, sleep-deprived fast on a remote mountain in Korea.

As you may know, going without sleep is much more difficult than going without food. After three days without sleep, I began muttering to myself; after five days, I was no longer able to control my body or my mind. It was in that delirious state, however, that I learned to peer into the place that lies beyond thought. I had to travel to the very edge of conscious awareness and then beyond. Only then could I access what has been called universal consciousness.

When I couldn't stand it any longer, I gave up—absolutely and completely, surrendering myself at the level of my soul. At that very moment, a voice rang out within me, saying, "My body is not me but mine." And I understood suddenly that it wasn't me who was hurting. It was only my body that suffered such pain. And I understood, too, that I had the power to end that pain and to achieve the peace I sought. My tool was my brain—the brain that wasn't me, but mine. As if to confirm that enlightenment, in the next instant I felt an explosion inside my skull, followed by a complete return to consciousness in which everything became sharply defined and very clear.

As I continued to learn and grow in the following years, I came to understand that this awareness doesn't require a huge amount of ascetic practice. It's simply a matter of surrender, which can be achieved in many ways. It is at the moment of absolute surrender of everyday consciousness that one encounters a world of non-consciousness—which is, paradoxically, a dimension of new awareness. Enlightenment, I believe, is simply becoming one with that consciousness, and it is the ultimate human experience. In such a state, you realize who you truly are, and I'm entirely convinced that this state of enlightenment is a function of the brain. It is stunningly physical and spiritual at the same time.

As you master your brain, push your own consciousness to its very limit with fundamental inquiries about your own existence. Let everything you think, feel, and do be a deep inquiry as you courageously move through your own life. You have to be willing to risk your whole way of life to make such inquiries, and to live the answers that they bring you.

When I discovered that enlightenment lay in the brain, I made the brain the new focus of all my visions, strategies, and plans. I also discovered that the world is attracted to people who have attained some level of enlightenment, not just in the spiritual realm but in any field. These people aren't weighed down by old and damaging information; instead, they radiate self-acceptance, compassion for others, peace, and tranquility. They are also fearless and filled with creative energy. Enlightened people understand that an easy life is not the same as a fulfilling life, so they pour their passion into efforts that benefit humanity and are also personally satisfying at a deep level.

In the past, many people viewed enlightenment as a gift of the very few, unattainable by most. But I believe that in the twenty-first century, a practical and grounded sort of enlightenment is more widely possible. I'm convinced that becoming enlightened isn't as difficult and doesn't take as long as people once believed. To experience a significant breakthrough, however, you must free your mind of obstacles and experience the courage it takes to face true liberation. You may long for freedom, but your brain is habituated to the prison of your limiting beliefs, so there's a strong tendency to cling to old patterns—even when they undermine your health, happiness, and peace.

My goals have been to make people familiar and comfortable with their brains, then to encourage them to begin living their lives as if they are already enlightened—because I now believe that when you live your everyday life as if you're enlightened, you inevitably raise yourself to a high level of awareness. I set my sights exclusively on these goals, adapting them and refocusing them with the principles of my Brain Education training. The more I considered the brain, the more I was moved to share my discoveries.

This book is the summary of what I have learned so far. I humbly offer you the messages that have emerged from my learning. I hope you find them valuable as you continue on your own journey of self-mastery.

THE FIVE STEPS OF BRAIN EDUCATION AT A GLANCE

BRAIN ORIENTED PURPOSE	BRAIN EDUCATION FIVE STEPS	EXPECTED BENEFITS AND RESULTS
Enhanced executive control and imagination	5 BRAIN MASTERING	Realizing the power of choice and action Authorship of life
Integrating brain functions and unleashing potential	4 BRAIN INTEGRATING	A sense of purpose More balanced and harmonious life view
Freeing the brain from negative memories and emotions	3 BRAIN REFRESHING	Positive outlook Self-confidence Emotional maturity
Making the brain more flexible and adaptable	2 BRAIN VERSATILIZING	Enhanced adaptability Increased creativity More resilient mindset
Awakening the brain-body senses	1 BRAIN SENSITIZING	Physical vitality Enhanced focus Attuned senses

CHAPTER 12

Everyday Application

The fundamental concepts of Brain Education can be applied in innumerable ways. Since everything we humans do is done with our brains, the basic principles of how the brain works and the Five Steps to a Power Brain can be used in all areas of our lives. This chapter focuses on the aspects that can be applied most effectively in your daily personal and work life.

Self-Healing

Many people believe that drugs, doctors, and hospitals cure disease. This appears to be common sense for most, and it seems odd to raise any objections. But strictly speaking, there's no drug or medical technology in the world that doesn't use the natural healing mechanisms already present in the body.

In fact, health is the most natural state of life. The body is designed to recover balance even when its systems are disrupted. Disease, we can say, develops when some aspect of our body's natural healing system is overactive, underactive, or malfunctioning in some way. All therapies—medication, physical therapy, or surgery—add something, subtract something, or stimulate something in the natural healing system to help it operate normally. And if the system fails, the treatment ultimately fails. People do what they can, but the final result ultimately is left to the system itself. Though we speak of "miracle drugs" and amazing advances in medical technology, the credit for any successful medical treatment actually goes almost entirely to the natural healing system in our bodies.

▸ Ways to Promote Natural Healing

When we're ill or in pain, we usually focus on our symptoms and try to eliminate them. We think that if we've eliminated the symptoms, the treatment has been successful. But when we do this, we ignore or fail to recognize the effects such treatments have on other organs, or on the system as a whole.

For example, the body develops a fever when it's under attack by bacteria or viruses. The fever itself is neither the disease nor the cause of the disease. In fact, the fever is a weapon that the body's defense system uses to fight its attackers. Of course, we have to take appropriate measures if the body's temperature rises too high, because that could damage important organs—including the brain. But too often, people take fever reducers even when a fever isn't severe, simply because it's inconvenient and uncomfortable. That's like taking away a weapon right when the body is fighting most fiercely. Clearly this is interfering with, not helping, the body's healing process.

Our goal should instead be to help the body recover its balance and rhythms, so that it can use its own built-in healing mechanisms. These mechanisms include pulse (thought waves), temperature, respiration (breathing), pH balance, energy balance, brain waves, and biomagnetic fields. Of these, the safest and easiest to control are respiration, energy balance, and brain waves.

Respiration is the best way to correct autonomic imbalance, as described in Chapter Five. Through breathing, we can increase the effectiveness of the parasympathetic nervous system, which brings rest and healing. Energy balance cools the head and warms the belly, enabling natural energy circulation to take place. This should happen automatically in a healthy body, but when it doesn't, it's possible to assist in the process—for example, by placing a warm pack on the lower abdomen. And by closing your eyes and concentrating on the feelings in your body, you can slow your brain waves to alpha-wave level and send positive intentions to the uncomfortable parts of your body.

▶ Attitudes that Promote Healing

What we call "compassion" is an attitude that contributes to healing the hurts and relieving the suffering of ourselves or others. The English word comes from Latin words meaning "to suffer with someone." To have compassion—which is something everyone has—is to have a heart that shares in hurt and sadness.

If you've worked with children, you might have noticed that sometimes they have stomachaches, get colds, are frightened, or suddenly develop fevers for no apparent reason. Very young children in particular have no way to complain of their discomfort other than crying, since they can't yet speak. A parent will stay up all night watching over their suffering child, with "a heart that shares in hurt and sadness." This is compassion—the concern we have and the energy we share with those who are hurt or suffering.

Take a look back on your attitudes about your own suffering and hurts. When our bodies are hurt, we first experience discontent and irritation. Next, we want to get rid of the symptoms as quickly as possible.

The first step toward letting healing happen is changing our discontent and irritation into an attitude of sorrow for what we've done, and then inviting in gratitude and love. Natural healing, in a certain sense, is forgiveness. It's forgiving the wounds my body has given itself, and it's forgiving myself for causing those hurts. The process of suffering includes being sorrowful for what I've done and then feeling gratitude and love regarding the pain and hurts my body is feeling. As I sense my body's feelings, it's good to say to myself or aloud, "I'm sorry. Forgive me. Thank you. I love you."

Symptoms are simply a language your body uses to talk with you. Through symptoms, your body is informing you that some problem has developed, and it's asking you for help. Taking painkillers as soon as you receive this message is like shushing your crying child when he or she asks you for help. We can't give our bodies the positive interest and energy they earnestly need for healing unless we recognize and acknowledge our symptoms. Without symptoms, in fact, we'd simply ignore our problems. We can learn many things through a dialogue with our bodies, and we can improve many of our health problems in a gentle, natural way if we take the time to listen and respond.

▸ Rethinking Pain

People think of pain as a bad thing, but really that's not true. Painkillers—which don't provide any actual healing—have become some of the best-selling medications at pharmacies because we lack the endurance to tolerate even trivial discomfort, and because we think pain should simply be eliminated without any consideration of underlying causes. Most of us pop an aspirin or ibuprofen pill without giving it a second thought.

If we think about this, though, isn't it normal to hurt when we have a health problem? How would we know we have a problem unless we hurt? How could you address a problem if you didn't know you had it? Pain is actually an important part of the body's warning system. The body and brain exchange information on hazards and emergencies in the body through the signal called "pain." Artificially removing that signal could disrupt this warning system and bring chaos to the body's natural healing system.

The size of the pain is generally proportional to the size of the risk and the degree of attention needed to deal with it. To put it another way, if the problem is significant, the pain is significant; when you have a lot of pain, you focus that much more on finding a solution. This is certainly common sense. Through this process, the body and brain cooperate to activate the internal systems necessary for healing.

If you have a problem in your body, it's normal to hurt, and you apply your mind to the source of that pain. The energy delivered through that mind is essential for healing. And the most powerful way to support the natural healing power within you is a heart that says, "I'm sorry, thank you, and I love you."

▶ Pain Is My Guide

What's the first thing you do when you feel pain or discomfort in your body? Most people shake, rub, or tap the area that hurts. Such movements are very effective for releasing stagnant energy and breaking up blockages. If you tap gently, energy will flow better and you'll feel refreshed. You may notice that some areas are tender or painful, which means energy is stagnant or blocked there.

But when I tell people to tap their bodies at a Brain Education workshop or a natural healing retreat, I find that some of them do it for a while and then stop. When I ask why they've stopped, most of them give me the same answer: "Because it hurts." But that pain is actually a signal telling them, "Yeah, this place is blocked." I advise them to continue tapping, accepting the pain and focusing on the feelings in their bodies. A great many people experience deep healing through this process.

I suggest that you change your thinking about pain: pain is not something to be avoided, but something to be followed. Pain teaches you what spots you should tap and open. Pain is a guide on your path toward healing. If you change your first reaction from complaining and irritation to "I'm sorry, thank you, I love you," you'll be able to heal the problem much more effectively. Furthermore, if you expand this attitude just a little, you'll be able to send the same sympathetic, helping energy to other people and other organisms that are hurting. As you do so, you'll be healing yourself while also healing others.

Changing Habits

Practically everyone has at least a few habits they want to change. But unless you're a very special person, you probably have more experience with failure than with success in trying to change your habits. That's why we end up listing the same goals for our New Year's resolutions every year. Why is that? Why are habits so difficult to change?

▸ A System of Habits

Where do habits exist? We commonly say things like, "My body is in the habit of doing such and such." However, habits aren't located in the body. Habits exist in our brains in the form of circuits, established networks of connections between brain cells.

When attempting a new pattern of behavior, we need to summon a lot of concentration. All the choices and behaviors associated with developing a new habit are controlled by the prefrontal lobes of the cerebral cortex, the brain's control tower. This area's attention is the brain's most valuable resource, and its rarest. If the same actions are repeated several times, the brain doesn't leave them to be continuously processed in the prefrontal lobes. Instead, information about such behaviors is stored in the operating system of the basal ganglia, a subsystem of the cerebral cortex. Information that's stored here gets processed virtually automatically, without the involvement of the prefrontal lobes. For example, you have to focus all of your attention when you first learn to drive, but once you're comfortable with driving, you can listen to music, drink coffee, and even use the telephone as you drive (though the latter certainly isn't advisable unless you have a hands-free system). Without thinking about the process of driving, you find that you've arrived at your intended destination and are parking your car.

Habit formation is a useful and essential system. We can save a great deal of time and energy by deferring to these stored processes. It becomes possible to focus our consciousness on more important things because we have a brain system for turning specific patterns of behavior into habits.

Certain habits, especially the ones we want to discard, are connected with specific rewards. Behaviors that you engage in when you're anxious—smoking a cigarette, shaking a leg, biting your nails, twisting your hair, or touching your nose—aren't easy to change, even when you know they're harmful or socially unacceptable, because you get some sort of reward from them. Drinking alcohol, overeating, being totally absorbed in a video game—indulging in habits such as these plays into your internal reward system.

The situations that elicit habitual behaviors can be different for every individual. For example, meeting the opposite sex causes certain habitual responses in some people, while others exhibit similar responses when they stand in front of a crowd. But regardless of individual differences, all such habits help the brain recover its chemical balance.

Feeling anxiety or some sort of craving means that at that moment, the brain is in a state of electrochemical imbalance. The habitual behavior triggers secretion of the hormones or neurotransmitters the brain needs to find equilibrium; chemical balance is restored, which causes anxiety to disappear. As this process gets repeated, an ever-stronger connection is formed between the brain's chemical response and the behavior, which compels the person to engage in the behavior again and again.

The brain's system of rewards also causes habits to grow stronger with time. Once created, the habit-reward circuitry is reinforced every time the behavior is used. If someone who's used to smoking a pack of cigarettes a day cuts back to half a pack, will their habit circuit for smoking cigarettes grow weaker? Unfortunately, current brain research says this is definitely not the case. Smoking even a single cigarette helps strengthen the circuit. This highlights an important illusion about changing habits—the illusion of "slow change." The most effective way—in fact, the only way—to weaken a habit circuit is to discontinue using it completely, however uncomfortable that may be.

Although a process for forming habits exists in the brain, there's also a process for changing them. Changing your habits is easier if you really understand the system by which the brain operates. Regardless of what habits you want to change, the following principles apply.

▶ Cooperate with Your Brain.

When we try to change our habits, we often choose to fight with our brains instead of cooperating with them. This example is a little extreme, but let's suppose that someone had tried all kinds of ways to quit smoking, without success. Finally, he has himself locked in a room so that he can't get near tobacco. The door is locked from the outside, and he can't go out even though he wants to smoke. What do you think he'll be thinking about the most? That's right—he'll probably think only about smoking.

Consider what this means for the brain. The experience and feeling of smoking tobacco is continuously being reproduced in this man's head, and a powerful current is continuing to flow in the circuits associated with that habit. He's fighting with his brain. This approach is going against the principles by which the brain operates, and as a consequence, it's unlikely to succeed.

The core functions of the brain—particularly the prefrontal lobes of the cerebral cortex—are attention, regulation/control, and choice. These three play important roles when we learn new patterns of behavior. They can also be used very effectively when we're changing existing patterns of behavior. First, recognize the moment when you're about to follow your pattern of habitual behavior (attention). Second, choose not to follow that pattern (regulation). Third, immediately move your attention to another pattern of behavior (choice)—or, if you don't have another behavior to replace it, simply inhale and exhale with a smile.

The moment when we're about to follow a habitual pattern of behavior is our best and only opportunity to change that habit. Recognizing that you're about to behave a certain way is like grasping the brain circuit that handles that habit. If you're aware of the impulse and choose instead to follow a different pattern, change takes place in that habit circuit. When you want to smoke, for example, you might decide to get a drink of water instead; or when you want to yell at someone, you could choose to go out for a walk.

Because chemical balance hasn't been restored by following the old habit, some instability may remain in your brain. Take a deep breath, and exhale with a gentle smile—and repeat this several times. The positive chemical reactions created by the oxygen from deep breathing and by the smile will help offset the instability.

▶ Have a Positive Attitude Toward Yourself.

When changing your habits isn't working and you keep going back to your old ways, your brain is already in a stressful state. So if you take a negative attitude toward yourself at this time, it's like rubbing salt in a wound. Don't your efforts to change and to become a better person show your sincerity about life? To put it another way, don't they mean that you're a decent human being?

It might be hard for you to recognize when you're about to follow a pattern of habitual behavior, then move your attention elsewhere instead. Even then, it's good to have an attitude of gratitude for the experience rather than criticize yourself.

When we follow patterns of habitual behavior, pleasure hormones are secreted in our brains, letting them temporarily recover chemical balance. However, that balance is shattered by the regret, guilt, and self-degradation that immediately follow, bringing a state of imbalance that is difficult to endure. The effects of positive attitudes toward oneself are much deeper, stronger, and long-lasting than the temporary, pleasant effects obtained by acting according to habit.

Try to recall the powerful current that flowed through your head and body at a moment when you felt proud of yourself. Having good thoughts about oneself creates powerful effects in the brain. So congratulate yourself when you've succeeded in following a different pattern—and when you haven't been successful, think of yourself as having learned what points are difficult. Have a positive attitude toward yourself in both cases, regardless of how things turn out.

▶ Seek to Serve a Greater Cause.

Sensual pleasure gives the brain temporary satisfaction. Positive thoughts about oneself, pride, and self-esteem give the brain greater satisfaction. The belief that you're serving a greater cause—a value greater than yourself—gives the brain satisfaction that's deeper than these two things put together. People often overcome their personal limitations through this power, and so can you.

You might wonder, "What in the world does a cause have to do with changing my habits?" But it means more than you might think. The world is already interconnected as a single whole, and the positive effects of changes you create in your life don't stop with yourself. For example, eating more vegetables than meat is good for your health, but it also reduces your environmental impact on the earth. Producing animal-sourced food requires more than ten times the water and energy it takes to produce of plant-sourced food, and it generates more than ten times the waste. If making changes in your lifestyle could reduce the stress you put on the earth by one-tenth, wouldn't that be a great enough cause to bring meaning to your life? There's a big difference between thinking that changing my habits is good for my physical health alone and thinking that it's good for me, it helps the earth, and it contributes to all humankind.

Provide this kind of information to your brain when you change your habits. Have a sincere intention and a sincere attitude about the meaning of your efforts, instead of just pretending to be happy about them. Your brain will be much more cooperative and will become an active participant in your efforts to change.

▶ Be Consistent.

Most of the stubborn habits you want to change weren't formed in just a day or two. They've been repeated over a long period, so the associated brain circuits are well established. That's why you can't expect to change them in a day or two. You must have a stick-with-it attitude.

Do you know how many times you fell down when you were learning to crawl, sit up, and then stand up? It takes most children one to two weeks to attempt and completely master standing for the first time. During that time, they repeat those movements with indomitable will and passion, never giving up until they succeed. A child might try to stand 100 times a day, and if it takes ten days to succeed, they'll have made approximately 1,000 attempts. This is something virtually every human in existence has done. This is the human spirit at work. You are a master of patience and will, having fallen flat on your behind at least a thousand times to learn one simple movement.

Don't give up just because you've attempted to change your habits several times and failed. Think to yourself, "Unless I've tried at least a thousand times, I'm not qualified to say whether I've failed or not." Whatever habit you want to change, consistency is the key to creating miracles.

Managing Stress

We know that almost all diseases are made worse by stress. The majority of doctor visits are stress related. We can't get rid of all the stressors in our lives, and we can't change our body's stress-response system, because that's essential for our survival. But we can better manage our stresses by observing the following guidelines.

▶ Maintain Energy Balance.

The optimum energy balance of cool head and warm belly lets you maximize the performance of your brain and body. That balance is reversed when you're under stress, resulting in a hot head and a cold lower abdomen. But you'll be less affected if you are able to maintain an energy balance with a cool head and a warm belly even when you find yourself in a stressful situation. Methods for maintaining this state, introduced in previous chapters, include Dahnjon Tapping, Intestinal Exercise, Brain Wave Vibration, and breathing to focus consciousness in the lower abdomen.

▶ Recognize Stress Early.

One of the most effective ways to deal with stress is to detect it before it reaches such a high level that it negatively impacts your body and mind.

Learn to observe and analyze your own energy state. You'll be able to discern the more subtle energy reactions in your body when you develop your energy sense.

Start by noticing where tension is held in your body. The stress response is usually felt first in the gut, chest, shoulders, and neck. You may get a feeling of something wriggling and rising up in your gut, or you may feel bloating, chest constriction and discomfort, stiffness and heaviness in your neck and shoulders, heat in some area of the body, and other uncomfortable sensations. Try to identify these sensations as soon as they occur, then release them by stretching, breathing, or meditating.

▶ Increase the Gap Between Stimulus and Reaction.

We all have our own reasons for reacting to stress in a certain way. But we're not machines that react automatically to stimuli. There are many ways to respond to a particular stimulus, and we can choose the most appropriate of those. Such choices, however, are only possible when there's a gap between stimulus and response. Rather than responding instantly when a stressful situation arises, pause first. Slightly increase the gap between the stimulus that's causing the stress and your own response to it.

But how can this be done? It's not as simple as telling yourself, "Don't react"—you're already in the middle of a stressful situation, and your mode of rational judgment isn't operating normally. You have no time to make yourself think calm thoughts, and self-judgments will likely only increase the feeling of stress.

Instead, the simplest and most powerful way to increase the gap between stimulus and response is to breathe. All you have to do is take three deep breaths before saying anything, doing anything, or making any judgments. Then, consider what options are available and choose your response. Following this one principle could keep you from saying things, doing things, and making decisions you might later regret.

▸ Focus on the Best Results.

If you end up in a stressful situation—for example, when having an argument with another someone—usually, you only have one thought in your head. You want to prove that you're right. Focusing on this leads you to act in ways that are contrary to your original intentions with this person. Even if you "win" the argument, you and the other person both feel bad, the work doesn't get done, and your relationship is strained. You'll likely find yourself under greater stress later as a result.

To prevent this, the moment you recognize that you're in an argument, ask yourself this question: "What is the best result I can create in this situation?" When you were seeking a way to beat the other person, you also asked your brain a question, unconsciously. You asked, "How do I knock out this guy?" Your brain responded with a method and a strategy. When you instead ask this new question—"What's the best result I can create in this situation?"—your brain will again start to provide answers, so many that it will shock you. By simply changing your attitude, you'll be much less stressed in an argument, and you'll find much better solutions to your problems.

Improving Concentration

What is it that normally has the greatest effect on your productivity or performance? Mood, physical condition, atmosphere—there might be many things, but for most people, the most important element is concentration. As we know from experience, there's an incredible difference between the quality and quantity of our work when we have focus and when we don't.

▶ Concentration Is Like a Muscle.

Although there are differences depending on the type of work, for employees working normal office hours, concentration generally is at its highest between 9 and 11:30 in the morning. As we get closer to lunchtime, we start to have many other thoughts, beginning with what we'll eat for lunch, where we'll eat, and with whom. After lunch, we're drowsy, our bodies become sluggish, and the whole office has lower energy.

Interestingly, if you give people a fitness test involving running, push-ups, and sit-ups at different times of the day—between nine and eleven in the morning, say, and between two and four in the afternoon—you'll find little difference in the results. But work efficiency does change depending on the time of day, because our ability to concentrate changes. Concentration is the most important element determining productivity, especially for work that demands a high level of mental activity, such as planning, analysis, integration, judgment, and brainstorming.

Concentration can't be maintained at a consistent level, even when it's normally the highest, for example from 9 to 11 am. Our attention spans are actually quite short. Our neurons become fatigued, just like when muscle pain develops and fatigue suddenly increases with the accumulation of lactic acid. As we use our muscle power to push beyond our muscular endurance, so too can we push to extend our length of focus. With practice, we can increase the length of focus, like a muscle gaining strength.

There are individual differences in how long a person can maintain concentration, just as muscle endurance is different for everyone. You can increase the time you maintain concentration if you continuously train your ability to concentrate, just as you can develop muscle endurance by training your muscles. Doing any old exercise for a long time doesn't develop muscles and improve muscular endurance. In the same way, doing work that requires concentration over a long time doesn't necessarily develop concentration. If you want to develop your muscles, you have to do muscle-building exercises. To develop your concentration, you have to do appropriate mental exercises. One of the most effective of these is meditation.

Meditation requires intense concentration. Even if you sit down purposefully to meditate, without full concentration it's easy to fall asleep or chase after distracting thoughts. Why doesn't meditation fatigue your nervous system as much as other mental activities do, even though you concentrate for the same amount of time? When we engage in mental activities like analysis or judgment, we focus on external stimuli, but meditation is concentrating on emptiness, on stillness, on the lack of stimuli.

Meditation for Developing Concentration

All the methods of meditation introduced in the Five Steps to a Power Brain can be wonderful exercises for developing concentration. All meditative practices that focus consciousness in one place—such as energy, the breath, a specific mantra or affirmation, or a particular object—help develop concentration.

The following two methods of meditation are so easy that they can be attempted by anyone, and they are powerfully effective. I hope that you'll practice them regularly. Through these simple techniques, you can accumulate the power of intense concentration as you let your mind and body rest and recharge. Developing concentration in this way helps you to maintain composure even in busy, stressful situations, because it's rooted in your breathing and in the energy center in your lower abdomen. Practice these methods regularly, and before long, people will notice that something has changed about you. They may even ask you for your secret.

▶▶ FEELING ENERGY

The easiest form of meditation for developing concentration is Jig-am training, which involves feeling energy with your hands (see page 122). After doing Jig-am training in a comfortable posture for about five minutes, lower your hands to your knees. Then, bringing your consciousness to your lower abdomen, do about a minute of deep abdominal breathing as you feel your breath. If you repeat this simple meditative practice just twice a day, you'll clear your mind, supply energy to your body and brain, and develop staying power in your concentration.

▶▶ COUNTING 100 BREATHS

This is training of a slightly higher level. After meditating by feeling energy as described above, lower your hands to your knees and feel your breath with your consciousness in your lower abdomen. In that state, start counting your breaths, with one inhalation and one exhalation as a single breath. Counting as you exhale, count 100 breaths as you slowly breathe in this way. If you lose count, start again from the beginning. Do you think you'll be able to do it well? It's not easy, but you'll find out for yourself.

It's difficult to count 100 breaths, so beginners should repeat counts of 10 instead. One, two, three...10. Then, again, one, two, three...10. Once you're comfortable with that, count 30 breaths, and after that's comfortable, count 100. Breathe as slowly, deeply, and evenly as possible. While you're counting to 100 breaths, don't move your body, if possible not even your pupils. After completing the 100 count, take three deep breaths and open your eyes. Being able to count 100 breaths without losing awareness indicates a very high level of concentration.

Although this varies from person to person according to how deeply they breathe, it usually takes at least 20 minutes to count to 100 without missing a breath. That's why it's good to do this when you have enough free time to focus comfortably.

Improving Job Performance

You've probably heard about the "law of 10,000 hours." It states that for someone to develop enough expertise to master her field, she must invest at least 10,000 hours in practice. Practicing three hours every day adds up to about 1,000 hours in a year, which means it would take about 10 years to reach 10,000 hours.

However, not everyone masters a field because they've done the same thing for 10,000 hours. Why, after doing the same work for nearly 10 years, does one person become the world's best in that field while another person does the same work without any great change? Time alone is not enough to master a certain field.

What other differences are there? Of course, there might be differences in innate ability, but what other elements create such great differences between individuals who invest the exact same amount of time in a pursuit?

▸ The Power of Reflective Replay

After a match, professional Go players reenact the game, whether they won or lost. They replay it from the beginning, placing stones in sequence—their own and those of their opponent. What's the reason for doing this? The game of Go allows a practically infinite number of moves. A stone can be placed in many different spots, even in the same situation, and the way the game unfolds varies greatly according to that stone's position. Players choose the position of each stone they place, but there are always many other positions they could have chosen.

During a replay, players can see possibilities they couldn't see while they were playing. Their state of mind is open, allowing them to see new things, not closed by the psychological stress of needing to win. The question they have in mind now isn't, "How could I have done better?" but

"Could I have done it some other way?" Through this process, they gain insight into moves they hadn't seen before, and that allows them to make better choices in their next game.

A similar principle applies to any activity where performance is central, from chess to vocal and instrumental music, figure skating, or gymnastics. For example, if pianists are unhappy with part of their performance, many of them will open the piano and bang on the keyboard as soon as they get the chance to be alone. They don't do that to relieve stress. They repeat the part they didn't like until they get the feeling, "Right, that was it." Their attitude is the same as that of a pro Go player doing a replay. They're redoing their performances not with a sense of self-reproach or inferiority, but with this question in mind: "Could I have done it some other way?"

This could be called reflection, and whether or not you do it determines whether you become a master. Someone without an obsession and passion for their own performance likely wouldn't want to replay a hard game of Go they'd just finished. And after a recital, a pianist might think, "It's too late now, anyway," and just want to go home, stretch out his legs to relieve stress, and maybe have a glass of wine. But one hour during which your brain reflects on its still-vivid memory of your performance can have the effect of 100 hours of ordinary practice done at another time. The circuits of the brain are changed by that hour invested in reflective replay.

This applies to everything you do. Washing the dishes, cleaning the house, giving the dog a bath, watering your flowers—there might be other, better ways of doing these things. The performance doesn't actually have to be repeated for reflective replay. You can also do it through your imagination. Whether in actuality or in your imagination, try to reflectively replay your actions, asking yourself without remorse and without conceit, "Could I have done it some other way?" In this way, we can raise everything we do to a greater level of perfection and achieve greater mastery in our everyday lives.

▸ Anticipation and Observation

Anticipation and observation form a set with reflective replay. The question to keep in mind is this: "How will I do it?" Whether you're giving a musical performance, a speech, or some sort of presentation, try it out in your imagination before the actual event with this question in mind. Many outstanding speakers, including Dale Carnegie and President John F. Kennedy, reportedly prepared for their speeches using this approach. They are said to have not just memorized the contents of their speeches, but vividly imagined their own expressions and gestures and even the reactions of the crowd, as if everything was happening before their eyes. Why not give this a try? Especially before a performance, when your concentration is high, this kind of practice has a shockingly powerful effect.

Speakers who've given their brains advance preparation like this can take the stage with thrilled expectation and confidence instead of fear and tension. They can direct the whole situation according to their own intentions—like a movie director or orchestra conductor—instead of simply reading their notes.

After preparing in this way, your attitude during the actual performance should be one of observation. You're both a performer and an observer. Ask yourself, "What am I doing?" Without any judgment about doing well or doing poorly, observe with close attention and an open mind what you're doing and what's happening. With sufficient observation, you can do a properly reflective replay after your performance.

Through anticipation, observation, and reflection, we prepare our brains before a performance, make them fully mindful during the performance, and enable them to find new possibilities with an open mind after the performance. These three are a set. Think about this: one individual practices anticipation, observation, and reflection for every performance, while another spends time in restless anxiety before a performance, has no idea what they're doing during the performance, and wants to completely forget it after the performance is done. The two live this way for ten years. How great will the difference between them be?

Character Education

Etymologically, education means "bringing something out." That's based on the belief that humanity has inherent good, positive, creative attributes which, when nurtured and allowed to develop, will benefit both the individual and the world. I believe this is the definitive essence and purpose of education. I would suggest that education should strive to be more than the effort to impart knowledge and skills. Rather, it should strive to develop in every single student all the positive potential that can benefit the world.

The time when education was centered on the acquisition of knowledge has passed. Knowledge is now something we search for easily on the Internet, not something we acquire. From the latest papers on how memories are processed in the brain to new hypotheses on the birth of the universe, from the temperature at which you should set your oven to cook the most delicious pumpkin pie to how to jumpstart a car with a dead battery, there's virtually no information we can't obtain through an Internet search. It's regrettable that our children spend so much time learning information they could get in a few minutes of online searching, yet don't really have much opportunity to learn the philosophy, experience, and qualities they need to take the lead in creating their own lives.

I think that education should focus on awakening the potential and creativity of the human brain. That potential is the true nature of Hongik, transcending individual interests and seeking to benefit others and the world.

I'm a parent of two sons, and I deeply share all parents' concern for their children. I want to provide the best education possible for our next generation. I've long believed that developing greatness within individuals, finding our true values, and awakening the spirit of Hongik are the ways to help our young citizens find the meaning of life and to awaken their latent passion to do good things for the world and for all life.

Because I wasn't able to find many people who agreed with my belief—or if they said they agreed, they didn't do much about it—I decided to attempt these educational reforms on my own. That's what drove me to develop the concepts, principles, and practices of Brain Education. I created a university in Korea to educate leaders and teachers to deliver Brain Education, and these leaders are now working in many schools in the United States, Japan, Germany, and Korea. In collaboration with the United Nations, the Brain Education school program is also being delivered in many developing countries in Latin America, Africa, and Southeast Asia.

In 2013, I established the Benjamin School for Character Education in Korea to realize what I think of as educational ideals. It's an alternative school that uses a free-school-year system, and it is characterized by the lack of a set curriculum, tests, homeroom teachers, school buildings, or schoolrooms. Escaping from traditional schools and classrooms, students make the world their school, have diverse experiences, and engage in service activities.

Students establish and complete in one year a challenging project that really holds their interest. This is the heart of the school's curriculum. The students find what they need to complete their chosen projects, and more than 500 professional mentors help them in this process. For example, a student who wants to become a performance director gets the kind of advice that comes from long experience by interacting with at least one mentor working in a related field, and they have the opportunity to plan and direct a performance. In the process of planning projects and bringing them to completion, students learn about themselves and the world. More than anything else, they come to have confidence and respect for themselves.

What has impressed me most is the type of projects the students choose. Even as they've been developing their own character, they've chosen projects that contribute to other people and their community. One student chose to paint a mural on more than 80 square meters of school wall. Covered in beads of sweat after working for several months, the student smiled brightly and said, "I'm doing work I want to do, and it makes me really glad to see that the work I've done makes others happy." I found this deeply moving.

My model for the Benjamin School for Character Education was Benjamin Franklin, one of the founding fathers of the United States. He overcame an unhappy environment and misfortune to become a self-made entrepreneur, politician, writer, and inventor. Although he had the benefit of a regular education only through the second grade, he taught himself everything he needed to know, serving as an example of how to use our brains. The main reason I named this alternative school after Franklin was that he made the goal of his life the growth of his own character, which he pursued through time management, ceaseless self-reflection, and self-development for his entire life.

Like many others who feel responsible for the quality of life in our homes and communities, I believe good education is our future and our hope for humanity. The recent violence and tragedies in U.S. schools have led many observers to say that the key to preventing additional tragedies is to help young people find deeper meaning of life. I completely agree, and I think this is far more important than creating more administrative procedures and regulations.

What makes our job easier is the fact that our children already have this attribute in their hearts: the spirit of Hongik, the inextinguishable passion to do good things for the world. We just need to guide them to find it. If people ask me what Brain Education is for, I would say it is for awakening this noble spirit.

AFTERWORD

Living with Your Power Brain

Nothing brings me greater joy than the sight of many people enjoying a new awareness of and affection for their brains. Seeing the smile on the face of someone who suddenly connects with these ideas is a big part of my fulfillment in life. When someone awakens to their truest potential and gains the confidence and mastery to live well, I celebrate. When anyone thrives and lives harmoniously, they actively bless all of our lives.

My goal is to help people gain wisdom, insight, and enlightenment and also to encourage them to teach the children in their lives about how they can achieve brain mastery. People of any age can be taught to approach their brains with love and respect, and when they act on this new information, their brains will open up to them.

The most precious gift we can give children is to let questions about the purpose of their existence grow naturally within them. We can then respond to their questions with the wisdom we have gained from our own life experiences. Of course, our answers won't automatically become theirs because we all have different life paths. But speaking with clarity and enthusiasm about our own life purpose inspires children to have confidence in their ability to find and express their own life purpose. We are raising children who will one day inherit the world. We must offer them every possible tool for positive change, and we must provide good examples of living our own fulfilling lives.

Having come to the end of this book, you understand that the life you have now is the life you have created, and what you experience is shaped by your thinking and by the emotions and actions that follow those thoughts. In order to create a different future, you must recover your creativity and learn to support your Power Brain so that what you focus on and act on is what you really want to experience.

You know that when you tune in to your brain, your brain will show you ways that you can focus your attention more deeply. You understand that when you find yourself unconsciously slipping into a pattern of staying on a narrow and difficult path, trapped in preconceptions and limited ways of thinking, you can shift to the wider vision of your Power Brain, and you can master your own consciousness. This new way of thinking requires discipline, but in exchange for that effort, you will experience ease and much less stress on the path to greater health, happiness, and peace.

You have also explored the beautiful truth of two paradoxical truths. You are not your brain, which you now know to be true because you are very much more than your brain. Yet you also know that you are your brain and that it is your connection to yourself, the world, and your creator.

You've learned that you don't need to be a brain scientist to comprehend your own brain and master it. You need only the tools provided here in order to experience more of your potential. I am delighted that the methods I've presented on these pages will be improved by new scientific discoveries and by the direct experience of people just like you.

We have a far-from-perfect understanding of the brain, and that is very good news. Every day, new advances draw us closer to understanding more of the brain, and, as that scientific work continues, so will the ways in which we expand our brain mastery with insight that comes from wisdom, enlightenment, and soul connection.

The world faces a lot of challenges right now, but, at the same time, we are also presented with a great opportunity for each of us as individuals and for humanity as a whole. For the first and only time in the history of our species, we have a chance to change the world and save the planet through our individual choices.

We as individuals have much more power than we think. We have brains with infinite potential, and we have within those brains a noble desire to do something good for the world. That noble desire pushes us to change for the better the ways we deal with other life forms and the earth. We can become Power Brains because we have this noble desire and this ceaseless passion to transcend all separation and to move beyond our limitations to embrace others and the entire world.

I hope that you take more than just ideas from this book. I hope you have experienced more of your brain and, as a result, have felt enthusiasm and energy for what you will do for yourself and others. It is my greatest hope that everything you experience will help you connect with your highest sense of self and that you will join the collective efforts of all the Power Brains that are happily creating the changes the world desperately needs.

ACKNOWLEDGMENTS

I would like to extend my sincere gratitude to all who have contributed to the creation of this book. In particular, I would like to thank Daniel Graham for helping transform my Korean into English. Phyllis Elving added an elegant and engaging style to the text with her editing.

From the beginning, Steve Kim and the staff of Best Life Media tirelessly helped me, from the original research and writing, to editing, to the final production. I am grateful for their creativity and editorial support. I also extend great thanks to Al Choi for the illustrations and to Kiryl Lysenka for his creative design of the whole book.

Thank you to my friends and colleagues in the worlds of science and spirituality all over the world for the inspiration you offer to this work and for the many opportunities you provide for these ideas and practices to grow and flourish.

Finally, I would like to thank all of the many thousands of individual practitioners who, through their diligence and dedication to their own self-development, have helped establish the efficacy of Brain Education.

RESOURCES

Individual Instruction

Sometimes, it's easier to study and exercise when you set aside a regular time to focus on increasing your health, happiness, and peace with the encouragement and help of others. To expand the breakthroughs you have experienced by reading *The Power Brain,* you may want to explore the variety of programs, workshops, retreats, personal coaching, and advanced-level trainings offered at any of the one hundred Body & Brain Yoga and Tai Chi centers in the United States.

National leaders in health and wellness, Body & Brain Yoga centers can be found in many major cities around the country. Their offerings include yoga, tai chi, meditation, and other mind–body training modalities based on Ilchi Lee's Brain Education methods. Find the center nearest you at bodynbrain.com.

Brain Education for Kids

Brain Education has been tailored to children, families, and the school environment so that healthy brain habits and brain mastery can be developed at a young age. Since 2006, Power Brain Education (PBE) has been offering this program through a variety of innovative on- and off-site trainings to more than five hundred schools, businesses, senior centers, non-profits, and community organizations all around the United States. It runs Power Brain Training centers and camps geared toward youth and their families, as well as Brain Education workshops for educators and parents. Hundreds of schools in New York, Arizona, and New Mexico have successfully integrated Brain Education into their curricula and school culture, and more are implementing it all the time. To find a program or location that's right for you, or to learn more about bringing Brain Education to your school, visit PowerBrainEducation.com.

Learn Brain Education Online

Founded by Ilchi Lee, ChangeYourEnergy.com is dedicated to providing online learning for lifestyle change and personal growth. Expert trainers with a wide range of talents and abilities share their experience through an expansive collection of courses, articles, webinars, and natural healing products based on Brain Education methods. Visit the website for advice and techniques on harnessing your infinite potential and developing a radiant and healthy body, mind, and spirit.

ABOUT THE AUTHOR

Ilchi Lee is an impassioned visionary, educator, mentor, and innovator; he has dedicated his life to teaching energy principles and researching and developing methods to nurture the full potential of the human brain.

For over thirty years, his life's mission has been to help people harness their own creative power and personal potential. For this goal, he has developed many successful mind-body training methods, including Body & Brain Yoga and Brain Education. His principles and methods have inspired many people around the world to live healthier and happier lives.

Lee is a *New York Times* bestselling author who has penned thirty-nine books, including *The Call of Sedona: Journey of the Heart*, *Change: Realizing Your Greatest Potential*, and *Brain Wave Vibration: Getting Back into the Rhythm of a Happy, Healthy Life*.

He is also a well-respected humanitarian who has been working with the United Nations and other organizations for global peace. Lee serves as the president of the University of Brain Education and the International Brain Education Association. For more information about Ilchi Lee and his work, visit ilchi.com.

INDEX

Page numbers with an i in italics indicate an illustration. Page numbers in bold indicate an exercise.

F

N

O

T

U

V

W